The CASSIA Spy Ring
in World War II Austria

The CASSIA Spy Ring in World War II Austria

A History of the OSS's Maier-Messner Group

C. Turner

McFarland & Company, Inc., Publishers
Jefferson, North Carolina

Library of Congress Cataloguing-in-Publication Data

Names: Turner, C., 1965– author.
Title: The CASSIA spy ring in World War II Austria : a history of the OSS's Maier-Messner Group / C. Turner.
Description: Jefferson, North Carolina : McFarland & Company, Inc., Publishers, 2017.
Identifiers: LCCN 2017036549 | ISBN 9781476669694 (softcover : acid free paper) ♾
Subjects: LCSH: World War, 1939–1945—Secret service—United States. | United States. Office of Strategic Services. | Espionage—History—20th century. | World War, 1939–1945—Austria. | Spies—History—20th century.
Classification: LCC D810.S7 T86 2017 | DDC 940.54/867309436—dc23
LC record available at https://lccn.loc.gov/2017036549

British Library cataloguing data are available

ISBN (print) 978-1-4766-6969-4
ISBN (ebook) 978-1-4766-2991-9

Front cover: Gustav Rüdiger (courtesy of Thomas Rüdiger), Helene Sokal (Zentrales Parteiarchiv of KPÖ; used with permission of Alfred Klahr Gesellschaft), Curate Heinrich Maier *(Gedenkbuch für die Opfer des Nationalsozialismus an der Universität Wien 1938),* and Franz Josef Messner (courtesy of Volker Sartorti); background map of Vienna, Austria and surroundings (iStock).

Printed in the United States of America

McFarland & Company, Inc., Publishers
Box 611, Jefferson, North Carolina 28640
www.mcfarlandpub.com

In memory of my father,
J.D. Turner

Acknowledgments

The author is particularly grateful to Dr. Siegfried Beer and Dr. Erika Thurner, without whose help and prior research (as recorded in the bibliography) this story would have been but a faint shadow of what it is. Dr. Beer, now retired, was a professor of contemporary history at Karl-Franzens-Universität Graz, which is also known as the University of Graz. An expert on the history of intelligence, he founded the Austrian Center for Intelligence, Propaganda and Security Studies, of which he remains director, and the *Journal for Intelligence, Propaganda and Security Studies*, for which he still serves as editor. Dr. Thurner is a professor at the University of Innsbruck and lectures on history and political science at institutions in Linz, Salzburg, Vienna, and Graz.

The author also thanks the following people—listed in order of meeting or correspondence—who generously shared their time and expertise, and in some cases their unique documents, photographs, and memories: Scott S. Taylor; Dr. Wolfgang Neugebauer; Dr. Winfried Garscha; Dr. Ursula Schwarz; Lt. Col. Karsten Damen; Mark D. Wolfe; Dr. Leslie Cullen; Andrea Hurton; Dr. Hans Schafranek; Dr. Herbert Posch; Mag. Thomas Maisel; Volker Sartorti; and Dr. Thomas M. Rüdiger.

With the exception of the Gestapo reports on the interrogations of Heinrich Maier, which Nicole Dieterich and Fernando Silveira Ruiz Diaz expertly translated, the author interpreted all other referenced German-language documents, articles, manuscripts, and Internet content, some in part and others in whole. Errors in meaning and word choice are solely the author's fault.

Table of Contents

Preface

Some tragic stories never really end. They linger in our memories, persisting through neglect and disregard. They may even haunt us.

This sad tale is Austrian and occurred during the Second World War. A smaller but still important part of it, though, was American. U.S. intelligence officers numbered among its most critical characters, and an American student risked his life to unearth the secrets of its end.

After the war, the story surfaced from time to time, but was recounted in abridgement or as a minor constituent of a broader study. In these scholarly and journalistic works, its timeless moral was often ignored or underplayed. Worse yet, its practical lessons fell victim to bureaucratic amnesia, which prevented their inclusion in the curricula of any U.S. intelligence schools.

The following account endeavors to correct these deficiencies, oversights, and lapses. It draws on a number of primary sources, some never before used and others never fully exploited. It also synthesizes a multitude of secondary sources, two of which preserve the results of singular interviews with key witnesses who are no longer alive.

What sprang from these efforts was an example of rare courage: A dozen men and women, united in cause and in friendship, who *chose* to stand against the ruthless Nazi juggernaut. Though none ever fired a shot, theirs was not a bloodless war. Half were executed, and the rest were left forever scarred.

In Austria's immediate postwar years, the survivors were often labeled as traitors. No matter, for they had never sought praise or prize; they asked no one to vindicate what they had done. And so they remained mostly silent. For them, Hitler's ignominious defeat had been reward enough.

> *Know you not that a good man does nothing for appearance sake, but for the sake of having done right?*
>
> —Epictetus[1]

Introduction

The shelves of bookstores and libraries are crowded with titles on the Second World War. A good many of these describe the activities of the Office of Strategic Services, the wartime agency that President Roosevelt signed into existence and tasked with stealing secrets from the Axis powers, supporting resistance groups behind enemy lines, and disseminating propaganda. Some are memoirs and others are biographies, with substantial offerings on the OSS's colorful leader, William "Wild Bill" Donovan, a veteran of the First World War and recipient of the Medal of Honor.

Books on the OSS often emphasize special operations. There are numerous volumes about the men and women who parachuted into France to assist the Resistance and to conduct sabotage, about the men who dropped into occupied Norway to target German heavy water production, and about the exploits of units that operated against the Japanese in Burma and China. Fewer, though, discuss the OSS's attempts at less spectacular but equally important work—handling the spies who took staggering risks to smuggle intelligence out of the Third Reich.

It is understandable why the bulk of OSS literature tips in favor of derring-do. Stories about intelligence-collection operations unfold at a much slower pace and involve significant periods wherein the "action" is comprised of document copying, agent debriefings, and report writing. Of course, danger lurks among all of these seemingly mundane activities, but the resulting tension does not always translate well to the page.

Fiction has done a better job at telling traditional spy stories. Contrived tales of espionage, even those supposedly inspired by real events, often draw from the standard repertoire of plot tricks: a spy photographing secret documents while her fanatical supervisor takes a telephone call in the next room; or an operative, traveling under alias and standing in line for a full-body search at a border crossing, gripped with fear for the possible discovery of the coded message concealed in his hollowed-out shaving brush. All of us have seen motion pictures in which beads of sweat form on the brow of the imperiled protagonist as he or she embarks on a hazardous mission or narrowly avoids detection. But the reality of spy work is much less spellbinding. It may be best likened to flying an airplane: 98 percent sheer boredom and 2 percent sheer terror.

Still, unembellished stories of the OSS's handling of spies can hold not only historical but also literary—or even cinematic—merit. The most compelling of them involve fascinating men and women who did the right thing at a critical moment and at great personal risk. And such stories aren't complete without a few worthy villains. It is the cast of characters, then, that makes or breaks a traditional spy story, and the heroes and scoundrels of the following tale could have been no more captivating if a talented Hollywood casting director had selected them.

Another component of a good spy story is location. Exotic settings may help to capture a reader's interest but, in the context of espionage, location has a more technical meaning. Intelligence agencies typically divide the world map into a few basic categories: permissive environments, denied areas (characterized by pervasive, persistent, and oppressive counterintelligence and security regimes, typically under centralized control), and war zones—each demanding unique elements of tradecraft. This story played out in all three.

Today's intelligence professionals sometimes forget that, during the Second World War, the U.S., British, and Soviet security services routinely conducted denied area operations that were as dangerous, complicated, and productive as the most sophisticated operations of more recent times. Ask these professionals to provide an example of a classic denied area operation and they will often reflexively mention a Soviet Cold War spy like Oleg Penkovsky, and will wax nostalgic on the arcane use of dead drops and microfilm and secret signals. Ask about war-zone operations and they will perhaps speak of the CIA paramilitary officers who slipped into Afghanistan some two weeks after the 9/11 attacks, linked up with the Northern Alliance, and set the stage for the eventual ousting of the Taliban from power.

But those feats, while sometimes of great geopolitical and historical significance, were made possible only by the audacious operations—the successes and the failures—that came before them. The operation described in subsequent pages was both: It began as a triumph but ended as a disaster.

As a case study of what can go right *and* wrong in an intelligence operation, it has few rivals.

In modern times, which are in many ways as difficult, divisive, and dangerous as were the years of the Second World War, intelligence professionals and their clients, the public, are obliged to study such historical lessons. While much has been said about learning from the past, none other than George Washington once gave us strong motive for so doing, to find our way to greater peace and security: "We ought not to look back, unless it is to derive useful lessons from past errors, and for the purpose of profiting by dear bought experience. To enveigh against things that are past and irremediable, is unpleasing; but to steer clear of the shelves and rocks we have struck upon, is the part of wisdom, equally incumbent on political, as other men, who have their own little bark, or that of others to navigate through the intricate paths of life, or the trackless Ocean to the haven of secury and rest."[1]

Dramatis Personae

In order of appearance.

Harald Frederiksen—an American student in Vienna
Fritz Molden—an Austrian Wehrmacht soldier
Allen Dulles—the American intelligence chief in Bern
Franz Josef Messner—an Austrian industrialist
Heinrich Maier—an Austrian Catholic priest
John Sekler—an Austrian resistance member
Helene Sokal—an Austrian communist and lawyer
Karl Seitz—a former mayor of Vienna
Theodor Legradi—an Austrian communist and company director
Oskar Maier—Heinrich Maier's uncle and colleague of Theodor Legradi
Barbara Issakides—a Viennese concert pianist
Franziska Messner—Franz Josef Messner's wife
Kurt Grimm—an Austrian attorney in Switzerland
Josef Joham—the director of a large Austrian bank
Walter Caldonazzi—an Austrian forestry engineer
Gustav Rüdiger—an Istanbul-based Austrian subordinate of Messner
Alfred Schwarz—an Istanbul-based Czech businessman
Lanning MacFarland—the American intelligence chief in Istanbul
Archibald Coleman—an American intelligence officer in Istanbul
Valerian Lada-Mocarski—the American intelligence chief in Cairo
Sigismund Romen—a Vienna-based German subordinate of Messner
Andreas Hofer—an Austrian police sergeant
Hermann Klepell—an Austrian Wehrmacht conscript
Dr. Josef Wyhnal—an Austrian Wehrmacht conscript

Wilhelm Ritsch—an Austrian Wehrmacht conscript
Clemens von Pausinger—an Austrian Wehrmacht conscript
Karl Fulterer—an Austrian apprentice lawyer
František Laufer—a Czech double agent working for Germany
Otto Hatz—a Hungarian double agent working for Germany
Lothar Kövess—a Hungarian double agent working for Germany
András György—a Hungarian double agent working for Germany
Margarethe Rotter—an Austrian agent of German Military Intelligence
Jack Taylor—a U.S. Navy lieutenant and an intelligence officer
Josef Niedermayer—a guard at a concentration camp in Austria
Franz Ziereis—the commandant of a concentration camp in Austria
Eduard Jacob Sekler—a Viennese actor
Eduard Franz Sekler—a Vienna-born Harvard professor
Kaiser—a Gestapo-Vienna officer

Comments on Terminology

Many of the terms herein will be familiar to readers who are steeped in the history of the Second World War, but for those who are not, and for purposes of clarity and standardization, a few definitions and explanations are warranted.

One of the most elemental terms is Nazi, which is often used as the modifier of a noun, such as in Nazi Germany, or in the plural, Nazis, to signify those people who were committed to or otherwise aligned with that ideology. Nazi is a contraction of *Nationalsozialistische* (a declension of *Nationalsozialist*), from *Nationalsozialistische Deutsche Arbeiterpartei*, or Hitler's National Socialist German Workers' Party. The term Nazi and its variants, such as Nazism, are commonly used in English-language literature and film. However, many European writers, orators, and filmmakers prefer NSDAP, the acronym of the party's full German name.

In the following narrative, Nazi will be used attributively in reference to Hitler's political party and its members, to the wider adherents of the party's ideology (characterized by pan–German nationalism, Germanic territorial expansionism, theories of racial hierarchy, and the Final Solution), and to the institutions that pledged fealty to Hitler's regime and its ideology. On occasion, in contextually appropriate instances, the term Nazis will also serve as a synonym of the wartime German nation, the broader European Axis powers, and the Third Reich, the aspirational great empire of Germanic peoples led by Hitler and inspired by his ideology.

The term Gestapo is likewise familiar to many readers. It is also a contraction but one that was widely used both inside and outside the Third Reich during the war. It was derived from *Geheime Staatspolizei*, the Secret State Police of the SS—the *Schutzstaffel*, the Nazi Party's main paramilitary organization.

The SS's intelligence and counterintelligence service was called the SD, the acronym of *Sicherheitsdienst*, which translates as Security Service. The SD was often in competition with the Abwehr—which means simply Defense—the military intelligence service of the German High Command of the Armed Forces (*Oberkommando der Wehrmacht*, often referred to by its acronym, OKW). In 1938 Vice Admiral Wilhelm Canaris (1887–1945) became the head of the Abwehr and remained in that position until Hitler disbanded the agency in early 1944. Many volumes have been written on Canaris's operations, his secret contact with the Allies, and his plotting against Hitler. In April 1945, about one month before Germany's unconditional surrender, Canaris was executed for committing high treason against the Third Reich.

Many readers will recognize the term Wehrmacht and will regard it as a synonym for the German Army during the Second World War. In reality the Wehrmacht included all three of the Third Reich's armed forces—the *Heer* (Army) and *Kriegsmarine* (Navy), as well as the Luftwaffe. However, in keeping with the vernacular definition of Wehrmacht, this book will primarily use that term when referring to the German Army, and will use Luftwaffe for specific remarks about the German Air Force.

Two British security services played roles in the following story. The first, which Ian Fleming made famous in his James Bond series of novels, was MI6. MI6 stands for Military Intelligence Section 6, and it is the British foreign intelligence agency. It is also called the Secret Intelligence Service and, as with its American counterpart CIA, is often referred to only by its acronym.

The second British service was the Special Operations Executive. SOE was formed in summer 1940 and was charged with conducting espionage, irregular warfare, and reconnaissance operations against the Axis powers. Because some of SOE's responsibilities overlapped with those of MI6, there was occasionally some tension between the two organizations. As another point of potential conflict, SOE and MI6 reported up two different chains of command: SOE through the Ministry of Economic Warfare and MI6 through the Foreign Office. In very general terms, for purposes of comparison, the Office of Strategic Services, the wartime intelligence agency of the United States, had one section, Special Operations, which shared many of SOE's mission objectives, and another section, Secret Intelligence, whose activities were more aligned with those of MI6. SOE was dissolved shortly after the end of the war.

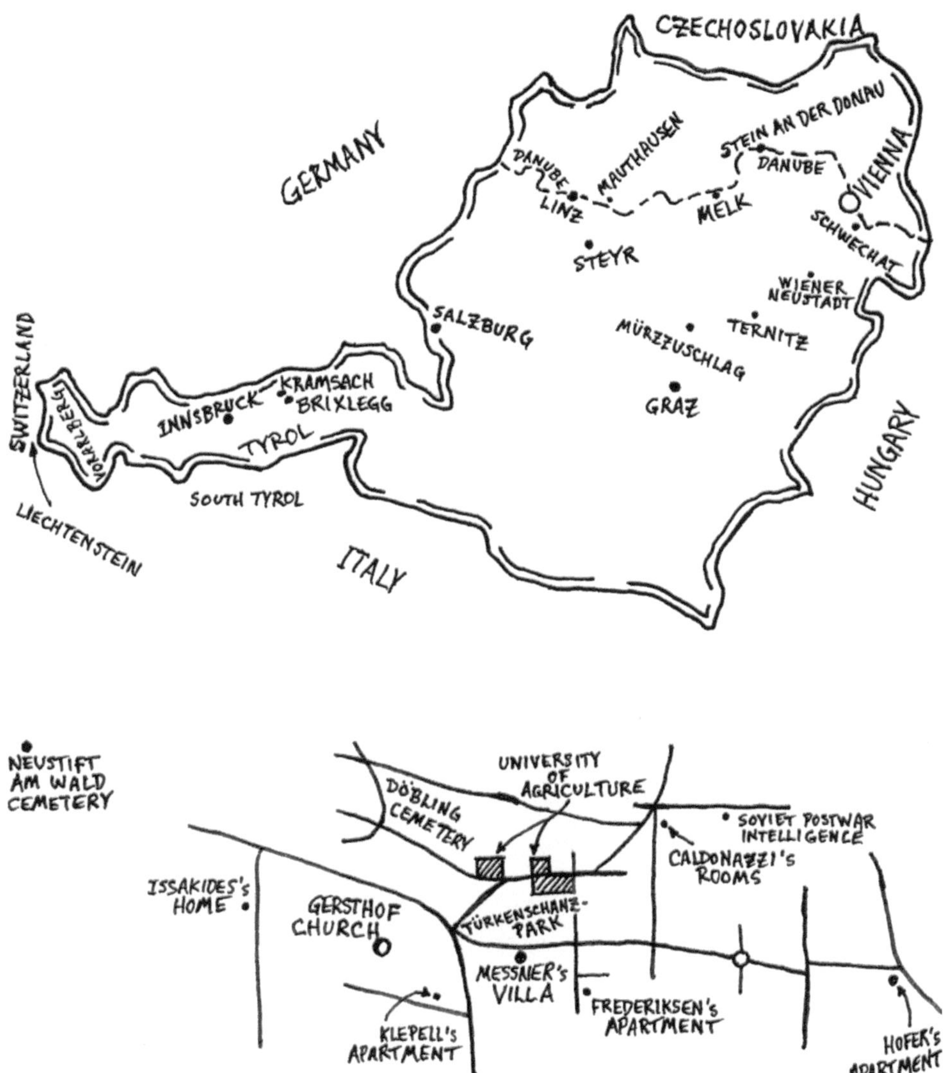

Top: Map of Austria, wartime borders; in the spring of 1939, Nazi Germany renamed the visible part of Czechoslovakia "The Protectorate of Bohemia and Moravia." _Bottom:_ Simplified map of a section of Vienna's 18th and 19th districts, centered on Türkenschanzpark (freehand sketches by the author; not to scale).

Noble deeds are most estimable when hidden.—Blaise Pascal[1]

Part One: The Communion of Nightfall

1

The Student

In April 1945, after the Soviet Red Army occupied Vienna, Harald Frederiksen was released from Gestapo confinement, only to be arrested by the city's new masters, snatched from his home at Gregor-Mendel-Strasse 26 in Vienna's 18th District, near a sprawling city park called Türkenschanz. The Soviets suspected that Frederiksen was an American spy, which he was, and that he had been left in the city to report on Red Army military activities and capabilities, which he had not.[1]

Unknown to the Soviets, Frederiksen's only clandestine duties had been to work against the Nazis. With the city's capitulation, those duties had expired, and with the closing of the city, Frederiksen's contact with the U.S. Office of Strategic Services, the forerunner of the Central Intelligence Agency, had been severed.

Soviet intelligence interrogated Frederiksen in appropriated offices at Chimanistrasse 21, fewer than 15 minutes by foot from his home, where his mother and sister, unaware of his physical closeness, worried yet again over his incarceration. Eventually, having extracted nothing of value from Frederiksen, the Soviets became less enthusiastic in their questioning, and then lost interest altogether. Perhaps the Soviets had begun to believe that Frederiksen was what he claimed—a hapless student, trapped with his sister and mother by the Anschluss, Nazi Germany's annexation of Austria in March 1938. They released him from custody but ordered that he restrict his movements to the city. Again a free man, Frederiksen immediately began looking for a way to escape to the West.[2]

In June 1945, he defied the Soviet order, slipped out of Vienna, and made his way up the Danube River. His first attempt to cross into the part of Austria controlled by the Western Allies failed, so he sneaked back a few miles down the Danube to Melk, a picturesque village nestled beneath a riverside promontory on which an ancient abbey stands. Here, Frederiksen came upon an Allied repatriation team that was looking for European and American prisoners of war, and sending them back home.[3]

Frederiksen asserted his citizenship, presented his papers, and was allowed to board a riverboat to Linz, where he spoke briefly to members of the U.S. Army Counter Intelligence Corps. CIC verified the basis of his story and shipped him farther west, to Salzburg, where he filed his first official report with the city's OSS contingent.[4]

Against all odds, this young university student had survived seven years in the Reich, in a city savagely disciplined by interrogation, torture, guillotine, firing squad, gallows, and gas chamber. Against all odds, he had thwarted the city's new overlords, the Red Army, who had also engaged in the odious ways of secret police forces, along with state-managed plunder and rapine. With these horrors and dangers behind him, with the prospect of family reunion before him, Frederiksen told his story to the OSS, from which he had received secret orders but whose officers he had never met until that day.[5]

Wartime photograph of Harald Frederiksen (courtesy Karsten Damen).

In the fall of 1944, Frederiksen reported, a sergeant in the German Army, the Wehrmacht, approached him. The sergeant's face was that of his dead friend, Fritz Molden.[6]

Molden had been reported as killed in action after partisans had ambushed his vehicle in the mountains of northern Italy, but Fritz, ever canny and resourceful, had staged his death and had stolen across the heavily guarded border of Switzerland.[7] Molden had then worked his way to an audience with the OSS chief in Bern, Allen Dulles, who some years after the war would become director of the CIA and, in an astonishing turn of events, Molden's father-in-law.[8]

Molden accomplished what few before him had: He convinced a wary Dulles that he was not one of the many opportunists who crossed OSS's threshold in those days, but that he was a true Austrian patriot. He was willing to work for OSS, to assume a Wehrmacht alias and to return to the Reich, where he would gather military, political, and industrial intelligence. He would also establish verifiable contact with what he claimed was a small but significant Austrian resistance movement called O5.[9]

Dulles and his staff had never heard of the group and were skeptical that it existed, but Molden asserted again that O5 was not only viable but was also eager for contact with the Western Allies.[10] The group's name, he explained, was derived from OE—the letter O and the fifth letter of the alphabet, E—a two-letter transcription substitute for special character Ö, which in this case stood for Österreich (Austria).[11] After the Anschluss, Nazi Germany referred to Austria as Ostmark, which translates as East Borderland (or, according to some sources, as Eastern March). In its name O5 expressed protest of this pejorative term and called for the restoration of an independent Austria, freed from Nazi domination.

Dulles and his officers assessed this brash young man and his claims, weighed the potential risks and payoffs of his proposal, and ultimately decided in his favor. Thereafter, Molden—designated as OSS agent K-28—traveled several times into Austria, and always did what he promised to do, and more. Over time, a deep trust grew between Dulles and Molden.[12]

In due course, Dulles assigned Molden a highly sensitive task. In 1943, Dulles explained, OSS had begun cooperating with a secret group in Vienna whose members were diverse—of virtually every political persuasion and from many different walks of life—but united in their staunch opposition to the Nazis. The group had collected and passed to the OSS all manner of intelligence, had engaged in anti–Nazi propaganda work, and had used ingenious methods to excuse conscientious objectors from front-line service in the Wehrmacht. Dulles referred to it as the "Messner Group," after one of its founding members, a Vienna-based industrialist named Franz Josef Messner.[13]

The group's cofounder, Dulles added, Catholic Curate Heinrich Maier, was equally as—if not more—important than Messner, for his unwavering morality and beliefs had defined the group's common purpose and had demanded loyalty among its sundry members. Maier, who held doctorates in scholastic philosophy and Catholic theology, was charismatic and eloquent, and enjoyed strong relationships with key figures from virtually every stratum of Viennese society.[14]

In fact, if not for Maier, there may well have never been a so-called Messner Group. The priest was the attractant that had drawn together the multifarious parts of the group, and his was the fair-minded philosophy that had kept it bound. His church was the group's crossroads, where dissimilar travelers could pass unnoticed and where, in the dark of night, Maier could preside over this secret communion of kindred souls.

With this preamble, Dulles let the other shoe drop: The group had been infiltrated and betrayed. The Gestapo had arrested about a dozen of the group's members, to include its primary couriers and some penetrations of the Wehrmacht and police. Everyone else had gone to ground, and OSS had lost all contact with the group. If you can, Dulles told Molden, use your contacts in Vienna to find the group's survivors, bring them into the umbrella resistance organization that you claim exists in Austria, and ascertain the fates of those who were arrested.[15]

And with that order, Frederiksen's fate was sealed, though at the time the young American was trying only to keep a low profile in Vienna, to avoid the Gestapo's brutal attention, and to continue secretly his medical studies, since Nazi authorities had barred him from attending classes.[16]

Audacious and brave, Molden once again crept across the border into his native Austria and used his fake orders to secure Wehrmacht transportation to Vienna. To address Dulles's special task, he enlisted the assistance of an old friend from his scrappy high school days before, during, and after the Anschluss. Molden had always been virulently opposed to the Austrian National Socialist Party, had attended anti–Nazi rallies, and had brawled in the streets of Vienna with Nazi-affiliated students. Not long after the Reich had annexed Austria, the Gestapo had arrested Molden, along with his young American friend.[17]

At the time the two boys were classmates at Döbling Grammar School and, though juveniles, they were held in the notorious "Liesl" prison, a nickname taken from Elisabeth-Promenade, the Habsburg-era appellation of the street fronting it.[18] After another serious brush with the Gestapo, and still more time in the Liesl, Molden secured an early release from prison by enlisting in a Wehrmacht punishment battalion, which after a brief period of training shipped out for the East.[19]

After dicey counterinsurgency work in the Pripet Marshes (in present-day Belarus and Ukraine) and subsequent other travels and adventures, to include fortuitous contact with Wehrmacht oppositionists, Molden was transferred to northern Italy. For Molden, as wartime assignments went, it was a plum job: He was fluent in Italian and had friends and relatives in the country. But it was not to last for long. When some of his past activities and associations began to surface and to cast suspicion on him, he fled into the mountains, where he planted his identity disc and papers on a Wehrmacht victim of a recent partisan ambush. Then, with great care and cunning, Molden sought out some of his Italian friends and, through them, the underground, which helped him to slip into Switzerland.[20]

So it was that Frederiksen found himself face to face with an old friend whom he thought he would never again see, and so it was that Frederiksen was indirectly tasked by OSS to find the remnants of the star-crossed Messner Group which, before its betrayal, was the OSS's most effective spy ring in Austria during the Second World War. To accomplish this difficult mission, Molden offered only one lead: a name, perhaps an alias—John Sekler.[21]

What follows is the story of that group, known to some historians as the Maier-Messner Group, to others as the Maier-Messner-Caldonazzi Group. (Walter Caldonazzi was a legitimist resistance figure who threw in his lot with Maier and Messner; he will be introduced later in this narrative.) During the war, a select few U.S. officials knew the group by its OSS codename, CASSIA, and it is chiefly using that name that this story will be told.

2

The Priest

Thirty-year-old Curate Heinrich Maier appeared often in a cassock, his black hair oiled and combed neatly back, his face serious, his eyes dark and penetrating. He was a man of abundant energy and, at Gersthof Parish Church in Vienna's posh 18th District, where he had lived and worked since September 1935,[1] he had earned the nickname "Hans Steam," to suggest a fully stoked locomotive thundering down the rails.[2] He was always willing to play football—soccer in the United States—with the parish's children, was always ready with a good joke, and always made time to listen to parishioners' concerns.[3]

During his first few years at Gersthof, Maier also taught religion at several Viennese preparatory high schools. But after the Anschluss, the Nazis abolished ecclesiastical instruction in Austria's secular schools, and by September 1938 Maier had lost his educational sideline.[4]

Maier's vows permitted only one mistress, the Gersthof Church, and she was a beauty. Built in the late 1800s, her architecture was common for the time—a hall-church design, in which nave and side aisles share almost the same ceiling height beneath a long, colonnade-supported roof. Gersthof's exterior was also typical for late 19th century Vienna: exposed red brick construction with a soaring bell tower. The tower's copper-sheathed spire was adorned with four clock faces, and its widened base served as the foyer of the main entrance.

The church dominated Bischof-Faber-Platz, looming over the square's stone-paved walkways, wood-slat benches, and leafy playground. From this central location, parishioners could hear the peals of the bell, calling them to mass, and could regularly synchronize their pocket watches with the tower's clocks. And it would be here that, unknown to all but a chosen few of his flock, Maier would trade furtive signals, hold discreet meetings, pore over stolen secrets, and dispatch international couriers.

In and around the church, the physical exertions of Hans Steam, while considerable, were nonetheless surpassed by the labors of his mind. In addition to his keen intellect, Maier also possessed finely honed instincts. He heard the drums of war early, long before most of his compatriots, and intuited that the coming conflict would be Austria's ruin.

Curate Heinrich Maier, circa late 1930s (from "Heinrich Maier" in *Gedenkbuch für die Opfer des Nationalsozialismus an der Universität Wien 1938*).

In the late 1930s Maier began to study for his second doctorate with the University of Vienna's Faculty of Catholic Theology. His approved dissertation topic—which he submitted in summer 1939—concerned the Catholic Church during the late Middle Ages.[5] On the surface Maier's research focused on the Church's struggle, at a time when plague, famine, and wars ravaged the world, to secure foundational religious rights from Europe's rulers. Beneath this scholarly veneer, though, Maier's study had great immediacy: He argued for the separation of church and state, and in so doing clearly advocated the preservation of the Church's independence. Maier's assertions, veiled thinly by historical reference, challenged the Nazis' intrusion into every facet of practical and spiritual life, and their routine disregard of basic human rights.[6]

But Maier's efforts went beyond the writing of academic allegory. By middle 1940 he had established contact with anti–Nazis of different—and in some cases opposing—persuasions. Using his vast and diverse religious, political, and social network, Maier linked up with various Catholic groups in Germany and Austria, with moderate members of Austria's rightwing Christian Social Party (known for its nationalism and for its leaders' anti–Semitic views), and with some prominent figures of the center-left Social Democratic Party of Austria.[7]

Of Maier's political associations, perhaps the most notable was the one that he forged with Felix Hurdes (1901–1974). Hurdes had been active

Gersthof Parish Church (taken by the author, 2016, from a vantage point near Döbling Cemetery).

in the Catholic youth movement and in political Catholicism before rising to a senior position in the Christian Social Party.[8] Between 1938 and 1945 the Nazis interned Hurdes twice in concentration camps for his vocal Austrian nationalism.[9] Because of his openly antagonistic relationship with the Reich, Hurdes may have been denied privileged access to intelligence, but his cooperation with Maier served to broaden the base of support for the priest's planned resistance activities.

But Maier didn't stop with his alliances in religious and political circles; he even managed to develop access to the Wehrmacht command in Vienna. Maier had long enjoyed a personal—and perhaps ecclesiastical—relationship with the family of Lieutenant General Heinrich Stümpfl (1884–1972), the Commandant of Vienna. Stümpfl, an officer after the Prussian model and as such deeply committed to his military duty, found

Nazi ideology distasteful. As Maier's friendship with the general grew, he revealed his intentions to mount an active resistance against the Nazis and to solicit help from the Allies abroad. Stümpfl not only approved of Maier's risky plans but also, as his high visibility would allow, passed Maier intelligence on the Wehrmacht's numbers, positions, status, and composition in Austria.[10]

With the exception of his friendship with Stümpfl, which because of the general's public profile was of limited utility, none of Maier's associations fostered any action; these religious and political groups seemed content only to discuss their opposition. So later that same year, Maier began looking for a new partner, for someone more aligned with his desire to follow ideas with deeds. In short order he found Franz Josef Messner, the director general of Semperit, a huge rubber company with branch offices throughout Europe.

Maier and Messner had first met in 1936 when Messner was attending a mass for a deceased relative at Gersthof Parish Church.[11] Messner's interest in Buddhism had sparked a conversation between them, which led to a sharing of ideas, then to an exchange of books, and finally to friendship.[12] Over time their discussions took a political turn. With the advent of the Anschluss, all lingering matters of Eastern philosophy were dropped in favor of more pressing concerns, and Maier confirmed that Messner numbered not among those who merely disapproved of the Nazis: He yearned to take decisive action against them.[13]

Messner was the perfect counterbalance to the humble, sociable priest. He was worldly, supremely confident, and bold. And Messner looked as if central casting had chosen him for the part. He was tall and broad-shouldered, with a bull neck and a shock of silver hair.[14] Here was a man, Maier thought, who had the courage and composure to face such hazards as would have made most others cower.

Messner's personal network of anti–Nazi sympathizers also complemented Maier's range of contacts. Messner's confidants—who included Semperit officials in Vienna, Budapest, and Istanbul—had access to the Reich's industrial, economic, and financial secrets. Perhaps his most unusual contact was Gusztáv Gratz (1875–1946),[15] a Habsburg legitimist who had once served as the Hungarian ambassador to Austria and briefly as the Hungarian Minister of Foreign Affairs.[16]

By the late 1930s Gratz had left public service and was working as the chief editor of a Budapest newspaper, but still enjoyed ready access to some senior government officials. In time Gratz would pay for his anti–Nazi activities. In spring 1944 after Germany had occupied Hungary, based on Gratz's suspected involvement in secret peace negotiations with the Allies, the Gestapo arrested him and shipped him to a concentration camp in Austria.[17]

Perhaps another reason that Messner and Maier formed a fast friendship was residential proximity. Messner lived a mere ten minutes' walk from Gersthof Church in an attractive 18th District villa at Hasenauerstrasse 61, which overlooked the duck ponds, winding paths, and profuse trees of Türkenschanzpark.

Messner's home was large and imposing, three stories towering over a manicured yard and garden, whose privacy was ensured by a tall, vine-laced wrought-iron fence. The house's mansard roof, plated with dark red tiles, had dormer windows spaced like gun ports below its hip. At the front of the house, the top of the foyer served as the floor of a long balcony with a sweeping view of the park. Even today one can easily imagine Messner standing there, arms akimbo, an expression of grim determination on his face, the fearless commander on the bridge of his ship as it plunged, inexorably, toward the rocks.

Unknown to Messner, a young American student, Harald Frederiksen, lived only a short stroll from his villa. But more than a few city blocks stood between them. Messner was 28 years older than Frederiksen, and they moved in very different social circles. Still, the two may well have passed one another on neighborhood sidewalks and on tree-lined pathways in the park, unaware that one day their destinies would converge.

At the villa and in the rectory, on the benches of Türkenschanzpark and in the booths of neighborhood coffee shops, Messner and Maier discovered, despite their many outward differences, that on the most important points they were likeminded: Both of them abhorred the Nazis and were ready to stop at nothing to eliminate this menace. When the inevitable war began, Maier confided in Messner, men of conscience would be required to do difficult, unpopular things, but such things would be necessary to spare innocent lives and to protect Austria's economic base, so that the country could be rebuilt to join again the civilized nations of the world.

Messner fully agreed, and then and there he threw in his lot with Maier, emphasizing for good effect that, as the trusted captain of a strategic industry of the Reich, he was also very well placed to follow through on his commitment. On this point Messner wasted no time in assembling "an intelligence network all over Central Europe through [his] personally picked managers of over twenty [Semperit] warehouses."[18]

While some of their neighbors were turning a blind eye to Nazi-orchestrated activities after the Anschluss, or were eagerly joining the party or the German military, or were assisting the Gestapo's ugly work, or were remaining indifferent to everything, Maier and Messner began secretly building a resistance organization. By 1942, they had established the group's core membership and had developed access to some key sources of intelligence. They were ready for action but still lacked one critical piece—contact with the Allied nations.

But Maier had a few ideas about how to remedy that deficiency.

3

The Communist

War often makes for strange bedfellows, none stranger than a man committed to celibacy and God, and a divorced woman committed to an atheistic ideology.

The woman was Viennese communist Helene Sokal,[1] who at 39 years old looked younger, and also quite bookish. Her short dark hair was usually parted and pinned back; her large, slightly downturned eyes seemed hesitant to meet another's; and her toothy smile hinted at a touch of awkwardness.

A critic of Austria's new Nazi regime, Karl Seitz, a former Social Democratic mayor of Vienna, facilitated contact between Maier's group and the leftist resistance organization to which Sokal and 62-year-old Theodor Legradi belonged. Seitz was acquainted with both Maier and Legradi, and thought that the two men's groups should be at least aware of one another, if not merged.[2]

Years later, however, Maier would tell the Gestapo a different story about his introduction to Legradi. In that version, Maier's uncle, Dr. Oskar Maier, a pharmaceutical scientist and the director of a Swiss-owned company in Prague, introduced him to his counterpart in Vienna, Legradi, probably in late 1941 or in early 1942. Maier added that in turn Legradi had introduced him to Sokal. Maier intimated that his uncle was unaware of his true reasons for wanting to meet Legradi; it seems that Maier was confident that he could both indemnify his uncle and lead his interrogators away from Seitz, who had already come to the Gestapo's attention. Regardless of the specific circumstances, the introduction between Maier and Legradi probably occurred in this general time-frame and resulted in a uniting of their two resistance groups.[3]

Sokal, a junior lawyer,[4] had assembled a coterie of excellent sub-sources committed to or at least sympathetic to the more radical elements of the leftist cause.[5] In addition to their political leanings, these sources were further spurred to action by Hitler's rabid anticommunism. In his book *Mein Kampf*, the Führer had singled out Marxism as the main enemy of Germany, and he even fused his two top nemeses when he wrote of the "Jewish doctrine of Marxism." Sokal's far-left associates and other contacts offered not only information of intelligence and propaganda value but would also prove crucial to Sokal's survival when the Gestapo began dismantling CASSIA.[6]

Among the most committed members of the Sokal-Legradi group was Eva Pawlin,[7] the wife of Communist Party of Austria (KPÖ) functionary (and metalworker) Theodor Pawlin, who was deeply involved in resistance activities and was the leader of KPÖ's organization in Lower Austria, the federal state that surrounds Vienna.[8] At some point the Gestapo got wise to Theodor's underground work and in early 1941 arrested him. In the fall of 1942, possibly around the time that the Sokal-Legradi and Maier groups were uniting, Theodor was convicted of treason, and he was guillotined on 15 January 1943.[9]

Eva was thus motivated to serve the cause of resistance by more than her ideology; she also yearned to avenge her husband's arrest and brutal interrogation, and later his death. Other members of the Sokal-Legradi group had seen kith and kin collared by the Gestapo, and were similarly inspired.

Legradi, a chemist[10] who had worked for Austria's "Epidemiology Service" during the First World War, was director of the Vienna branch of the Swiss company Wander AG, which was—and still is—known for its development and production of the drink Ovaltine (Ovomaltine in Continental Europe), but which was also involved in the pharmaceutical industry. Through his professional contacts, Legradi had developed access to the activities of the chemical industry in the Reich and to pharmaceutical research at the University of Vienna.[11]

One wartime German document asserted that Legradi had been born Theodor Pollack but at some point had changed his surname, and that because of this diversion his genealogy was uncertain. In Austria, the surname Pollack—spelled alternately Polack, Polak, and Poláček—is typically thought to be of Czech origin but to signify the presence of Polish ancestry. This same document further speculated that Legradi might have also been in possession of a Swiss passport. While the details of Legradi's ethnicity and citizenship were apparently quite fuzzy, his family status was described in clearer terms: He was married and had one adult son who was a businessman in Brazil.[12]

In summer 1942 Sokal secured permission from the Reich to visit

Switzerland—probably through Legradi's contacts with Wander's home office in Bern. Maier then drafted a message for Allied intelligence and instructed Sokal to memorize it. This was around the same time that 18-year-old Frederiksen learned of his acceptance into the University of Vienna Medical School, and he was unwittingly placed on an intersecting course with CASSIA.

When Sokal (possibly accompanied by Legradi) arrived in Switzerland, she followed Maier's guidance and sought out Catholic theologian Dr. Otto Karrer, whose political leanings and character Maier knew and trusted.[13] Once she had an audience with Karrer, Sokal recited the message and asked him to convey it to the "Anglo-Americans."[14]

Later, when pressed for a reason why he had selected Karrer, a man with no special connections, for such a delicate mission, Maier provided the history of his interaction with the man, intimating that he had chosen him because he'd had no other ready alternatives for contact on neutral soil. Maier explained that back in 1939 he had traveled to Switzerland to explore the possibility of studying at the University of Geneva. During the trip, he had visited Lucerne, where he had sought out Karrer, a theological writer of some standing and whose work he admired. Although Maier claimed that they had not discussed politics, he admitted that Karrer had expressed his concern for Austrians who had been forced into Swiss exile after the Anschluss. In the end Maier was allegedly left with the impression that Karrer might be sympathetic to anti–Nazi causes.[15]

The message that Sokal carried to Karrer was simple, cautious, and short on specifics, but still effectively conveyed its point—a diverse but united resistance group existed in Austria and was ready to act: "Mutual suffering has brought the Austrian nation to the point of overcoming its ideological differences. The parties, on both the left and the right, now find themselves on a common platform. They all support an independent and democratic Austria. We will be ready, once the war is over, to take our place in the newly ordered European family of nations and wait for your call as soon as the time is right."[16]

As Sokal had requested, Karrer delivered this message to the British Consulate in Lucerne, for onward passage to Sir Stafford Cripps, whom Sokal had misidentified as the British Foreign Minister. (During the war Cripps served as British Ambassador to the Soviet Union and Minister of Aircraft Production, but never as Foreign Minister.) Sokal also asked Karrer to pass a copy to Soviets, for delivery to Soviet Foreign Minister Vyacheslav Molotov.[17]

In the future, however, other members of CASSIA of different political persuasions were to feel no such compunction to include the Soviets. In fact, in the coming years Messner would worry that Soviet influence over the Austrian resistance was too great and should be countered by the Western Allies.[18]

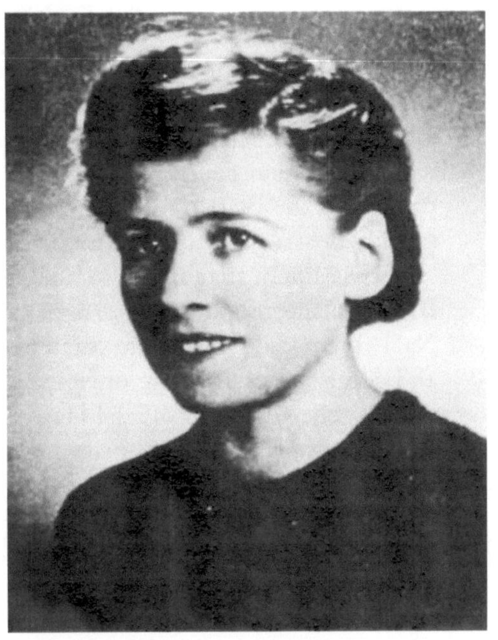
Helene Sokal (Zentrales Parteiarchiv of KPÖ; used with the permission of Alfred Klahr Gesellschaft).

London later acknowledged receipt of the message with a BBC radio broadcast of *Sendung für Österreich* ("transmission for Austria"). During the war BBC's External Services sent many such messages to resistance groups throughout Europe, often beginning them with the signature line "This is London calling…." Then, on at least one Wednesday evening beginning in late October 1942, BBC sent the Austrians a follow-up phrase, which Sokal had devised and also passed to Karrer: *Mai zuerst 1942* ("May 1st, 1942," which was—not surprisingly for Sokal—International Workers' Day), presumably as a simple reassurance that the Allies were still interested in engaging with the group.[19]

After the war Sokal claimed that the group had never established contact with the Soviets, and that "when we later reconstructed the events of that time, we found no evidence that the message had ever been delivered to Moscow."[20] However, an OSS cable dated 5 February 1944 recorded an antipodal perspective: "The group [CASSIA] already has received a number of Russian liaison officers, who are working with them."[21]

As for the British, it appears that, other than sending radio messages, they did not pursue direct contact with the group. (Please see Appendix II for details on a group member's efforts in 1943 to engage the British.) During the war, British military and intelligence officials in Switzerland assumed that most volunteers from the Reich were provocateurs.

The British had good reason to suspect treachery. For example, in November 1939, the Germans captured two British intelligence officers who had been lured to a meeting near Venlo, The Netherlands, with operatives posing as German military opponents of Hitler. Hitler then used the "Venlo Incident" to buttress his claim that Britain was behind an assassination attempt against him, and to justify his invasion of The Netherlands, which had been neutral, in the spring of the following year.[22] Because of this reflex, the British turned away many such volunteers—some of whom quickly beat a path to the Americans' door.[23]

It is likely that many, if not most, of these volunteers were, as the British suspected, opportunists or fabricators or information-peddlers or Nazi-directed double agents, each with his or her own goals, some personal and some national, some obvious and some obscure. However, a few of them, such as Abwehr official Hans Bernd Gisevius and German Ministry of Foreign Affairs official Fritz Kolbe, after being spurned by the British in Switzerland, turned to OSS, specifically to Allen Dulles, and proved not only to be genuine but also to be incredibly valuable sources of intelligence on the Reich.[24] So too would be the case with CASSIA.

In an 8 May 1944 secret cable, Allen Dulles summed up the situation as follows: "I have the feeling from my dealings with Zulu [the British] that their services, because of the leg-pulling they suffered in gloomy times of 1940–1941, are unaware on occasion of the degree to which the situation has been reversed, even in the field of intelligence. Several of my finest sources would have been lost to me had I pursued their course."[25] Lending credence to Dulles's claims, according to the official history of the OSS, British intelligence recognized that in at least one case its loss had been OSS-Bern's gain when it "rated [agent Fritz Kolbe] the best intelligence source of the war."[26]

Maier was undaunted by British and Soviet indifference. If they weren't interested in the group's services, maybe another of the Allies would be.

4

The Musician

For the second attempt at contacting the Allies, Maier decided to use a new courier: Barbara Issakides.

Like Messner, Issakides was Maier's neighbor. She lived at Scheibenbergstrasse 61,[1] a few blocks from "Saint Leopold," as Maier's Gersthof Parish Church was also known. Issakides, a respected concert pianist, performed recitals around Europe. Issakides's musical pedigree was impeccable. She had trained at the *Wiener Musikakademie*, the Viennese Academy of Music, under such eminent teachers as Viktor Ebenstein (1888–1968), Emil von Sauer (1862–1942), and Friedrich Wührer (1900–1975).[2] As for her literal pedigree, she was a member of an ethnically Greek family that had founded a successful rug store,[3] Orient-Teppiche Issakides, at Fleischmarkt 13 in Vienna's 1st District, tucked in beside the old Holy Trinity Greek Orthodox Church.[4]

After the war, though she often refused—politely—to speak about her resistance activities, in the late 1970s an American author managed to interview Issakides and to see photographs of her from the CASSIA years. He described her as having had a classic Grecian face and raven hair with a shock of white running through it. This description—together with such observations as "striking," "darkly regal," and "possessed of extraordinary presence"[5]—contrasts with pictures of Issakides in old age, in which she looked more like a slightly plump grandmother, a kind smile on her lips, her thick silver hair pulled back and neatly coifed.

As with most other members, Issakides came to CASSIA through Curate Maier, whose boundless energy made him a familiar figure in the neighborhoods around the Gersthof Parish Church. Issakides had no particular interest in politics but found the Nazis and their ideology distasteful.[6] Recognizing the great potential in her ability to travel

The Issakides family home, Scheibenbergstrasse 61 (taken by the author, 2016).

internationally, Maier, in his inimitable way, sniffed out Issakides's true feelings about Hitler's regime, which for furtherance of her musical career she certainly kept hidden, and then he recruited her into CASSIA.[7] And it was Maier who, as part of his plans to send a second message to the Allies, introduced Issakides to Messner,[8] who had identified a new prospective intermediary for the group in Switzerland.[9] Before long, in addition to a natural disdain for the Nazis, other motivations grew within Issakides: deep admiration for and stubborn devotion to these two men.[10]

Issakides, Maier thought, would make an excellent emissary for the group, and so too would Messner, since he routinely traveled outside the Reich, visiting Semperit's European offices and foreign firms with which his company maintained trading and financing arrangements. Together, they could serve as CASSIA's intelligence conduit and its lifeline to the Allies.[11]

According to Maier's plan, when a natural opportunity arose, one or both of them would travel to Switzerland and would establish contact with the Allies. Then, Messner and Issakides—and perhaps suitable others—would execute the terms of what Maier hoped would be the resulting agreement: the delivery of high-level intelligence to Western intelligence services, which would strive to guide American and British bombing missions to war-related industries and other military targets; and in return, CASSIA would ask the Allies to spare civilians and civilian life-support infrastructure.[12]

Maier's quiet patience paid off. Issakides told him that, in November 1942, she would perform a program of Chopin compositions at a concert in Switzerland, and that she was willing to use this trip to advance the group's cause. It was an ideal opportunity, Maier thought, to deliver another message to the Allies.[13] He immediately began to prepare Issakides for the task—helping her to memorize the lines that he had drafted, and giving her instructions on how to make contact with the new intermediary.

Later, in Zurich, after a well-received performance, Issakides slipped out of the theater and made her way to Austrian Kurt Grimm's apartment in the Hotel Bellerive au Lac, which gazed over the northern end of the city's scenic lake. The hotel was—and still is—a five-minute stroll south of the Zurich Opera House, where Issakides may have performed that night. Grimm, a wealthy expatriate lawyer licensed to practice in Switzerland, was a prominent (and slightly chubby) figure in the country's Austrian émigré community.[14]

Once she had a private audience with Grimm, Issakides delivered Maier's message—apparently similar to the first message, but with a more explicit offer to provide intelligence on the Reich and a more specific request for subsequent clandestine contact. Issakides asked Grimm to pass the message to the Western Allies.[15]

Grimm was the perfect choice for this task. He had corresponded with Allen Dulles before the war, when both men were practicing attorneys, and had been one of Dulles's most trusted interlocutors since the OSS chief's very first days in Switzerland. But Grimm was more than a confidant: He maintained well-placed sources in Austria and routinely provided valuable intelligence from them during his long discussions with Dulles.[16]

When he was in his middle thirties, Grimm had emigrated from Austria to Switzerland in 1938, the year of the Anschluss, and for the next seven years he dedicated himself to working against the Nazis.[17] In the summer of 1944 Grimm formalized his role in the Austrian resistance when he co-founded O5's *Verbindungsstelle Schweiz*—the Swiss Liaison Office.[18] This Zurich-based post, which after the war the OSS described as having opened in late 1944, seems to have primarily operated a courier service, facilitating the exchange—with Swiss oversight—of messages between the Western Allies and resistance-minded Austrians.[19]

For the pianist's part in this intrigue, she had knocked on Grimm's door not by luck but by design. The exact sequence of events that preceded Issakides's trip to Zurich differs among primary accounts and secondary analyses, but the following version appears to be likely: Earlier in Vienna, one of Messner's close business associates, Josef Joham, the director of large Austrian bank Creditanstalt-Bankverein,[20] had disclosed to Messner that Grimm, a former Creditanstalt employee, was cooperating with the Western Allies in Switzerland. Once Joham was convinced that Messner and his cohorts were willing to play an active role in the defeat of Nazi Germany, he had contacted Grimm, vouching for the group's intentions and advising him that one of its emissaries—Issakides or Messner—would soon attempt to make contact with him in Zurich.[21]

Joham's presumptive revelation to Messner about Grimm's secret work would not have been foolhardy. Joham and Messner had known each other for years and had engaged in a broad range of confidential business matters. They had met in the 1930s before Messner had taken command of Semperit, when Messner had been working with Creditanstalt to restructure and modernize the company.[22] During this time Messner may have also become acquainted with Grimm, who was then serving as a senior advisor to Joham.[23] So effective was Messner's renovation of Semperit that later he was named its general director,[24] a position that put him on more equal footing with and in the same sphere of influence as Joham. (After the Anschluss and the Third Reich's subsequent takeover of several vast Jewish-owned companies, to include Creditanstalt from the Vienna branch of the Rothschild family, Semperit was ranked as the second largest company in Austria.[25]) As a consequence of their dealings, Messner and Joham had developed a relationship founded, at least in part, on mutual trust.

Joham was one of only two senior executives at Creditanstalt whom the Nazis had retained after their purge of the company in 1938.[26] But in him they had not chosen wisely. Joham, who remained in Vienna throughout the war, served as one of Grimm's sources, and thus one of OSS-Bern's sources, on the Reich's finances and industries. In 1943 Dulles assigned Joham—whose surname in some OSS records appears as "Johan"—code number 680,[27] thereby officially recognizing him as a regular source of intelligence.[28]

One prominent Austrian historian observed that Joham had cooperated—through Grimm—with the Allies prior to the Moscow Declaration of 1943, which "reminded" Austria that "the final settlement" of the war would consider any role that Austrians played in their own liberation.[29] So even before the tide of the war had definitively changed in favor of the Allies, Joham was passing intelligence on "strategic bombing targets and on the effect of bombing raids on armament-related industrial sites."[30]

Issakides and Grimm took to the grave the details of exactly what happened during their first meeting, but this much is known: Grimm received Issakides in his quarters and accepted from her Maier's message to the Allies; he agreed to meet again with Issakides, Messner, or other members of the group who traveled to Switzerland; and after the meeting, he passed Maier's message to OSS-Bern chief Allen Dulles.

What happened after Dulles received the message, however, is a matter of historical record: The OSS stepped onto a path that would lead to its best intelligence-gathering operation in Austria, and the members of CASSIA stepped onto a path that would lead to catastrophe.

Part Two: The Confession of Splinters

5

The Merchant

Late in the summer of 1943 Issakides returned to Switzerland, but she was not alone. Messner went with her. And this time she carried more than another cautious message from Maier. Issakides and Messner, taking a weighty but worthy risk, smuggled a batch of high-level tactical and strategic intelligence out of the Reich.[1]

For his part, Messner likely traveled on a business-trip pretext to visit Rubber Investment AG in Zurich, which was part of the Semperit Group of companies.[2] Issakides's stated purpose for leaving Austria probably concerned her schedule of international performances.

Meanwhile, back in Vienna, 19-year-old Frederiksen was becoming acquainted with a fellow medical student who was working with a Yugoslav resistance group. Through this student and other resistance members, Frederiksen began developing contacts in the underground that would later qualify him to go looking for the survivors of "The Messner Group."

For this dangerous mission to Switzerland, Issakides's partner was ideal—urbane, world-wise, and unflappable. Born in Austria's western state[3] of Tyrol, Messner was a man with an exotic past. After serving as an officer in the First World War, he pursued an itinerant career in business, working in Vienna, Innsbruck, and Dakar, Senegal. Then, in 1925, he moved to the Brazilian state of São Paulo, where he assiduously studied and invested in the coffee industry.[4]

A year later, having earned a reputation as a coffee expert, Messner returned to Vienna and opened a business that specialized in importing a variety of goods from Brazil. Shortly thereafter he co-founded and held one-third interest in a second firm, *Brasil-Kaffee-Gesellschaft* (Brazil Coffee Company). Messner and his partners spared no expense on this company's location. It was sited in the city center on Stephansplatz, fronting ancient

Saint Stephen's Cathedral, whose intricate Gothic architecture and soaring south tower—which rises almost 450 feet (more than 135 meters) above the square—dominate and define the Viennese skyline.[5]

Franz Josef Messner, circa 1940 (courtesy Volker Sartorti).

Also in 1926 Messner increased his direct investments in Brazil, purchasing a coffee plantation, cotton and castor bean farms, livestock, and an orange grove in Pedra de Guaratiba, a neighborhood in western part of Rio de Janeiro. So enamored had Messner become of his adopted country and apparently it of him that in 1928 he began service as Brazil's honorary consul and commercial attaché. And to consummate the affair, in 1931 he was naturalized as a Brazilian citizen.[6]

Like his friend Curate Maier, Messner was also a man of letters. In his thirties he had gone back to school and, drawing on his work experience, had written a dissertation on coffee production in the Brazilian state of São Paulo.[7] The University of Vienna accepted Messner's thesis, and on 2 July 1934 he received his doctorate.[8] Henceforth his name would appear on many documents as Dr. Messner or with the *Eszett* replacing the double S as Dr. Meßner.

That same year, 1934, Messner began working as a top-flight industrial consultant on the restructuring of several Austrian companies that had been rocked by the Great Depression and were in desperate need of modernization if they were to survive. Messner quickly earned a reputation for being fair, efficient, and effective in this difficult work, and in 1936 he was hired by Creditanstalt-Bankverein—in other words, by the bank's director, Josef Joham—to restructure and renovate Semperit, of which Creditanstalt was majority shareholder.[9] So successful was Messner's overhauling of Semperit that in 1937 he was named its director general and was awarded a yearly income equivalent in 2016 purchasing power to more than U.S.$650,000.[10] Semperit was a vast concern, operating seven large plants and a score of warehouses from Duisburg in far western Germany to Krakow in southern Poland.[11] Messner was now counted among the most powerful industrialists of Austria.

In a time defined by great austerity and frequent inattention to labor rights, Messner immediately set to work improving his employees' working conditions. He ordered the construction of modern lavatories and a well-equipped cafeteria and infirmary; he founded an on-site company park; he offered health insurance (which was extended to employees in all Semperit subsidiaries) and childcare; and he instituted wage reforms.[12]

But Messner didn't spend all of his time behind his desk, hunched over blueprints, ledgers, proposals, and internal memoranda. In early June 1939, at the behest of the Reich Ministry of Economy, Messner returned to Brazil, supposedly flying a leg of the trip on a Zeppelin dirigible.[13] (Messner may have taken a European flight of the *Graf Zeppelin II*, which left service in August 1939. Germany completed its last airship flight to South America in 1937.) In the Amazonian city of Manaós (now called Manaus), with the help of a local German expatriate named Carlos Dreyer,[14] Messner negotiated a deal under whose terms Germany purchased 3,000 metric tons (about 3,300 U.S. tons) of natural rubber, a resource critical to Germany's war machine, and arranged for its shipment to Germany by sea.[15]

At the time of Messner's visit, Brazil was still neutral and traded equally with both Allied and Axis powers. It was not until 1942 that, after a series of moves that favored the Allies, Brazil first severed diplomatic ties with the Axis powers and then, after German U-boats sank several Brazilian ships, declared war on them.[16]

Messner remained in Brazil for a few months, probably checking on his investments, basking in the sun, and sipping caipirinha cocktails. In 1940, his business and leisure in the southern hemisphere concluded, he boarded Italian steamer *Conte Grande*[17] bound for Europe. In the mid–Atlantic the French—which, along with the British, had declared war on Germany in September 1939—captured the vessel, impounded it at the colonial Port of Casablanca, and arrested Messner. Perhaps around this same time, Messner's precious shipload of rubber was sent to the bottom of the sea, courtesy of British or French naval action.[18] Given Messner's anti–Nazi predilections, he was certainly not heartbroken that all of his hard work in Amazonia had come to naught.

In Casablanca—according to one account—Messner was tried (presumably for arranging the sub-rosa rubber deal between Brazil and Germany), convicted, and sentenced to death.[19] Another version of the story suggests only that he was held for 30 days in a Casablanca prison and another ten days in a "desert fort"—a reference that hints of a Foreign Legion outpost.[20] But both accounts agree that, after France signed her armistice with Germany on 22 June 1940, Messner was freed from captivity.

Messner was whisked by airplane from Casablanca to Spain, where he was reunited with his wife, known by the crisp sobriquet "Franka," but whose birth name would have daunted even the voluble—Melchia

Franz Josef and Franka Messner's villa, Hasenauerstrasse 61, Vienna (taken by the author, 2016).

Franziska Theresia Kristinus.[21] The couple then flew back to Vienna, and by middle August 1940 Messner was again sitting in the Semperit director-general's chair, which was probably leather, overstuffed, and parked behind a massive and elegant hardwood desk. In a stroke of luck that would help his clandestine endeavors, Messner discovered that his ordeal in Morocco had bolstered his pro–Axis credentials.[22]

There is speculation that Messner may not have been only a worldly and adventurous man, but also a ladies' man. Some accounts suggest that Issakides and Messner had, at least by the time of their joint visit to Switzerland, begun a love affair.[23] Issakides, in her late twenties, was single but Messner, in his late forties, with no children, had been married since 1922 to the aforementioned Franka, who was three years his junior.[24] A Third Reich document from the fall of 1944 seems to be one source of this conjecture. In it Messner is described as having "mastered the piano keys from top to bottom," which may be a ribald metaphor of his alleged relationship with Issakides.[25] However, this and other references are unsubstantiated, ambiguous, and open to interpretation; they do not—and probably cannot—specify if the relationship was in fact romantic, or if the couple used the appearance of an affair to explain their traveling together, as cover to conceal their clandestine agenda for CASSIA.

In Switzerland the couple retraced Issakides's steps a few months before to Grimm's apartment in Zurich's Hotel Bellerive au Lac. Innuendo has also suggested, again without substantiation, that this hotel was the rendezvous for the romantic liaisons of Messner and Issakides.[26]

What Issakides and Messner accomplished during this trip was preserved in a Gestapo report, drafted less than a year later: "In September 1943, Maier and Messner decided to divulge further details on the [Reich's] main armament factories to the enemy powers, on the one hand to demonstrate the Austrian resistance's contributions to an [eventual] Allied victory and on the other to prevent the enemy air force's destruction of industries important for peacetime production and the destruction of demilitarized cities."[27]

The Gestapo was spot on about the intentions of Maier and Messner, but a bit off target on the date, possibly because those CASSIA members under interrogation in the middle of 1944 were attempting to obfuscate one of the group's biggest intelligence coups: the timely provision to OSS of crucial intelligence that, on the night of 17/18 August 1943, had helped almost 600 British bombers—in a mission called Operation HYDRA—to strike the V-weapons facility at Peenemünde on the Baltic Sea.[28]

The raid's damage may have set back V-weapon development and production by only a matter of weeks, but that delay was sufficient to ensure that the Germans would be unable to use these weapons to target the buildup to and the execution of the Allies' massive D–Day operation. In fact, the first V-1 fell on London on 13 June 1944, a full week after the commencement of landings at Normandy.[29]

Founded in the late 1930s under a slightly different name, the Peenemünde Army Experimental Establishment (*Heeresversuchsanstalt Peenemünde*, or HVP) was located on the Baltic Sea island of Usedom. HVP designed, developed, and tested Nazi Germany's advanced *Vergeltungswaffen* or "vengeance weapons," which included the V-1, the world's first combat-deployed cruise missile, and the V-2, the world's first long-range guided ballistic missile.[30] These were the kinds of futuristic weapons that could well alter the course of the war, and as such were among the highest priority targets for the Allies.

CASSIA's first confession to the Allies had contributed to turning parts of this remote top-secret facility into smoldering piles of splinters. And it was a portent of similar things to come.

Although CASSIA focused on intelligence that could inform aerial bombing missions, its members occasionally stumbled across other bewildering types of information. As a case in point, at one of his first meetings with Grimm, Messner reported that large numbers of Jews were being executed at a concentration camp called Auschwitz-Birkenau.[31] At the time the Allies were just beginning to understand that the Auschwitz camps were methodically murdering people, but not until war's end would the staggering body count be revealed: more than one million souls, about 90 percent of whom were Jewish. In fact, the Nazis had designated Auschwitz-Birkenau, also called Auschwitz II, the very camp that Messner had highlighted, a death camp—a facility designed expressly for systematic mass executions.

This camp, Messner said, was part of a network in Poland that included Monowitz, where German chemical conglomerate IG Farben had built a synthetic rubber factory, which operated with slave labor. Through his access to Reich rubber production, Messner explained, he had learned about Monowitz and the rest of the Auschwitz complex. Supposedly, when Grimm passed this report to Dulles's office, because of the great scale and ghastly nature of the activities it described, Messner's information was initially met with disbelief.[32]

These insights might have been new to some of the Allies, but not to

Messner. He was already quite familiar with the plight of Europe's Jewish population. Not only was he aware of the mass murders at Auschwitz, but he was also resisting pressure to surrender Jewish members of his own workforce to the Nazis. By the fall of 1942, months before he met with Grimm, Messner's correspondence with Third Reich officials suggested that, on the surface, he was toeing the party line with regard to Semperit's remaining half-Jewish employees: Messner noted that, per Nazi directives, he had limited the authority of those workers and had not allowed any of them to transfer to Semperit offices or subsidiary companies abroad.[33]

But the flashing subtext of Messner's assertions was that he was still employing half-Jewish employees in Vienna and other countries at a time when many people with even fractional Jewish ancestry were either in or en route to concentration camps. Probably by demonstrating that these workers were crucial to Semperit's continued production of strategic materials, which included not only processed natural rubber but also *buna*,[34] a copolymer synthetic rubber, Messner had successfully avoided having at least some of his ethnically Jewish subordinates fall victim to the Holocaust.

At the meeting in Zurich, Messner told Grimm that this first tranche of reports revealed only part of what the group was doing. It had also been secretly drafting, printing, and distributing anti-Nazi leaflets. These were very risky activities that put the group's members in the streets, laden with incriminating documents; if caught *in flagrante delicto*, they would suffer extremely harsh penalties. Messner then provided a few examples of this propaganda. Some fliers denounced Hitler and his henchmen as "traitors of the German people" and called Hitler's militarism the "shame of our century."[35]

While incidental collection of intelligence and the distribution of propaganda were important, Messner acknowledged, the group wanted to begin operating more deliberately.[36] Some CASSIA members had access to, or could develop access to, key strategic industries beyond Messner's rubber company: steelworks that were producing arms and ball bearings, and factories that were building tanks and aircraft. Messner's claims were not mere rhetoric; in the coming months, he would follow through on his promise, and would provide to the Allies sketches of and production figures for all of those industries.[37]

But, as always, the devil was in the details—how to get such intelligence into Allied hands securely and in a timely fashion, so that bombing missions could act upon it. But it was Messner this time, not Maier, who had an idea for meeting those exigencies. His idea was excellent, but it would prove to be not only a solution but also the group's undoing.

6

Intelligence Esoterica—A Brief Analysis of Intelligence Reporting on Peenemünde

Details on intelligence gathering before the attack on Peenemünde differ among historical references.

Some accounts suggest that Dulles pieced together the facts on the Peenemünde facility from three different sources: Abwehr penetration Hans Bernd Gisevius, Messner, and a scientist whom Grimm had recruited, Ernst Kraus, the director of the Vienna office of Siemens-Schuckert, a German electrical engineering company that would be integrated into Siemens AG about two decades after the war. (Like Joham, Kraus may have also passed intelligence directly to his friend Messner. One of Messner's established sub-sources, OSS codename CARNATION, may be identifiable with Kraus.[1]) According to this version, in May 1943 Gisevius provided general information on Germany's development of a rocket-propelled missile, Messner provided drawings of and technical details on the V-2 ballistic missile, to include its speed and the explosive yield of its warhead, and Kraus noted that Siemens-Schuckert had delivered components to a district called Peenemünde on the island of Usedom in the Baltic Sea.[2]

OSS-Bern's stream of reporting on V-weapons began in early February 1943 when agent 490—German businessman Walter Bovari—reported that the Germans were producing a new secret weapon. Bovari described the device as a "flying contraption perhaps in the form of an aerial torpedo," for which he suspected one of his factories in Germany was providing a small part.[3] Although at the time the report appeared little more than fodder for the credulous, in the U.S. War Department's official history of the OSS, Bovari—who was described not as a German but as a "Swiss industrialist"—is credited with providing the very first intelligence on the V-1 flying bomb to the Allies.[4]

In late May 1943 Abwehr officer Gisevius offered some much-needed clarification. According to the OSS's official history, "the Germans had developed what [Gisevius] understood to be a new heavy missile employing the rocket principle" and the weapon was in "limited production somewhere in Pomerania." Then, in late June 1943, "Gisevius and another source [not further identified] brought details on the rocket [to Dulles], and an Austrian source [Kraus or Messner] fixed the location of the assembly plant and testing ground at Peenemuende."[5] An "Austrian source," possibly the same agent who specified the facility's location, was also credited with providing "much of the technical information on the rockets."[6]

In a classified message dated 24 June 1943, citing a previous report, Dulles reported details on the German rocket's dimensions, weight, propellant, and manufacturers, and on the location of the rocket's assembly and testing facility—"in Pomerania at Tpeonemuende [Peenemünde] between Greifswald and Swinemuende [present-day Swinoujscie, Poland]"—which is exactly where the facility was. Dulles attributed these crucial details to "a well placed but non-technical source," who, through cross-referencing cables, the editor of this historical collection concluded was Gisevius, agent 512.[7]

While Gisevius did, in fact, provide locational information—"Pomerania," as noted earlier—it seems less likely that he also had access to precise scientific data on the V-weapons program. The source of this information instead smells much more like either Kraus or Messner, though of the two only Messner would qualify as a "non-technical source." Furthermore, these were the same details—the V-2 rocket's dimensions, weight, propellant mixture, and component manufacturers, along with some refinement and amplification—that CASSIA would submit a few weeks later, in September 1943, to a different OSS office.[8]

If one takes these points into account, the presumptive attribution of the report to Gisevius, while accurate from an archive-analysis perspective, is perhaps misleading. Dulles may have purposefully obfuscated the true source as an added security measure; he may well have blended information from three—or more—sources when drafting that report (this option seems quite likely); or he may have simply made a mistake. A final possibility is that CASSIA's contributions to the Peenemünde targeting package were comparatively minor, although one could argue effectively that there is sufficient direct and circumstantial evidence to dismiss any such exclusionary verdict.[9]

Subsequent declassification regimes have suggested that additional human sources (both British and American), aerial reconnaissance, and code-breaking operations contributed substantially to the pinpointing of Peenemünde. However, it is a matter of historical record that Dulles's report of 24 June 1943 contained not only the weapon's specifications, but also the accurate location of its assembly and testing facility.

Even with mounting evidence from diverse quarters, British intelligence agency MI6 still suspected that Dulles's sources were part of a clever German disinformation campaign designed to waste Allied time and resources. The British continued to adhere to a statement they had first made on 29 April 1943: "It is clear that a heavy long-range rocket is not an immediate threat."[10]

This statement was in some respects true, in that German V-weapons wouldn't be fully operational and available in large numbers for more than a year. However, from an intelligence-collection perspective, based on the fact that the British had no forthcoming deterrent, the Germans' rapidly progressing rocket program was not only an "immediate threat"—which in jargon implies the impending possibility of harm—but also, particularly in the case of London, it represented an imminent and immutable reality.

There was some postwar squabbling about which Allied source provided the most critical piece of the Peenemünde puzzle, but after the passage of so many years it now seems that there is more than enough credit for everyone who played a role. Regardless of who deserves the grandest accolades, in terms of Dulles's contributions, which should be shared with CASSIA, Gisevius, and Kurt Grimm's sub-sources, after the war U.S. President Harry S. Truman awarded Dulles the Medal of Merit—at the time the highest civilian decoration in the U.S.—in part for his wartime reporting from Bern on the location of the Peenemünde V-2 rocket-production facility.[11]

7

The Forester

Messner was the first but not the only Tyrolean to join CASSIA. In late 1942 or early 1943 Maier met forestry engineer Walter Caldonazzi. But unlike Messner, who strode confidently onto the stage of international intrigue, with silver mane flashing in the lights, Caldonazzi, his dark hair just beginning to thin up front, limped along the backdrop, bracing against a cane.[1]

In addition to cutting a different figure, 27-year-old Caldonazzi also brought another political perspective to the group. He and some of his fellow members of Amelungia, an Austrian Catholic student fraternity, were so-called legitimists who yearned to restore the monarchy under Otto von Habsburg (1912–2011), the heir apparent of the family dynasty that had once ruled the Austro-Hungarian Empire and an enemy of the Reich who lived in exile in the United States. In practical terms, though, some of these legitimists harbored a less hardline monarchist perspective, and also endorsed the administration of former Chancellor Engelbert Dollfuss that had ruled from 1932 until 1934.[2]

In 1933, about a year after becoming chancellor, as Austria's political situation became increasingly unstable, the diminutive Dollfuss, a member of the conservative Christian Social Party, dissolved the parliament, outlawed the Austrian Nazi party, and began to impose an autocratic regime. In May 1934, after implementing an authoritarian constitution, Dollfuss assumed full dictatorial powers, which marked the beginning of Austrofascism. Dollfuss's moves outraged Austrian Nazis and frustrated their political ambitions, and in response they assassinated him on 25 July 1934 during an attempted coup d'état.[3]

That some members of Amelungia would consider Dollfuss's political lineage to be a suitable alternative was only natural. The late chancellor, one of Austria's first victims of Nazi aggression, had belonged to affiliated Catholic fraternities during his schooldays.[4]

With these two Tyroleans in the ranks of CASSIA, and others poised to join, a digression from the storyline is warranted, to provide a touch of salient background on this region, whose scenery is reminiscent of that portrayed in the 1965 film *The Sound of Music*, which was set in and around Salzburg, some 30 miles—50 kilometers—northeast of the Tyrolean state boundary. But first a few orienting words about the family roots of Caldonazzi and Messner.

Caldonazzi was born in 1916 in Mals, sometimes spelled Malles, a German-majority town in the region known as South Tyrol, which until the First World War was part of Austria, but which later was ceded to Italy.[5] After the war, Caldonazzi's father, Rudolf, a gendarmerie sergeant in Mals, moved the family to Kramsach, a town in Austrian North Tyrol.[6]

Caldonazzi attended high school nearby in the Austrian town of Kufstein, the administrative seat of a district by that same name in the Austrian state of Tyrol. Messner hailed from Brixlegg,[7] a town in Kufstein district just across the Inn River from Kramsach. In short, these two men were of the same elemental stuff, were from a culture of common experience, were raised a stone's throw from one another, and were likely aligned—despite Messner's dabbling in Brazilian ways and interest in Buddhism—in their basic worldview.

This view was shaped by history. In accordance with treaties signed secretly during and publicly after the First World War, North and East Tyrol fell within Austria, and South Tyrol went to Italy. The Kingdom of Italy formally annexed South Tyrol in 1919, and over the next few years, as Italy increasingly embraced fascism, it strove through heavy-handed methods to Italianize the area. In 1939, as many European borders were being redrawn, Adolf Hitler and Benito Mussolini agreed that South Tyrol would remain Italian—the Third Reich pledged not to annex the area as it had Austria—but that the German-speaking population of South Tyrol would be allowed to choose between staying and thereby accepting Italianization, or moving to the Third Reich, which by this time included Austria. Some South Tyroleans and Austrian Tyroleans viewed this agreement—which allowed Mussolini to retain a German-majority area that was culturally and linguistically aligned with the Austrian Tyrol—as a betrayal, and were thus inclined at least to disfavor, if not to resist actively, the Nazi cause.[8]

Caldonazzi had more than his Tyrolean lineage and loyalties to lure him into CASSIA. He found substantial common ground too with Maier. Caldonazzi was a devout Catholic and, like Maier, was a member of a Catholic fraternity at an Austrian university. In 1937, while studying at Vienna's University of Agriculture,[9] Caldonazzi had joined Amelungia,[10] while Maier had joined a similar Catholic student fraternity called Nibelungia, presumably when he was attending the University of Vienna.[11] After the 1938 Anschluss, the Nazis had banned such fraternal organizations, but demonstrating their disdain for Hitler, their courage, and their willingness to take risks to preserve their principles, Caldonazzi and some of his Amelungia brothers continued to meet secretly and to engage in nationalistic and monarchical discussions, which were, from a Nazi perspective, seditious.[12]

But what of that limp and cane for a man only in his late twenties? In 1933 a teenaged Caldonazzi suffered serious leg and hip fractures while boarding a train, presumably by falling from a station platform. (It was a disability that in a few years would excuse him from service in the Wehrmacht.[13]) Despite this setback, less than a year later he entered the University of Agriculture, eventually earning a diploma in forestry engineering. After graduating, he worked briefly as an assistant at the university, and then found permanent employment at a private forestry firm in Vienna.[14] Caldonazzi—his pale eyes brimming with steely resolve—wasn't the kind to let a crippling accident stand between him and his dreams.

As with the other members of CASSIA, location seems to have also played a key role for Caldonazzi. The University of Agriculture, which sits astride the border between the upscale 18th and 19th Districts around Türkenschanzpark, is a five-minute walk from Messner's villa and some 15 minutes by foot from Maier's church. Caldonazzi also lived nearby: He rented rooms in a house that was a short walk east of the university at Cottagegasse 94 in the 18th District.[15]

While the exact circumstances of his first contact with Maier are unknown, given Caldonazzi's devotion to the Catholic faith, it is likely that he attended the nearby Gersthof Parish Church, listened to Maier's edifying sermons, and then struck up a conversation with the priest that revealed a common outlook on the war. Another theory is that Maier heard—presumably from his network of sources—about Caldonazzi's band of legitimists and sought him out with a proposal that the two groups should join forces.[16] What happened next, however, is less speculative.

Caldonazzi visited Maier several times in the Gersthof rectory and the two men engaged in conversations that ranged from religion to politics, where they found much agreement and many shared objectives.[17]

Over time, after assessing Caldonazzi's attitudes and opinions and disposition, heard within and without the confessional, Maier decided to bring him into the CASSIA fold. Maier subsequently visited Caldonazzi in his office at the forestry firm and, among other CASSIA-related business, they discussed the need to begin producing anti–Nazi and antiwar fliers, to counter Hitler's propaganda machine and to shine the light of truth on Hitler's folly.[18] Some of Caldonazzi's educated and eloquent comrades seemed perfectly fit for the task.

Caldonazzi threw himself into his new calling. In Vienna and the Tyrol he drafted and disseminated anti–Nazi leaflets and "agitation" tracts. He forged contact with resistance groups in the Tyrolean municipality of Wildschönau and in Brixlegg, Messner's hometown.[19] During visits to nearby Kramsach, where he was raised, Caldonazzi and his father organized a resistance movement among workers in the Achenrain Brass Works, a factory established in the 17th century.[20]

Caldonazzi focused on Achenrain not only because it was in his hometown and because his father knew some of its employees. He also understood that brass was indispensible to the German war machine. The metal's uses were as multitudinous as they were matchless—shell casings, gearwheels, ball bearings, pipes, tubing, and valves. Brass was critical for those applications in which metal-on-metal sparking and corrosion must be avoided at all costs—not only for ammunition cartridges and maritime applications but also for pipes, tubing, and pumps designed to convey explosive or flammable substances, and the tools and other implements used to manipulate such objects.[21]

From his firsthand observations and from collaborating workers, Caldonazzi also collected intelligence on some of the Reich's key armament factories. Using this information he drafted figures on production numbers, jotted down locations, and sketched maps of factories' layouts.[22] CASSIA's couriers carried these materials to the OSS, which in turn passed any actionable intelligence to Allied bombing commands for consideration as targets on future air raids.[23]

In short order Caldonazzi proved to be a vital member of the CASSIA team. But as one's importance increases in an intelligence operation, so too does one's culpability. Before the final shot of the war was fired, Caldonazzi was to learn this lesson, painfully.

8

The Associate

Secure and timely communications with an agent are the linchpin of every intelligence operation. Even if an agent has excellent access and is highly motivated, that agent's intelligence value will only be realized through the professional execution of a well-designed communications plan. A bad plan may do more than devalue an agent's contributions; it may well put an agent behind bars … or worse.

An agent handler—also called a case officer or operations officer—must receive an agent's intelligence and operational details without these communications being detected. The handler must, in turn, be able to convey securely guidance, collection requirements, and support. In a clandestine relationship, support takes many forms. A good case officer acts accordingly as an agent's employer, financial advisor, psychiatrist, friend, marital counselor, and religious guide. And the agent and his or her handler must be able to exchange such information on a timely basis, so that developing events do not move beyond the intelligence, making it obsolete.

Messner was not a trained intelligence officer, and OSS had provided him no guidance, but he instinctively understood that communications would either make or break CASSIA.

Messner and Issakides had already accomplished a very difficult step. They had made initial contact with OSS and in so doing had demonstrated the group's access to key intelligence and a willingness and an ability to pass it secretly to OSS. But now the real work would begin, and the next steps would be just as difficult, if not more so.

Messner's answer to the communications conundrum was manifest as a man: Gustav Rüdiger.[1] Rüdiger—whose birth name was Josef Wenzel Rüdiger—had chosen the nickname Gustav[2] because an older brother who had died in infancy was also named Josef. And so Rüdiger's family honored his wishes and called him only Gustav or, as a term of endearment, "Gustl."[3]

Messner had dispatched Rüdiger to Turkey in early 1941 to assume management of Semperit's subsidiary in Istanbul, *Semperit Lastik Sirketi* (Semperit Tire Company).[4] Rüdiger enjoyed not only Messner's full confidence and trust in business matters, but also his friendship. In fact, by the time of his arrival in Istanbul, Rüdiger was likely aware of, if not yet involved in, the resistance plans of Messner and Maier.[5]

Rüdiger had landed in Turkey as a 46-year-old bachelor. He was successful, highly intelligent, and very well connected, but he owed none of these things to a privileged birthright or education. Gustav had always pulled himself up by his own bootstraps.[6]

When he was still young, Rüdiger's father—a restaurateur in Vienna's exclusive 1st District—had died and Gustav had begun working fulltime to support his mother and siblings. When the First World War began, as the family's primary breadwinner, 20-year-old Rüdiger had avoided military service—a development that had suited his pacifist tendencies. Then, in the interwar years, through his industry and acumen, Rüdiger had landed a job as a senior executive at *Marconi-Werke* (presumably the Austrian branch of Marconi's Wireless Telegraph Company).[7]

Rüdiger's work at Marconi may have led him to business dealings with Messner and, over time, their interactions may have led to friendship. When Messner reached the uppermost rungs of the corporate ladder, he invited a few confidants to join him. And so Rüdiger became a member of the Semperit team and, not long after that, of CASSIA.

In August 1941, some three months after his 47th birthday, Rüdiger returned to Vienna and married his fiancée, Margaretha "Gretl" Ender, in Saint Stephen's Cathedral, not far from the storefront of Messner's *Brasil-Kaffee-Gesellschaft*.[8] Margaretha was one of three daughters of Otto and Maria (née Rusch in Switzerland) Ender, a politically influential family that hailed from Austria's far western state of Vorarlberg.[9]

Rüdiger's new father-in-law had even briefly perched on the pinnacle of power in Austria. Otto Ender (1875–1960) had served as the ninth chancellor of Austria for about six months between December 1930 and May 1931. His administration had been ousted soon after the bankruptcy of Creditanstalt-Bankverein, which played a key role in events that led to the Great Depression. But before leaving office, Ender, working with the bank's owner, the Rothschild family, had rescued the institution. (In 1931, after Creditanstalt had been stabilized largely under state control, Josef Joham joined the bank's board of directors.) Ender had then served in the middle 1930s as a "minister without portfolio" during Dollfuss's Austrofascist regime and then had taken a senior position in the administration of Dollfuss's successor, Kurt Schuschnigg.[10]

After the Anschluss, the Third Reich removed Ender from office and, along with other former regime loyalists, the Gestapo arrested and imprisoned him. In fact, at the time of his daughter's marriage to Rüdiger, Ender may have been incarcerated; his wife, Maria, may have stood alone for the family at the wedding. Ender was later sent to Dachau concentration camp, from which he was freed in 1945 by advancing Allied forces.[11]

After the wedding, Rüdiger and his bride returned to Istanbul, and he resumed work at *Semperit Lastik Sirketi*. Fourteen months later, in October 1942, the couple returned temporarily to Vienna for the birth of their first son, Thomas. Thomas's imminent arrival, which was two months premature, had so concerned his parents that they wanted Austrian doctors to oversee the delivery. But Thomas was born without incident, and the new family went back to Istanbul.[12]

Then, in late 1942 or early 1943, shortly after Issakides's first meeting with Grimm, Messner asked Rüdiger to begin looking for a more readily serviceable link to the Allies. In the coming months, Rüdiger's role in the group would be of such importance that he would hold the very lives of the other members in his hands.

Gustav Rüdiger, July 1943, during a visit to Vienna (courtesy Thomas Rüdiger).

Rüdiger was not only the right man for the job, but he also lived in the right place. Turkey's neutral status during the war made the Semperit office in Istanbul essential; there, the Reich could still make deals to acquire strategic materials. Consequently, Messner traveled frequently to Istanbul to confer with Rüdiger and to negotiate with other companies. These trips, Messner and Maier realized, would give him the necessary cover for carrying intelligence to a location where it could be passed directly to the Americans. At Messner's urging, Rüdiger, carefully using his network of contacts, began looking for an entrée to one of the Allied intelligence services, and in this endeavor Istanbul's setting, wartime population, and other inimitable attributes helped him.

During a war, the great advantage of a neutral city like Istanbul is that it is open for business to everyone; there, no one suffers discrimination. A neutral city's great disadvantage is that it is open for business to everyone—not just those involved in legitimate enterprises but also those who specialize in skullduggery and intrigue and deception and other offences, large and small. In Istanbul during the Second World War, enemies lived and traded side by side, sometimes in the light, sometimes in the shadows. It was not a place for the earnest, the gullible, or the naïve.[13]

This permissive environment was due to more than the city's neutrality; geography and history were also contributing factors. Istanbul straddles the Bosporus Strait, which connects the Sea of Marmara and the Black Sea (into which Vienna's Blue Danube ultimately spills), and which brings Atlantic Ocean commercial fleets and navies into the belly of East Europe. As a result, Istanbul has been a strategic commercial—and thus military—site since the days of the Silk Road. The Strait, however, is more than a canal for seagoing vessels and an historical terminus for caravans; it also rends the continent, leaving Europe on one side and Asia on the other. During the war, this openness and exoticism attracted adventurers as sweet aromas lure bees, and enticed swindlers as foul pungencies lure flies.

It was in this freewheeling city, whose air carried the scents of both great opportunity and great danger, that Rüdiger plied his official and unofficial trades. He proved to be adept at both. But Rüdiger's prowess would take CASSIA only so far. For the rest of the journey the group would need to rely on the OSS.

Rüdiger's furtive probes led him in 1943 to a shadowy Czech businessman named Alfred Schwarz who ran a network of agents for Allied intelligence.

9

The Middleman

Thirty-nine-year-old Schwarz had lived in Istanbul since the late 1920s. Proficient in German, Turkish, and English as well as his native Czech, he had come to the city as the representative of an established company but had later struck out on his own and had built a successful business.[1]

Trained as an engineer, Schwarz specialized in producing and marketing industrial, agricultural, and maritime machinery, and enjoyed profitable commerce in Germany, Austria, and Czechoslovakia.[2] Among the several companies that he represented in Istanbul was the Chicago Pneumatic Tool Company[3]—a U.S. firm that designed and manufactured pneumatic implements (to include a "hot dimpling machine" that used very high heat and pressure to shape rivet heads for wartime aeronautical applications), compressors, drilling equipment, and diesel engines. Since the early 1900s the company had enjoyed robust international sales and had even opened a few offices abroad.[4]

After the war began, supposedly spurred by German predations on his homeland and persecution of his fellow Jews, Schwarz volunteered to Istanbul representatives of British intelligence, who were intrigued by his wide range of contacts in the city, particularly by his close friendships with influential German exiles.[5] In short order the British—it seems that both MI6 and the SOE were involved in his handling—formally recruited Schwarz and assigned him codename LEONARD.[6]

For MI6's part in the case, Schwarz appears to have been handled by its Istanbul office—led by Head of Station Colonel Harold Gibson—from 1942 to 1943.[7] The gross insubordination that later became the hallmark of Schwarz's behavior would not have been possible with the likes of Gibson. He was an experienced operator who had served in Prague and maintained a stable of trustworthy contacts—through which he could readily check out any agent's claims—across Eastern Europe.[8]

In the spring of 1943, shortly after the OSS arrived in the city, Schwarz's MI6 overlords asked him to help the Americans with their fledgling efforts.[9] Then, as OSS's Istanbul office was still being set up, Schwarz signed a formal agreement with its new chief, Lanning MacFarland, pledging to put his network and skills at OSS's disposal. MacFarland was as dazzled by Schwarz's cosmopolitan flair as Schwarz was shocked by MacFarland's easy ingenuousness.[10]

As was the case with many OSS officers, in practical terms, MacFarland was an operational neophyte. He had little intelligence training and no experience. A Harvard-educated vice president of a Chicago bank, MacFarland had served in the First World War first as a volunteer ambulance driver and, after the United States entered the conflict, as an Army captain. Apparently impressed with his postwar relief work in the Balkans, the OSS had offered him a job.[11]

The official history of the OSS outlined what the agency had initially ordered MacFarland to do in Istanbul: "[I]n April 1943, an OSS representative [MacFarland] arrived to establish a mission for (1) organized interrogation of travellers, (2) counter-espionage, and (3) operations into Hungary, Bulgaria, and Rumania. [MacFarland's] cover of Lend-Lease representative was supported by his previous experience as an American banker."[12] Schwarz stood ready and seemingly able to help MacFarland with all of these objectives, with an emphasis on number three, which Schwarz—with OSS's blessing—would expand to include additional target countries such as Austria.

With the bargain clinched between MacFarland and Schwarz, OSS christened its new agent DOGWOOD, the codename that OSS would also use when referring to Schwarz's network. For his part in the deal, Schwarz made available to OSS his existing array of contacts, from which he had previously gathered information for MI6 and probably for various Zionist groups, and with little instruction and inquiry from OSS, he began looking for and recruiting new sources.[13] In a matter of weeks he had assembled a large pool of sub-agents who hailed from a variety of countries, possessed diverse backgrounds, and pursued a wide range of vocations.[14] Quantity is what Schwarz delivered and quickly, and quantity is what OSS took with little regard for quality.

In contemporary intelligence jargon, Schwarz was a principal agent—a paid agent who handles a number of secondary agents. Oftentimes a principal agent has personally recruited some or all of the secondary agents and may have the requisite cover for action to continue meeting them. Also, a principal agent is usually the most familiar with his or her secondary agents' needs, impulses, motivations, and overall disposition; may have earned the loyalty of—and may even have genuine friendships with—the secondary agents; and may therefore be best situated to deal effectively with them. Further, in some cases, secondary agents remain unaware of a principal agent's true affiliation—the intelligence service for which a principal agent is secretly working, and which those sub-agents may find distasteful.

These factors sometimes trump the dunning doctrines of counterintelligence, which define and quantify the risks of connecting multiple sources, particularly those that are naturally disparate, to a single point of potential failure. Such precepts argue for operational and case-documentary compartmentalization, much as a ship's bulkheads provide sealable barriers in the event that one compartment is breached, thereby allowing a compromised vessel to stay afloat. Wherever the rules are relaxed, counterintelligence experts warn, danger begins to seep in, and then disaster will surely follow.

In summary, the use of principal agents to gain access to intelligence from webworks of secondary agents is rarely the preferable way to operate, but on occasion it is the only way. Typically, an intelligence service is willing to stomach an increase in risk that is proportional to the appraised value and anticipated yield of the information in question.

Among the many sub-agents whom Schwarz brought to OSS was a man who would become one of the most productive sources of the DOGWOOD network. Schwarz had first met this agent several months before his introduction to MacFarland, when he was still working for the British. At the time, the man in question, an Austrian named Gustav Rüdiger, the director of the Semperit office in Istanbul, had been discreetly searching for a middleman[15]—someone who could securely facilitate contact between the group of Austrian spies that he represented and Allied intelligence.

The official postwar history of the OSS recorded that Rüdiger had found Schwarz through an Austrian "radio" businessman who, by a stroke of luck (good at the time, bad later), was apparently an existing sub-source of the British LEONARD network.[16] This businessman was Josef Lehrner,[17] a senior manager with the Netherlands-based Philips & Company,[18] renowned internationally—then and now—for its development and manufacture of technological products. In the 1930s, when Lehrner was living in Brazil and representing Philips's interests in South America,[19] the company had earned the distinction of becoming "the world's largest manufacturer of radios and radio tubes," which explains his bland descriptor in OSS's history.[20] Lehrner and Rüdiger had been friends since before the war, liked to have a good time, and apparently shared a certain joie de vivre.[21]

Rüdiger had listened closely to Lehrner's testimonial. After all, on the surface, Schwarz—the point man for an agent network that he managed at the behest of Allied intelligence—appeared to be exactly what CASSIA needed. What Rüdiger didn't know is that Schwarz's enterprise had grown unwieldy, and that its master not only undervalued the game's rules of compartmentalization, simplicity, and discretion but that he often thumbed his nose at them.

As spies have always been wont to do, Rüdiger and Schwarz had probably circled one another for a while (even with Lehrner's good-natured brokering), each taking the measure of the other man, each building his own assessment. Both men had tried to elicit telling insights while remaining as circumspect as possible, and had run a few formal and informal checks. It was an ancient dance; time had not altered but only refined its steps.

At some point, once sufficient trust existed between them, the two men had entered into a clandestine agreement. After Rüdiger was officially on Schwarz's books, British intelligence had codenamed him STAR.[22]

Rüdiger had wasted no time in convincing Schwarz that he needed to speak directly to the British, to solicit their patronage of a diverse group of anti–Nazi Austrians. In his subsequent discussions with MI6 and SOE, Rüdiger had referred to this group as the "Action Committee" (*Aktionskomitee*) and had claimed that it included prominent Social Democrats and Christian Socialists. From the outset, however, the British had doubted the group's legitimacy and intentions, and had even suspected that Rüdiger may have used the names of some well-known Austrian politicians without their knowledge.[23] (Please see Appendix II for more details on Rüdiger's contact with British intelligence.)

Rüdiger's proposal may well have included some embellishments, but his group was real and diverse, and did include influential people. To wit, between the networks of Maier, Messner, Legradi, and Sokal, the group's supporters included noteworthy Social Democrats and Christian Socialists, Catholic clergy and laymen, communists, a senior Wehrmacht officer, a member of the Hungarian elite, and leaders in the fields of industry, economics, finance, chemistry, and pharmaceuticals. And the group was only in its formative stages; Caldonazzi and his devoted friends were on the verge of expanding its access and activities beyond all expectations.

Rüdiger hadn't been discouraged by Britain's blasé response. Taking a page from the playbook of the indefatigable Maier, he had pressed on, and when Schwarz had signed up with OSS, so too had Rüdiger, and he became a sub-agent of the Americans' rebranded DOGWOOD network.

"Radio" businessman Lehrner was one of the first DOGWOOD sub-agents to meet directly with the OSS, and once he had won the designated handling officer's confidence, he wasted no time in highly recommending the services of his old friend Rüdiger. However, other than introducing Rüdiger to Schwarz, endorsing him to OSS, and setting up an initial meeting between Rüdiger and the OSS handling officer, Lehrner—whom OSS codenamed PERIWINKLE—seems to have played no further role in CASSIA.[24]

OSS-Istanbul, not yet knowing exactly what they had in Rüdiger or in the group of Austrians whom he represented, assigned him codename STOCK, after a common flower sometimes called ten-weeks stock.[25] It was a protocol that would be repeated again and again: Everyone affiliated with the DOGWOOD network would be codenamed after flowering plants.

10

The Handler

MacFarland—who is referenced in OSS documents by his nickname, "Packy," or by his official OSS code number, 550—was not a seasoned field operative but he strove to dress the part. He often wore a trench coat and fedora, the accouterments of enigmatic movie characters such as Rick Blaine (played by Humphrey Bogart) in the 1942 film *Casablanca*. To add a point in MacFarland's favor, though, he seems to have realized his shortcomings in skill, if not those in fashion, for he quickly designated OSS officer Archibald Coleman as Schwarz's primary point of contact. OSS then assigned Coleman the codename CEREUS after the night-blooming cereus cactus, formally linking him to the DOGWOOD network. Coleman thus became—once again in intelligence jargon—Schwarz's handling (or case) officer.[1]

Coleman had more experience at clandestine operations than did MacFarland, but he was by no means an accomplished veteran of this esoteric trade. Earlier in the war the OSS's predecessor, the office of the Coordinator of Intelligence, had assigned him first to Mexico, whose government asked him to leave, and then to Spain, where his own ambassador asked him to go.[2]

Such diplomatic expulsions are not unprecedented but are rare. Back-to-back removals are rarer still. Most intelligence officers enjoy long careers without having ever been ousted or withdrawn. Depending on the circumstances, one truncated tour might be considered an unlucky or unavoidable occurrence, but two, particularly two in rapid succession, suggest chronic flaws in Coleman's approach to intelligence work. MacFarland was nonetheless impressed with Coleman's background, even if upon closer inspection his past performance had been at best dubious.

After his aborted tour in Spain, which ended in June 1942, Coleman had cooled his heels for almost a year before being sent to Istanbul in the spring of 1943. Coleman's cover job—both his cover for being in Turkey and his cover for some of his sub-rosa OSS work—was as a correspondent for *The Saturday Evening Post*,[3] a widely read and well respected bimonthly U.S. magazine (perhaps best known for its slice-of-life Norman Rockwell covers) that published a wide variety of fiction and nonfiction pieces.

By coincidence, on 29 May 1943, about the time that Coleman showed up in Istanbul, *The Saturday Evening Post* published an issue whose cover featured the now-famous Rockwell painting of Rosie the Riveter. Muscular red-haired Rosie, clad in overalls and a denim shirt, sits during her lunch break at an aircraft factory, a ham sandwich in one hand and a foot propped on a copy of Hitler's *Mein Kampf*. A pneumatic riveting hammer rests on Rosie's lap. The hammer is one of the signature products of the Chicago Pneumatic Tool Company, which Schwarz had represented for many years in Istanbul.[4]

In MacFarland's eyes, Coleman's ostensible job as a journalist offered an advantage: It would allow him to meet some sensitive contacts, particularly those from the Reich, for whom a visit to the OSS office in Istanbul's U.S. Consulate would be ill advised, if not downright lethal. As for maintaining secure contact with the existing and prospective agents of the growing DOGWOOD network, MacFarland ordered Coleman to work with Schwarz and to develop other suitable cover arrangements.[5]

Schwarz's solution was to open a branch office of Western Electric Company, a large U.S. business now mostly remembered for the electrical equipment-supply hegemony that it enjoyed through the Bell Telephone/AT&T family of companies. Schwarz apparently surmised that he could insinuate DOGWOOD's activities into the great flurry of "legitimate" business that was emanating from his offices.[6]

Before long DOGWOOD and its agents were communicating by post (to include the use of mail drops sponsored by other supposedly unrelated concerns), telephone, and telegraph. For its part, OSS-Istanbul arranged for the OSS facility in Algiers to transmit coded radio messages to deployed DOGWOOD agents. DOGWOOD also found creative ways for its agents to photograph documents and to secrete them in innocuous—but slightly modified—items such as toiletries, clothing, and pencils.[7]

OSS-Istanbul lacked officers who were fluent in German, so MacFarland—through Coleman—devolved responsibility to Schwarz for identifying and assessing prospective agent candidates. OSS-Istanbul still performed background checks, known in operational parlance as "traces," on nominated individuals, but the quality of these investigations appears to have been uneven at best, and deplorable at worst. As one OSS officer said in a postwar interview, "We didn't have all that much time and facility to check out people. We took what time we could spare to check their stories."[8]

Also of questionable quality were many of DOGWOOD's intelligence reports. Neither Schwarz—who collected all of the intelligence, and wrote and processed most of the reports—nor Coleman was proficient at the difficult work of winnowing possible facts from the vast chaff of speculation, opinion, and gossip that the network's agents provided. And neither of them grasped the importance of striving to corroborate such presumptive truths, and of establishing the information's "sourcing"—its provenance, method of acquisition, and chain of custody before it had reached OSS's hands.[9]

Schwarz acted as a purposeful impediment to these key intelligence processes. He simply refused to provide to OSS the necessary details on his sub-sources: "Neither OSS-Istanbul nor the Washington office, however, knew the identity of Dogwood's subagents. Dogwood insisted on concealing them, fearing leaks from careless OSS personnel or intercepted [radio] transmissions."[10]

After the war, however, in its damning appraisal of DOGWOOD's counterintelligence profile, the U.S. War Department would blame not Schwarz's zealous pursuit of operational security, but OSS-Istanbul's lack of handling savvy: "Since the mission chief [MacFarland] exercised no control over 'Dogwood,' the latter would not reveal his sub-sources, merely assigning them various code names on his reports."[11]

Despite Schwarz's noncompliance on this point, and OSS's concerns about the quality of some of his reporting, OSS-Istanbul continued to rely heavily on DOGWOOD's production. The numbers were impressive, and MacFarland certainly felt substantial internal and external pressure to keep the DOGWOOD tap fully open.

Early in its association with OSS, CASSIA—as represented by Rüdiger—contributed to these stress levels by passing some very high-profile intelligence. In September 1943, a few weeks after Messner's report to OSS-Bern had helped the British bombing of Peenemünde, Rüdiger provided further insights on the V-2 ballistic missile, to include precise details on its fuel mixture, dimensions, speed, range, and methods of construction. Rüdiger also outlined the locations and activities of the different facilities that were contributing to the weapon's manufacture.[12]

Then Rüdiger added some intriguing—and highly unsettling—insights on the Reich's production of artificial-rubber plates with which the German Navy planned to sheathe some of its submarines, to evaluate the plates' effectiveness as a countermeasure to Allied anti-submarine sonar systems.[13] These were the types of alarming reports that were given to senior U.S. policymakers and stimulated in them a gnawing hunger for more of the same.

In its heyday, DOGWOOD may have controlled around 67 agents,[14] some of whom were singletons, reporting directly to DOGWOOD, while others, like CASSIA, were organized "chains" or rings of agents, which totaled, perhaps ominously, 13.[15] This vast network often produced more than 80 intelligence reports a month, many on tactical—and, therefore, potentially actionable—subjects. Some of this information addressed the Allies' most pressing requirements, to include details on the Wehrmacht's order of battle, Reich industrial facilities and production, and political opposition personalities and movements inside Germany.[16]

One researcher put OSS-Istanbul's gross output at 1,500 intelligence reports,[17] and in its official history of the OSS, the U.S. War Department estimated that, from the second half of 1943 to early 1944, more than 700 of those reports had come solely from Schwarz, who had attributed that intelligence to some 60 of his nebulous sub-sources.[18] One can only imagine how the heavy return-flow of accolades for these kinds and quantities of intelligence must have influenced and burdened MacFarland, making the success of OSS-Istanbul ever more dependent on DOGWOOD.

It was into this messy, overextended, poorly controlled situation that an unsuspecting Messner walked. Ever mindful of his security, and how it affected his good friends back in Vienna, Messner took precautions for his first meeting with DOGWOOD.

As arranged through Rüdiger, Messner visited a technical school in Istanbul—what would be considered an in-pattern activity for the head of company that produced synthetic rubber. At the school he dropped in on a German teacher who ostensibly happened to be speaking with another businessman—Alfred Schwarz. The German teacher, who was actually one of Schwarz's agents, then allowed the two men to hold an operational meeting in his office at the school.[19]

Establishing initial contact with a prospective agent is always tricky. Unbending adherence to security protocols would prevent any such contact from ever happening, since risk is unavoidably involved. But before any intelligence gathering can occur, contact must be made. So, in this case, two men who weren't supposed to know each other, who had no reason for meeting, needed not only to make contact but also to engage in a substantial conversation in a private location, away from curious eyes and ears. The solution involved a third, unrelated party—the teacher. If this teacher had been a German double agent, or in an inopportune moment had let an intriguing detail slip, the contact between Schwarz and Messner would have been blown from the very start.

For these reasons, the plan that led to the first meeting between Messner and Schwarz was not ideal, but given the circumstances of both men and the lack of meaningful guidance from OSS-Istanbul, it may well have been the only workable arrangement. Field operations are, after all, about tradeoffs: One must take calculated risks to get the intelligence one needs or desires.

Messner and his group thus became part of the DOGWOOD network, and OSS assigned them the codename CASSIA[20]—after the yellow-flowering shrub known also as candle bush. (CASSIA was Messner's codename, but just as OSS had referred to "his" spy ring as the Messner Group, so too it often called the entire group CASSIA.) Then, on 3 February 1944, unaware the ground was already giving way beneath his feet, Messner signed a formal agreement with OSS, as represented by MacFarland's field supervisor, OSS-Cairo chief Valerian "Valla" Lada-Mocarski (1898–1971), codename JUNIPER, to assist the Allies in the defeat of Germany, which would allow Austria to reestablish itself as a free and independent country.[21] (Please see Appendix III for the full text of the 3 February 1944 Memorandum of Agreement between CASSIA and OSS.) Lada-Mocarski, a prewar banker in the United States whose father had been a senior Russian Imperial Army officer, had come to Istanbul specifically to negotiate the terms of the agreement with Messner.

For its part in the arrangement CASSIA pledged to continue providing intelligence on Germany and disseminating anti–Nazi propaganda, and to begin preparing to support Allied irregular action—in advance of conventional military operations—on Austrian soil.[22] To this end, in late March 1944 OSS Headquarters endorsed an operation—codenamed REDBIRD—that would infiltrate a two-man parachutist team from OSS-Algiers into Austria, where members of CASSIA would receive them. OSS Headquarters instructed the point men for REDBIRD, OSS-Algiers officers Joseph Rodrigo and Gerry Van Arkel,[23] that the mission had no "authorization to carry on political transactions" with the Austrian resistance and that it should be strictly limited to "performing intelligence work." Related communications on REDBIRD suggested that, to coordinate the prospective drop and reception, OSS needed to deliver, post haste, a clandestine radio transmitter/receiver to CASSIA.[24]

Very few of us can fathom the courage that it took for Messner, on behalf of the entire CASSIA group, to sign a contract with the American intelligence service. After only a couple of meetings and a stroke of the pen, the group had documented its high treason against a draconian police state, one of the most ruthless that the world has ever known. Everyone was now playing for the very highest stakes, and it was anyone's guess who, in the end, would be holding the winning hand.

11

Intelligence Esoterica—A Closer Look at CASSIA's Intelligence Reporting

As the war dragged on, the Allies wrested control of the seaways, gaining the upper hand against Germany's surface fleet by late 1942 and against its U-boats by middle 1943. Then, key countries—to include Brazil, where in 1939 Messner had acted as a Reich purchasing agent—sided with the Allies, and Germany lost access to its sources of natural rubber in Latin America and Asia.[1]

During this critical time, even before Messner scratched his name on the OSS contract, CASSIA began to entrust troves of rare intelligence to DOGWOOD. The group gave OSS the first intelligence on the Reich's production of synthetic rubber, which the dearth of natural rubber had made essential.[2] Among these reports were accurate details—to include geographic coordinates, production estimates, and descriptions of unique overhead features—on three Reich rubber-processing facilities: two in Germany, one near the town of Hüls and another near Schkopau, and a third in Poland (the forced-labor plant at Monowitz). CASSIA also reported on a new factory at Monowitz that was producing carbon black, an important reinforcing agent used in the production of synthetic rubber; this facility had replaced a carbon-black plant—located near the German city of Dortmund—that British bombers had destroyed.[3]

In addition to this information and the previously discussed intelligence on V-weapons at Peenemünde, CASSIA is also credited with providing OSS accurate drawings of the Tiger I, an advanced German heavy tank.[4] CASSIA's access to the Tiger I came from Nibelungenwerke, the Reich's extensive tank-production complex located in Sankt Valentin,

Upper Austria,[5] and possibly from Maier's contact with Wehrmacht Lieutenant General Heinrich Stümpfl, the Commandant of Vienna.[6]

Nibelungenwerke primarily manufactured the Panzerkampfwagen IV medium tank, but was also involved in the development of the Ferdinand, which was later designated the Elefant, a tank destroyer built on the hull of a discontinued Tiger I variant. Nibelungenwerke thus held schematics for both the Tiger I and the Ferdinand/Elefant.[7]

Still, despite this commendable track record, some researchers have charged that Messner made every effort to spare Semperit facilities from Allied air raids.[8] It is probable that both assertions are true. Messner provided key intelligence on synthetic rubber- and arms-production facilities, *and* in keeping with CASSIA's stated goal of trying to preserve sectors of Austrian industry for rebuilding the country after the war, he almost certainly attempted to save some of his factories and other locations from destruction.[9]

But a man does not risk his life against the likes of Hitler's merciless Reich simply to keep his business running at full capacity. Some merchants are brave, but they do not charge into the fires of hell to ensure maximum profitability; they do such things for principles much grander than a bottom line.

Take Joham, for example, the director of Creditanstalt bank, who remained firmly anchored in Vienna, never strayed far beyond his natural access and patterns of movement, and conveyed his information only through intermediaries and cutouts, with whom his contact either had airtight pretext or was deniable. Joham's secret cooperation with the Allies was very risky, of course, but Messner was engaged in much more dangerous work—hands-on and higher profile activities for which he put his life on the line, time and again.

Because of Schwarz's refusal to provide details on his sub-sources, OSS questioned some of CASSIA's reporting, considering it too vague or suspecting that it might be feed material[10] that the Germans had fobbed off on OSS through witting and unwitting sub-sources. But other pieces of the group's intelligence were well received, and were appraised as being "extremely valuable … reliable, and relevant."[11]

However, as is too often the case, the loudest—but not necessarily the truest—voices seem to have attracted the most attention. Several OSS and U.S. Army Air Force analysts continued to express vehemently their suspicions about CASSIA's intelligence, and in some cases dismissed it outright. And their perspectives and opinions—which only in proper measure and context would have added value—were given much more weight and airtime than they deserved.

A perfect example of this criticism involved a CASSIA report on Allied air raids that had damaged the Messerschmitt aircraft-production complex just outside Vienna and had forced the company to relocate to three former textile factories outside the city.[12] Based on interpretations of aerial reconnaissance photographs, some USAAF analysts contended that in November 1943 the Messerschmitt factory had been destroyed but never rebuilt; it was not under repair as CASSIA had asserted. As for those textile mills, where, according to CASSIA, production of fighter planes had been shifted, the analysts claimed that those locations were doing nothing of the sort: The mills were still producing cloth for military uniforms and had no connection whatsoever to the Messerschmitt factory.[13]

But inconsistencies in official records concerning USAAF's appraisals of this intelligence have in turn led to varying postwar conclusions about those assessments.[14] According to the CASSIA report in question, which was likely collected from uncontrolled sub-sources with indirect access, Messerschmitt had dispersed its operations from a single large facility in Wiener Neustadt to smaller factories in Pottendorf, Ebreichsdorf, and Bad Vöslau.[15] OSS's official postwar history cites this report but provides an antipodal USAAF assessment: "Fifteenth Air Force photo-reconnaissance checked on this hint [i.e., dispersion of Messerschmitt operations to the three specified smaller towns] and verified it."[16]

This failure of USAAF and OSS to speak with one evaluative voice—not only between but also within organizations—illustrates the great difficulty of imposing measurable structure on intelligence that is naturally nebulous, convoluted, and shifting. Some CASSIA reports came directly from members of the group, others from regular sub-sources of members, still others from one-off sources of unknown reliability. Only Schwarz and Coleman were in a position to ascertain the origin(s) and circumstances of each collection, and to qualify the resulting report(s) with complete acquisition and context details. But neither man—and here, as handling officer, Coleman (or his designated backup, MacFarland) was particularly negligent—dedicated himself to this exhaustive, exhausting, and essential work, which some modern intelligence agencies include as priority competencies in the broader concept of "collection management." Without such supplementary information, intelligence reports cannot be accurately evaluated, and without such assessments the planners and shooters of the military cannot act appropriately on the intelligence. In professional intelligence organizations, past and present, collected information without ancillary clarification is typically regarded as little more than rumor.

In 1949 the U.S. War Department documented that an OSS officer with regional responsibilities had reached the same conclusion. Because Schwarz refused to reveal details on his sub-sources, "The Reports Office in Cairo was therefore unable to evaluate the intelligence material. The large majority being vague hearsay, the Cairo Reports Officer at one point refused to process or disseminate the material as intelligence at all."[17] Further muddling the appraisal process was the fact that Cairo was only receiving part of the network's total intelligence production; because many DOGWOOD reports addressed "top priorities," they were often sent directly from Istanbul to OSS Headquarters.[18]

Condemnations of CASSIA didn't stop with the group's intelligence on the Messerschmitt plant. USAAF also charged that CASSIA's reports had exaggerated activities of the Heinkel Aircraft Works at the Luftwaffe base at Schwechat,[19] a suburb of Vienna.[20] The Schwechat factory complex—often called Heinkel-Süd to distinguish it from Heinkel-Nord at Rostock, Germany—was deeply involved in designing and manufacturing advanced combat aircraft, and as such was a priority intelligence-collection target for the Allies.

It was at Heinkel-Süd that between 1943 and 1944 the company produced the He 219, a sophisticated twin-engine night fighter that proved effective against Allied heavy bombers and a respectable foe of the de Havilland DH.98 Mosquito, Britain's formidable twin-engine, multi-role airplane.[21] When considering the He 219, one might reasonably conclude that on occasion the exact production numbers for a facility may be less important—particularly if such intelligence is highly compartmentalized and thus beyond the reach of most agents—than what is being made there. Still, the USAAF criticism may well hold some water; CASSIA may have provided faulty production numbers for the He 219. However, there is no evidence that the group purposefully inflated these estimates.

CASSIA sub-sources probably collected this intelligence based on indirect access to certain Heinkel documents and on some firsthand observations of the aircraft's production line. (In its less sensitive areas, Heinkel-Süd employed thousands of slave laborers and prisoners of war, and it is possible that some of these workers incidentally collected information that found its way to CASSIA.) However, Heinkel-Süd was never able to manufacture the He 219 at full capacity. These limitations were due not to technical or labor problems at the factory or to damage from aerial bombing, but to high-level Luftwaffe bickering. Some senior Luftwaffe officers saw the He 219 as a redundant model for their inventory, despite its clear superiority to older night fighters such as the Junkers 88, and successfully lobbied to have its production decreased.[22] CASSIA had no access to the Luftwaffe high command and could only base its estimates on what sub-sources were able to observe at Heinkel-Süd or to elicit from workers there. These are precisely the kinds of collection details that can place a piece of intelligence in its proper context.

In yet another appraisal of CASSIA reporting, USAAF concluded that the group's information was often "inaccurate" and "vague," and that sketched maps were so distorted and otherwise erroneous as to be "useless." OSS took these denunciations at face value, and declared that the discrepancies and CASSIA's alleged attempt to pass the Allies "exaggerated figures" on Heinkel-Süd meant that all of the group's intelligence was suspect and should be handled accordingly.[23]

But as one author has correctly observed, CASSIA's members were inexperienced at espionage, had received no instruction—not even the most basic—from OSS (which itself was staffed with a great number of intelligence novices), and were simply making honest mistakes on quality control. Many of CASSIA's sub-sources, those with direct access to such tactical intelligence, were low-ranking members of the German military with no proficiency at estimating the numbers of passing or mustered troops, current and projected production figures at factories, and battle damage from air raids. None of these frontline collectors were cartographers or artists or graphic designers, so their maps were often not to scale or were otherwise distorted.[24]

(It should be noted that Caldonazzi and one other CASSIA member studied engineering at the University of Agriculture and almost certainly possessed at least a basic proficiency in drafting dimensional specifications of mechanical devices. But these skills would not have necessarily aided them in accurately drawing maps, particularly when such maps were derived from ground-level observations and, in some cases, from second-hand source reporting.)

USAAF analysts, whose world of targets snapped into crisp focus at around 15,000 or 20,000 feet, did not fully understand the workaday complications, messiness, demands, and danger of running a secret intelligence-gathering organization in the heart of an oppressive, sadistic police state. And at the time OSS did not—and, because of its officers' inexperience, perhaps could not—offer any helpful clarification on these points.

One researcher on CASSIA, drawing on the expertise of a contemporary intelligence professional, observed that "the information contained in damage reports by the [USAAF] was notoriously unreliable and … the Air Force had a tough time in justifying the effectiveness of its raids on industrial sites." In other words, USAAF analysts often based both their praise and their condemnations on flawed information.[25]

And there was another problem with the conclusions of the USAAF analyses and with the OSS responses to them: They argued that CASSIA was purposefully misleading the Allies. The charges ranged from CASSIA's being under German control to Messner's attempting to eliminate his competitors.

The suspicion of hostile control was valid, but only as a suspicion and not as a conclusion, and as such it should have been fully and competently investigated and then it should have been dismissed. The second charge should have also been considered, since it would have been only natural for Messner to attempt to preserve the very thing—Semperit—that was both funding CASSIA and giving him access to intelligence.[26]

OSS even recorded Messner's perspective on this point in its after-action analysis of the CASSIA operation, citing one of Messner's earlier statements: "To bomb Semperit, [Messner had] said, would be to kill off the Resistance group." But Messner's logic was ignored and instead OSS focused on his suggestion that the Allies should instead target his chief competitor, Germany's Continental AG, which as it turns out *was* heavily involved with chemical conglomerate IG Farben in the production of synthetic rubber for the Wehrmacht.[27] As one researcher observed, "It made solid common sense that [the CASSIA members] did not wish to have the factories of their own company bombed."[28] In other words, Messner's efforts to spare Semperit and to target Continental did not mean necessarily that the group was wittingly engaging in some kind of state-sponsored treachery or other underhanded activity. Such common sense, however, was absent in most analyses of the operation.

Once again, as a case study, CASSIA offers an abundance of lessons. Agent handlers and analysts should never leap to any conclusions. They should, of course, recognize legitimate problems, but then they should work diligently and objectively toward identifying the likely causes of such problems. When agents make errors, as they inevitably will, a professional intelligence organization—beginning with the designated handling officer—must act immediately to determine the reason or reasons for such lapses. The handling officer, supported by the resources and expertise of his or her agency, must strive to generate a comprehensive assessment of the involved source's operational information and intelligence production, and must delve again and deeply into the source's psychological disposition and motivation for cooperating.

Throughout this time-consuming and arduous process, the handling officer must remain both unbiased and highly alert for any signs that suggest the presence of counterintelligence issues, to include any indications that a source might be fabricating for personal gain or might be under hostile control. Then, the officer and his or her agency must launch an intensive investigation into the nature and consistency of these signs, to determine *over time* if a source is A) deficient in critical skills but trainable, B) hopelessly unsuitable, or C) intentionally misleading the handling organization for reasons that are personal (e.g., for financial gain or to protect friends) or institutional (i.e., at the behest of and with guidance from a rival security service).

Instead, OSS failed to deal methodically and impartially with CASSIA's inconsistencies, and appears to have lumped together several of CASSIA's smaller (but still important) concerns with the mounting and much more serious troubles of the greater DOGWOOD network. By focusing on the possibility that CASSIA was manipulating the relationship for then-undetermined reasons, and failing to look after the counterintelligence health of the greater DOGWOOD network, OSS discounted a rich source of intelligence while absurdly ignoring the real problem. In an ironic twist, the very officers who lambasted Schwarz for reporting hearsay were often prone to disseminate little more than hearsay in their assessments of CASSIA's intelligence.

Now, decades after the guns have gone quiet, after extensive research on Allied and Axis documentary holdings, it is evident that CASSIA was not under hostile control, was not attempting to mislead the Allies, and was not operating with any other agenda. CASSIA made a few fairly typical mistakes in its collection and reporting efforts but, in the final analysis, none indicated duplicity. From a counterintelligence perspective, all of CASSIA's errors—even those that Messner may have committed to spare certain facilities—were of benign origin and were correctable through the skillful application of agent-handling techniques.

12

The Snitch

In the early 1940s, a man with a dark purpose began to stalk Messner.

His name was Sigismund Romen and he was an executive at Semperit. He was also a strident Nazi and, as one might imagine, a vocal anti–Semite. He was born in the Rhineland, the part of far western Germany that runs along the middle and lower Rhine River. He had come to work in Vienna before the Anschluss, and at the time had enjoyed a discreet, cooperative relationship with the German Embassy,[1] which under the sinister leadership of Ambassador Franz von Papen (1879–1969) was a veritable beehive of activity, supporting Austrian Nazis, laying the groundwork for the coming annexation, taking careful note of every voice of dissent.[2] (After leaving Austria in 1938, von Papen served as the German ambassador to Turkey from 1939 to 1944. He and his subordinates were well aware of, and in some cases had key roles in, the cloak-and-dagger activities that played out in Istanbul during the war.)

At first Romen diligently assisted his boss, Messner, and may have used his German Embassy contacts to that end. However, at some point Romen had begun to suspect that Messner held certain anti–Nazi beliefs, and this realization must have at first rankled him.[3] Later, as he stewed over the fact that he was subordinate to a man whose loyalties he had come to question, a man in charge of a strategic industry in the newest "province" of his homeland, he became enraged.

Anger and hatred drove him to secret accusations. In May 1943 Romen posted a missive to Reich Minister of Propaganda Josef Goebbels in which he alleged that Messner was involved in subversive activities. Romen's poison pen letter seems to have prompted Gestapo-Vienna to bring him in for further questioning, but since Romen could provide no proof of his claims, he was released and the Gestapo pursued no rigorous action against Messner.[4]

But Romen persevered. He maintained his furtive observation of Messner, and after a few months added a new target: Rüdiger, the Semperit representative in Istanbul. More by luck than by skill Romen was honing in on two hidden enemies of the Reich.

By the fall of 1943 he had filed four lengthy accusations with Gestapo-Vienna. "[Messner] has worked for the Nazis," Romen wrote, "but if he had some poison, he would prefer to kill them."[5] Such were his incendiary but inconclusive charges against his superior. But despite his submissions' hefty word counts, Romen was apparently failing to give the Gestapo any actionable leads.

At this stage the Gestapo may have added Messner and Rüdiger to its long list of suspicious Austrians, those of uncertain loyalty to the Reich, and may have even made some routine inquiries, but not much else appears to have come of Romen's ranting. One might ask why the Gestapo didn't immediately put Messner under intense scrutiny; it is true, after all, that the Gestapo often arrested and interrogated people on the basis of similarly groundless accusations. But one must remember that Messner was in a position of importance and had already "proven" his reliability, having negotiated the rubber-supply contract with Brazil and for his efforts having been arrested, held captive, and possibly sentenced to death by pre-occupation France. Further, Romen, whose literary voice apparently came off as a bit hysterical, was a very ambitious man who likely coveted his boss's job. The Gestapo surely realized this possible motivation and factored it into their assessments of him.[6]

Even so, some of Romen's claims were disturbingly close to the truth. He told the Gestapo that in 1941 Messner had supposedly thought about "arranging" for the British to bomb synthetic rubber factories, to further the Allies' efforts and to shorten the war, and that Messner was using his foreign business trips to meet with people opposed to the German cause. Some of Romen's shots in the dark struck quite close to the bull's-eye.[7]

But cautious and capable Messner wasn't going to be blindsided by the perfidious likes of Romen. Among the senior executives and clerical staff at Semperit, Messner had his own counterintelligence tripwires in place to alert him to any potential insider threats.[8]

When he learned about Romen's cooperation with the Gestapo, Messner thought first not about himself, about fleeing Austria and going into hiding, or about defecting to the Allies. Instead he thought about the other man in Romen's sights—his good friend, colleague, and co-conspirator Gustav Rüdiger. If Rüdiger were left unaware of this lurking threat, the Gestapo might well ambush him on one of his business trips back to the Reich. Messner had to let Rüdiger know what was afoot.

After the war, Rüdiger recalled when Messner had told him about the snitch: "In February 1944, Dr. Messner visited Istanbul for discussions with officers of the Allied General Staff [sic], on which occasion Dr. Messner told me that my frequent traveling and activities abroad had attracted the attention of Mr. Sigismund Romen (a confidential informer [of the Gestapo]), and to ensure the safety of all members of the group, and not least of all to look after my own security, Dr. Messner advised that I must prepare for a long stay abroad until I receive a signal from him that I could safely return [to Austria] or until the Nazi regime had collapsed."[9]

But unknown to Messner, Romen's denunciations alone didn't spur the Gestapo to action. An established German source had begun to report on CASSIA—and not just on Messner and Rüdiger, but also on the entire group. And this source's reporting wasn't shrill, personal, and unsubstantiated; it was calm, measured, and objective, and included a wealth of hard evidence.

13

The Policeman

In summer or autumn of 1943, Caldonazzi introduced Maier to a valuable candidate for membership in CASSIA. Twenty-eight-year-old Andreas Hofer, born in the Tyrolean state capital of Innsbruck, was a district police sergeant,[1] had many acquaintances among soldiers in the Wehrmacht, and enjoyed great freedom of movement.

Hofer, who originally joined the police in 1938, had also served in the Wehrmacht, pulling frontline duty for four months before being declared medically unfit due to sciatica and neuropathy. He returned to Vienna—more specifically to his wife and three children—and resumed his job as a policeman.[2]

Hofer's appearance differed from that of the stereotypical policeman. He didn't have a brush cut, deep frown, cynical stare, and heavy jaw. Hofer's face was lean, with sad eyes and downturned brows, full lips, a cleft chin, and a high forehead from which his dark hair was brushed straight back but was always a bit unkempt. As stereotypes run, Hofer looked more like a musician or a poet.

Regardless of his appearance, the spirit of resistance coursed through Hofer's veins. He was a direct descendant and namesake of famous Tyrolean independence fighter Andreas Hofer (1767–1810).[3] Perhaps young policeman Hofer was inspired by one of his forebear's most famous lines: "I will not purchase my life by a lie."[4] In a chilling augur for one of his progeny, the historical Andreas was eventually captured and executed.[5]

As noted previously, most members of CASSIA lived in the same general neighborhood, and Hofer was no exception. He and his family occupied one of the 143 apartments in a subsidized housing block at Philippovichgasse 1,[6] now called Klose-hof, which was an easy 15-minute stroll due east of Türkenschanzpark and about the same distance southeast of Caldonazzi's rooms at Cottagegasse 94. Almost certainly Hofer played with his children in nearby Währing City Park and warned them to stay clear of the adjacent Old Jewish Cemetery, which since the Anschluss had moldered in shadows and sorrow beneath a tangle of trees and vines, behind high walls and padlocked gates. (Today the cemetery molders still and is off limits to all but a select few, among whom the author did not number.)

Along with Caldonazzi, Maier met Hofer several times in the Gersthof Parish Church rectory, and over time delicately turned their long discourses toward the subject of politics. By prompting but not leading Hofer in these discussions, Maier began to get a sense for the man's opinions on topics of increasing sensitivity, and over time ascertained where Hofer stood on the question of Nazi rule of Austria and what Hofer wanted for the country's future.[7]

Maier expressed sympathy about Hitler's betrayal of the Austrian Tyrol. His disdain for Hitler's ceding of Austrian claims on South Tyrol to Mussolini resonated strongly with Hofer. With such common positions established, Hofer became more candid in kind. Once Maier felt that sufficient trust had grown between them, he revealed the existence of a secret organization in Vienna—while not admitting his prominent role in it—and that its "Central Committee" was working to correct these and other injustices that the Nazis had wrought.[8]

In the end, Hofer signed on with CASSIA. He would soon join a small band of other young men, mostly brought into the fold by Caldonazzi with Maier's blessing (probably both literally and figuratively), and together they would embark on some of the group's most dangerous work.

14

The Soldiers

About the same time that Hofer joined CASSIA's ranks, Maier also agreed to bring in Wehrmacht conscripts Hermann Klepell, Dr. Josef Wyhnal, Wilhelm Ritsch, and Clemens von Pausinger. With the additions of these four talented men, CASSIA's clandestine work would reach new heights.

Caldonazzi was responsible for spotting these men, all opposed to the Nazis in particular and to the war in general, and for introducing them to Maier for further assessment and, eventually, for recruitment into the group. Another key reason that the soldiers committed themselves to this dangerous mission was their great esteem first for Caldonazzi and later for Maier, who were not only charismatic but also highly principled, and whose steadfast faith commanded that they work against evil, no matter the risks involved.

Twenty-five-year-old Klepell lived in an upper-floor apartment at Ferrogasse 16,[1] two blocks from Maier's Gersthof Parish Church. His father was an innkeeper[2] and a former 18th District socialist councilman.[3]

Klepell looked much older than his age, with a stocky build and prematurely receding hairline, but his dark, friendly eyes gave him away. In them was a twinkle of youthful mischievousness. When he joined CASSIA, Klepell was a corporal in the Wehrmacht, but before his conscription in late 1942, he had been a candidate for an engineering degree at the University of Agriculture, Caldonazzi's alma mater.[4]

At 40 years of age, Dr. Wyhnal was the old man of the bunch. He was a corporal in the Wehrmacht Medical Corps, but before the war, after studying medicine in Vienna, Graz, and Paris, he had been a physician.[5] Dr. Wyhnal's pale eyes, sad and thoughtful, set in a lean face, lent his countenance a certain melancholy. His overall appearance was reminiscent in some ways of jazz legend Chet Baker, whose angular face was similarly etched, but by hard living. Dr. Wyhnal's knowledge of toxins, infections, and pathology would lead the group in a new direction.

One wartime German document alleged that, during his studies in Paris, Wyhnal "temporarily joined the foreign arm of the National Socialist Party," but as with other members of CASSIA, his association with Nazism may have been perfunctory, to retain authorization to continue his studies. Further, Wyhnal's father was described as a Reich railroad employee, a position that may have demanded the son's party membership.[6]

The possibility remains, of course, that Wyhnal, like many other Austrians, may have been initially enticed by the alluring promises of Hitler to rehabilitate the country's flagging economy and to restore the reputations of Germany and Austria that had been sullied by the First World War. But ultimately, the possible Nazi affiliations of Wyhnal and other CASSIA members are beside the point. These men not only voiced their opposition to the Nazis, but they also took decisive—and very risky—action against the Reich.

Ritsch, also a corporal, was a 28-year-old former doctoral student. Forced to abandon his studies when he was conscripted in 1940, Ritsch was later diagnosed as suffering from neuropathy and was limited to garrison duty.[7]

But despite his Wehrmacht uniform, Ritsch looked nothing like a soldier; his was the mien of a scholar—prominent nose, untamed dark hair, pencil-thin mustache, and casual bearing. One could easily picture him at the lectern, slightly disheveled and wearing a tweed jacket, in a theater packed with university students. It is much more difficult to imagine him goose-stepping on a parade ground, outfitted with a rifle and steel helmet.

Ritsch had been born in Brez (Bretz or Britsch in German),[8] a town of fewer than 1,000 people in South Tyrol.[9] Like Caldonazzi's family, which had relocated to North Tyrol after the First World War, the Ritsches had also moved to Austria but had settled in the country's westernmost state, Vorarlberg, which is bordered by Germany, Switzerland, Liechtenstein, and North Tyrol. As another point of commonality with Caldonazzi, Ritsch's father had also served in the gendarmerie.[10]

Ritsch may have once been a member of "the Nazi student alliance."[11] As with the case of Dr. Wyhnal, Ritsch may have joined in name only to continue his studies unmolested, or because he was at first beguiled by Hitler's rousing vision of renewed Germanic national strength and international influence. But these are only speculations. What is certain is that

Ritsch saw through the lies and, though he had none of the special talents or connections that often presuppose efficacy in espionage, he had the courage and commitment to work against the Reich.

Von Pausinger, as evinced by the nobiliary preposition *von*, was from a titled family.[12] His father was Clemens von Pausinger Frankenburg (1855–1936), a once-famous portrait artist.[13] The younger von Pausinger may have been born in Brittany, France, in the small village of St. Enogat, not far from St. Malo[14]; perhaps von Pausinger Frankenburg had been commissioned to paint a portrait in the area. By the time that he joined CASSIA, the younger von Pausinger was married and had two children.[15]

A 1944 German court document recorded that from 1931 to 1934 von Pausinger had been a member of the *Vaterländische Front* (Dollfuss's Austrofascist party), and at that same time had also belonged to two paramilitary groups—the *Heimwehr* (Home Guard) and the *Freiwilliges Schutzkorps* (Volunteer Protection Corps). This same document asserted that in 1938 von Pausinger had applied for Nazi Party membership,[16] but just as with Wyhnal and Ritsch, if von Pausinger did associate with the Nazis early on, whether to protect his or his family's position, or because he was initially intrigued by Hitler, he later sought not only to break with the party but also to undermine it.

When he joined CASSIA, von Pausinger was a sergeant in the Wehrmacht, but in civilian life he had held the lofty title of "Assessor of Law," which attested to his having acquired his Juris Doctor degree in 1938, to his having passed the bar examination, and to his being fully qualified for a profession in law.[17] His involvement with CASSIA would provide the ultimate test of his skills in writing legal briefs.

In addition to—or perhaps related to—his Wehrmacht service, in January 1942 von Pausinger began working for a Viennese translation and transcription company that held a contract with a surveying agency.[18] It is possible that this job gave him access to intelligence of interest to the Allies.

One last individual, Karl Fulterer, apparently provided some assistance to Ritsch's subversive activities, but it is unclear if he was a formal member of CASSIA or if he even fully comprehended what Ritsch was doing.[19] Thirty-one-year-old Fulterer was born and raised in Dornbirn, Vorarlberg, the same state where Ritsch had grown up. Fulterer was described as holding a Juris Doctor degree, and as being an "apprentice lawyer." Fulterer had been excused from military service due to an unspecified physical impairment from a past accident.[20]

This group of new recruits, overseen by Caldonazzi and Maier, wasted no time in planning and executing subversion, intelligence-gathering, and propaganda operations.

On at least two occasions, Hofer arranged for Dr. Wyhnal, a specialist in bacteriology, to inject anti–Nazi district police officers with medicines or other substances that precipitated high fever, to excuse them from their duties or from conscription into the Wehrmacht. At some point Dr. Wyhnal—again apparently at Hofer's behest—administered a fever-inducing substance to a young man who was being drafted into the Waffen-SS, the armed part of the *Schutzstaffel* that saw heavy combat during the war. Dr. Wyhnal also facilitated the development of infections, inflammation, and fever in some men by packing "bacterial cultures" and other contaminants into open wounds—delicate procedures that, if performed improperly, could have resulted in gangrene or septicemia.[21]

After helping some of his colleagues and friends, Hofer himself began to worry that he might be again conscripted and sent back to the Eastern Front. So, around Christmas of 1943, Dr. Wyhnal injected turpentine into Hofer's ankle joint, which likely caused acute inflammation and scarring of connective tissues—effectively hobbling him. Although the procedure certainly carried the risk of causing permanent damage to Hofer's ankle, it nonetheless served its intended purpose: Hofer was admitted to the hospital for treatment of his debilitating "condition." Then, in early 1944 Dr. Wyhnal administered a second dose of turpentine to Hofer because the effects of the first injection were beginning to wear off.[22]

With assistance from Hofer and Ritsch, Dr. Wyhnal performed similar acts on likeminded Wehrmacht regulars and conscripts in advance of their military fitness examinations in an attempt to disqualify the men from active duty—particularly from frontline service. At every planning session for these operations, and at some of Dr. Wyhnal's actual "treatment" sessions, Caldonazzi was present.[23]

In a very risky move, Dr. Wyhnal, Klepell, Hofer, and Ritsch initiated contact with some French prisoners of war, who were probably serving on work details in and around Wehrmacht installations or as forced laborers in factories, and began providing them information and other undefined assistance to facilitate their escape from the Reich, presumably to neutral countries such as Switzerland. These four CASSIA members provided similar such advice and help to sympathetic Wehrmacht soldiers who wanted to flee Austria.[24]

But CASSIA didn't commit these subversive activities at the expense of traditional intelligence gathering. Beginning in the fall of 1943, the group also began to collect sensitive details on arms-production factories in Steyr,[25] Wiener Neudorf, and Wiener Neustadt. Corporal Klepell, his engineering studies interrupted by the war, was largely responsible for these efforts. He had natural access to the Wehrmacht's Survey Office, from which he took copies of the factories' procurement plans, along with a site plan of the Steyr factory. He passed this sheaf of valuable documents to Messner, who delivered it to OSS on a trip to Switzerland or Turkey.[26] Klepell's intelligence then served as the basis of OSS report number 359: "Steyr Armament Works."[27]

Never one to sit on the sidelines, Caldonazzi also lent a hand to this work. He loitered around the Schoeller-Bleckmann factory in Mürzzuschlag,[28] keeping his eyes peeled and ears open for intelligence. The company, known for its steelworks, was heavily involved in arms production for the Reich. While Caldonazzi's access to the facility was probably limited, he was nonetheless able to write a description and to sketch a map of the factory.[29] OSS subsequently submitted Caldonazzi's intelligence in report number 339: "The Schoeller-Bleckman [sic] Works at Muerzzuschlag."[30]

Not to be bested by their fellows who were stealing secrets, other CASSIA members turned their attention to the dissemination of propaganda. In July or August 1943, around the same time that Klepell began taking Wehrmacht documents, von Pausinger and Ritsch—the latter possibly using a typewriter that Fulterer had provided—produced copies of at least three fliers with anti–Nazi and antiwar messages. Then in September 1943 Ritsch furtively posted the handbills in downtown Vienna.[31] The messages[32] condemned Hitler and his military ambitions, and called for the people to rise up in resistance:

> During the last two months, the eastern campaign has cost Hitler 1.5 million men—Austrian, German—it is time to take a stand! Cast aside your individual political beliefs and come together as one. Hunt the Nazi clique to hell and give our country its longed-for freedom!
>
> Why an even longer war? On all fronts the war is failing. Only a madman or criminal like Hitler still speaks of "victory." The inevitable end is coming. Why should thousands more sacrifice themselves? It is time for us to free ourselves from this tyranny. Unite for a common goal: the destruction of Hitler, the greatest, most accursed criminal of all time.

The third leaflet called Hitler and his henchmen "traitors to the German people," and charged, "You [Hitler] and your criminal clique have ruined us all. Your game is over and the people are now calling for revenge."[33]

In a city ruled by fear, with informants lurking in every shadow and around every corner, this act—in the spirit of similar acts that preceded it, particularly those carried out by Caldonazzi—was incredibly courageous. A modern equivalent would be a band of North Koreans distributing fliers in downtown Pyongyang that describe dictator Kim Jong-Un as a criminal and a tyrant, the Communist Party as illegitimate, and Kim's belligerence toward the U.S. and South Korea as counterfeit and harming the populace, and that encourage the people to rise up and to overthrow him and his cronies.

Very few people, then and now, have a fraction of the mettle—"the sand" as some Americans say—that CASSIA's men and women had in abundance.

Part Three: The Eulogy of Triumph

15

The Professional

On occasion, between his visits to Istanbul, Messner still traveled to Switzerland, sometimes with Issakides. One significant trip occurred in December 1943, some two months before Messner autographed Lada-Mocarski's terms, when Kurt Grimm, CASSIA's facilitator in Zurich, introduced Messner and Issakides to his U.S. intelligence contact, OSS-Bern chief Allen Dulles.[1]

Dulles's appearance alone would have reassured the couple. With his silver hair and mustache, strong chin, friendly but incisive eyes, rimless round glasses, tailored suit, and fine briar pipe, he possessed the air of both a patrician and an intellectual. At 50 years of age, the oldest man in the room, Dulles was a paragon of maturity and dependability, but he also exuded an abundance of enthusiasm and energy.

It is uncertain if the meeting took place in Grimm's apartment in Zurich's Hotel Bellerive au Lac or in Dulles's ground-level rooms at Herrengasse 23 in Bern—a secluded location, about a block from the River Aare, accessible not only from the street but also through a system of footpaths.[2] A postwar appraisal of OSS-Bern's operations suggests that Dulles's residence, while not anonymous, in that it was officially associated with Dulles, was nevertheless well situated for fairly discreet contact: "Meetings with sub-agents were held, after blackout, at the mission chief's [Dulles's] house, where surveillance was almost impossible."[3] Wherever they met, Dulles was impressed with Messner and his "envoy," Issakides, the young concert pianist who had been responsible for establishing the first link to Allied intelligence through Grimm.[4]

Although Dulles had been the first OSS officer to make contact—albeit indirectly—with CASSIA and to collect the group's initial offering of valuable intelligence, he acknowledged that MacFarland's crew in Istanbul had operational primacy on the case. After all, it was through Rüdiger and DOGWOOD that contact was now being maintained and quantities of intelligence were being passed.[5]

Even so, Messner noted that he and Issakides would continue to visit Switzerland, and they wanted to use that country—and Dulles's good services therein—as an alternate means of contact, a backup or accessory to CASSIA's arrangements with OSS-Istanbul. Dulles agreed, and then warned (diplomatically, one must assume, without disparaging his OSS colleagues) that Istanbul was a nest of spies, with information being sold to the highest bidder, or worse still to more than one bidder, and was thus a very dangerous place to operate.[6]

What Dulles refrained from saying is that he handled operations very differently from the way that MacFarland did. OSS-Istanbul, in congruence with the city's rowdy wartime atmosphere, ran its operations loosely and aggressively, but Dulles's work in Switzerland was more careful, discreet, methodical, and mindful. Perhaps "mindful" was most important quality of Dulles's operations. He understood the delicate political and security circumstances of his hosts, the Swiss, and this awareness guided the way that he conducted his OSS business.[7]

As the conflict wore on, the Swiss realized—as did Dulles—that Hitler would be eyeing their country's unexhausted resources and bulging banks and additional Alpine routes to the Italian Front, and that, as his greed and desperation grew, the Führer would be looking for any excuse—such as Swiss preferential treatment of Allied intelligence services and Swiss tolerance of anti–German operations being handled in and launched from Switzerland—to dismiss the country's claims of neutrality and to roll across its borders. And from a more workaday perspective, since his arrival in 1942, Dulles had relied on the Swiss for honoring his "diplomatic" credentials and allowing him to live in their country, and on the Swiss security services' circumspect but crucial assistance—which in some cases simply meant turning a blind eye—to his operations.[8]

Of course the Swiss grasped that Dulles's agents alone would not decide the war's outcome, since Germany's eventual defeat was likely and growing likelier still. But they realized too that some of his sources were so well placed that they might contribute to a quicker end to the war, thereby removing the Wehrmacht menace from their borders.[9]

Some Swiss officials also understood just how many people were dying every day in combat, forced labor camps, and death camps, and among affected civilian populations from starvation, exposure, and disease. This already-staggering tally, they knew, would only rise as the war careened toward an inevitable last stand on German soil. With such grisly arithmetic in mind, some of Dulles's Swiss counterparts viewed any shortening of the war—whether by months, weeks, days, or even hours—to be of paramount importance; they reasoned that, if Dulles's agents could help to hasten the Reich's collapse, even if slightly, then Switzerland should not frustrate his good efforts.

Dulles also differed from MacFarland in that he proved a quick study when it came to learning how best to run intelligence operations. In terms of formal training, Dulles was no less an intelligence neophyte than was MacFarland. But in 1916, after taking a master's degree in international relations, Dulles entered the U.S. diplomatic corps and served in Austria and Switzerland during the First World War, sometimes collecting confidential information, as his duties required, on Germany, Austria-Hungary, and the Balkans. At war's end he joined the U.S. delegation to the Paris Peace Conference as a low-level advisor on Central Europe, and then in 1920 he was assigned to the U.S. embassy in Constantinople (Istanbul). Two years later Dulles returned to a job at the U.S. Department of State in Washington DC and on the side went to law school, leaving the government in 1926 to become an attorney in New York City. But Dulles kept his hand in the field of foreign affairs: He was a member of the Council on Foreign Relations, the private think-tank and publisher of great repute. Even in his day job, Dulles exercised skills that would serve him well in Bern. His lawyer's mind was schooled in and exercised with the practical application of logic in the solving of complex problems.[10]

He also enjoyed fairly productive relationships—though with occasional tension—with his British counterparts in Switzerland, and from them learned more about the curious trade of intelligence, in which the British had gained extensive experience in the far corners of their empire.[11] He likely gained further insights on clandestine work from some of his expert sources, primarily Abwehr officer Gisevius, who knew well how to look after his operational security. All in all, by training, experience, and disposition, Dulles was much more suited to clandestine work than was MacFarland, whose pre–OSS résumé consisted of service as a wartime ambulance driver, a U.S. Army captain, and a banker.

After his first meeting with Messner and Issakides, Dulles assigned new codenames and a code number to CASSIA—DIANA, OYSTERS, and 840—to differentiate OSS-Bern's interactions with the group from those of Istanbul.[12] Dulles correctly assumed that OSS's encoded radio and telephone communications[13] were vulnerable to German interception and decoding, and used a system of alternating codenames and numbers in transmissions, to confuse and mislead any potential eavesdroppers about the sources of his reports.[14] So heavy was OSS-Bern's burden of enciphering and deciphering messages that, with Swiss permission, Dulles seconded into OSS service six or seven U.S. aviators who had been forced to land in Switzerland and put them to work as cipher clerks on a round-the-clock rotating schedule.[15]

After his first face-to-face meeting with representatives of the Austrian group,[16] its diverse members united by a righteous cause, Dulles reflected on this strange "agent trio"—two unlikely emissaries, a musician and a merchant, dispatched to Switzerland by, unlikelier still, a Viennese priest.[17]

16

The Mole

His real name was either František or Bedøich Laufer, but he also answered to Fritz, Friedrich, Direktor Schröder, Ludwig Meyer (or Mayer), Ludwig Hermann, and Karl Heinz. He was either Jewish, half-Jewish, or, according to his papers, Aryan. He was either skinny or fat. He was either an agent of the Abwehr, the Gestapo, the SD, the OSS, the Czech underground, or Zionists. He may have been blond, unless he had jet-black hair or was completely bald. He was definitely tall. Possibly. Well, if he wasn't short, he was certainly tall.[1]

One thing about Laufer is clear and irrefutable: He was a scoundrel of the highest order. He looked out only for himself, and was willing and ready to stab anyone in the back—literally or figuratively—to gain advantage or coin. He was a survivor.

On the other hand, Sigismund Romen, the snitch, at least chose a side. As history has judged him, he was not on the right side—right meaning both just (or at least more just, as war is at best an ambiguous setting) and correct, which one could translate not only as valid but, in this case, perhaps also as victorious. But Romen was consistent. Despicable, yes, but consistently so. Laufer was not: He blew with the day's breeze, and had a ready alias and persona to take advantage of every potential shift in wind speed and direction.

Laufer wasn't alone, of course, in his dirty trade; he wasn't the only man or woman during the Second World War who engaged in a game of double cross. (In Laufer's case, make that triple or quadruple cross.) But in terms of treachery he was a maestro, the scummiest in a world filled to the very brim with scum. The sordid streets and alleys of let's-make-a-deal Istanbul were perfect for him. There, he felt at home. But the city gave him more than just comfort. It also provided him the inspiration, opportunity, and resources to compose his magnum opus.

Laufer's status with the German security services was different from that of Romen. Laufer was categorized as an official undercover agent, designated in some documents as a *V-Mann*. In German intelligence jargon, *V-Mann* is short for either *Verbindungsmann*, a term that emphasizes the controlling service's clandestine link into a targeted group, or *Vertrauensmann*, a term that speaks to the confidential nature of the agent and his or her work. Regardless of the preferred root word, a *V-Mann* is a formal agent, recruited and responsive, whom a controlling service uses to infiltrate enemy organizations.

But what of the vitriolic Romen? The Gestapo classified him as an informer, a person of unknown or untested reliability who has provided—and may provide again—some information of potential interest, which the informer has collected incidentally or naturally, and perhaps incompletely. Probably because of Romen's unconcealed personal hatred of Messner, his blind ambition, and his fragile vanity, the Gestapo likely deemed him unsuitable for delicate *V-Mann* assignments and elected not to formalize its relationship with him.[2]

The consensus is that Laufer began his career as a *V-Mann* in 1940, in his hometown of Prague, at the age of 40. When the Germans marched into Czechoslovakia, Laufer's half-Jewish ancestry marked him for deportation to a concentration camp. But turncoat Laufer—one might imagine the reptilian sibilance of his silver tongue—convinced the city's new masters that he would be of much greater value to them as a clandestine agent.[3]

The Abwehr, German military intelligence, was the first, but by no means the last, to bite. Laufer, who had worked as both a waiter and a petty criminal, found himself standing in court in 1940, presumably because of his efforts in the latter profession. Impressed with Laufer's sophistic skills and mindful of the vulnerability that his half-Jewish designation presented, Abwehr Captain Erich Klausnitzer[4] recruited Laufer to infiltrate the Czech underground in Prague.[5] To secure his loyalty, the Abwehr removed the deportation order and issued Laufer doctored papers that identified him as an Aryan.[6] One wrong move, of course, and the papers would be revoked, and slack-jawed Laufer would find himself in a crowded cattle car bound for a most unpleasant destination. For the Abwehr, the papers comprised an effective, if crude, means of controlling its new agent.

Over time, something akin to trust—or perhaps more like mutual assured destruction—grew between the Abwehr and Laufer, and before long, usually disguised as a businessman, he was being dispatched on missions to Zagreb, Belgrade, Budapest, and Istanbul. At some point,

Laufer returned to Prague, and probably without the Abwehr's knowledge (so much for that "trust"), he began working as an agent for its rival service in the SS, the SD.[7]

According to one reference, the Gestapo or the SD "impressed" Laufer to work for them under the threat that his loved ones would suffer if he chose not to cooperate, but it seems much more likely that the greatest pressure that Laufer felt stemmed from his desire to keep his false Aryan-attestation papers, and thereby to avoid being tossed into a concentration camp.[8] Regardless of what influences were being used and who was using them, Laufer was a coldblooded opportunist who gave as well as he got, and the sands on which he chose to live and work were constantly shifting—usually, through his scheming, in his favor.

Eventually, the Abwehr—probably this time without the SD's knowledge (touché!)—sent Laufer to live in Budapest, where he targeted the Czech underground cells that were operating there. By infiltrating the underground's key courier connections,[9] particularly the Budapest-Vienna route, Laufer was able to identify a number of Czech resistance members and supporters, whose arrests the Abwehr then arranged.[10]

Despite these arrests, despite reports that he was cozy with the Germans, despite his lavish spending, Laufer didn't merely survive—he thrived.[11] Every time a charge against him surfaced, every time suspicion fell on him, Laufer was ready with an eloquent, credible, and assuring explanation that reversed all doubts and soothed all frayed nerves. Laufer understood the power of telling people what they want to hear.

In summer 1941 the Czech underground sent Laufer to Istanbul to retrieve a tranche of funding.[12] It would be the first of many visits to the city and, always looking for efficiencies, Laufer also used the trips as opportunities to sniff around for Allied intelligence activities. It is quite possible that, by this time, Laufer had also begun working with Gestapo-Vienna; after all, because of his Abwehr assignment to penetrate the underground's Budapest-Vienna courier route, he spent much time in the capital of Ostmark province, formerly known as Austria.[13] So it is also possible that Gestapo-Vienna gave him a juicy lead, courtesy of snitch Romen, that led him to Rüdiger and then, by shadowing or tricking him, to his handler.

Another theory is that Laufer may have needed no outside help with finding Schwarz. According to this version of the story, the two men had been friends since childhood in Prague, and Schwarz trusted Laufer implicitly.[14] Regardless, Istanbul was swarming with spies and information peddlers, so even without help from the Gestapo or absent a shared adolescence with Schwarz, it wouldn't have taken Laufer long to find a fellow Czech, a prominent Jewish businessman who was running—and not very secretly—a large, lucrative network of agents for the Americans in Istanbul. That man was, of course, Alfred Schwarz, the OSS principal agent known as DOGWOOD.

Awed by Laufer's worldliness and hoodwinked by his honed chicanery, Schwarz, always looking to expand his empire, recruited him as a subsource in early July 1943.[15] Schwarz described his agent as "an objective, realistically minded, serious man, extremely enterprising and not without a certain adventurous vein."[16] Schwarz was partially correct: Laufer *was* enterprising and adventurous. Later, confronted by another agent's claims that Laufer was a traitor, Schwarz simply dismissed the charge and countered that Laufer was his "best agent."[17] For its part, which wasn't much, OSS-Istanbul—as usual lockstep with Schwarz and otherwise fully blinkered—assigned Laufer the codename IRIS.[18] And just like that, Laufer was on his way to the biggest accomplishment of his shady life.

Once again Schwarz refused to reveal the background of his new subsource, and once again OSS's X-2 branch (counterintelligence) was denied the chance to conduct any meaningful checks on Laufer. Without full traces on Laufer, OSS remained unaware of his possible connections to other parts of DOGWOOD, and of the degree to which Schwarz was comingling different, unrelated lines of the network's reporting.

As it turns out, the OSS probably *did* have some derogatory information on Laufer. Back in November of 1941, more than a year and a half before Laufer signed on with DOGWOOD, an informant had told a U.S. diplomat about Laufer's work for the Germans against the Czech underground, but a clerical error prevented X-2 from retrieving the report and potentially associating it with Schwarz's new agent.[19]

Laufer wasted no time in ferreting out the disparate other parts of DOGWOOD. By late 1943 he was definitely cooperating with Gestapo-Vienna—in addition to continuing work with the SD and the Abwehr—and was reporting on DOGWOOD in general, and CASSIA in particular.

To compromise CASSIA, Laufer simply waited for Schwarz's lax security to reveal at least one member's identity, or a solid clue to such an identity, and then Gestapo-Vienna's flatfoots did the rest—through physical surveillance, telephone tapping, and informant reporting—until connections between the group's members emerged.[20] Meanwhile, the other German security services, which had a hefty presence in Istanbul, mobilized their resources and began unraveling clues to the city's CASSIA-related personalities and activities. By early 1944, the Gestapo had compiled thick dossiers on all of the primary culprits and was preparing to take action against them.

Put succinctly—and lamentably—by a surviving CASSIA member, who later reflected on those dark days, "a spy had crept into the Maier Group toward the end of winter 1943/44."[21]

17

The Arrests

January and February often find Vienna under leaden skies. Murk descends on the city; lines and edges blur. The stunted days are worn down shorter still. The smooth blanket of Christmas snowfall becomes patchy, pockmarked, and stained. Muddy slush forms along pathways.

As the barometer plunges, so too does the city's collective mood. Faces darken and harden. Courtesies are observed, but more curtly. Melancholy stirs and persists until the first thaw of spring.

Vienna was wearing her winter's shroud when CASSIA suffered her first casualty: The Gestapo placed Walter Caldonazzi under provisional arrest on 15 January 1944.[1] Jostled by his grim escorts, Caldonazzi limped into Gestapo Headquarters, the former Hotel Métropole on Vienna's Morzinplatz, and later into a Liesl cell. He was never again to walk as a free man. After more than a month of further investigation and harsh interrogations, the Gestapo solemnized his arrest on 25 February.[2]

Three days later, on 28 February 1944, Hofer was arrested.[3] The Gestapo found especially distasteful and egregious Hofer's status as a fellow policeman, whose absolute loyalty the Reich demanded, and his alleged assistance to French prisoners of war, sworn enemies of the state. His time at Morzinplatz and in the Liesl would be particularly unpleasant.

Around this same time, the University of Vienna expelled 20-year-old Frederiksen from medical school for interfering with an SS recruiting lecture on campus. His protest was a risky move but luckily he avoided arrest. His involvement in the resistance had not yet been detected.

With the beast now wounded, the Gestapo was ready to plunge a harpoon into its head, and for that deathblow they had the perfect Queequeg[4]—František Laufer.

CASSIA's downfall began with OSS's clumsy attempt to fulfill its obligations to the group, as defined by the agreement that Messner had signed with Lada-Mocarski. CASSIA had made good on its promise by providing high-level intelligence and distributing anti–Nazi propaganda, and now OSS needed to reciprocate by giving the group a radio, ciphers, transmission instructions, and funding.[5]

In OSS-Istanbul's signature style of poorly planned and badly executed operations, the DOGWOOD network handler, either Coleman or his backup, MacFarland, let Schwarz direct the show. Always one to throw caution to the wind, to open all compartments when the ship was leaking, and to cross four live wires simultaneously, Schwarz tasked two other DOGWOOD agents, JASMINE and JACARANDA, neither of whom should have known anything about CASSIA, with delivering 100,000 Reichmarks[6] and a radio transmitter/receiver to a third DOGWOOD agent, Messner, in Budapest in early March 1944.[7]

For this radio set OSS had grand ambitions. Once CASSIA had established two-way, real-time communications, OSS would arrange to parachute-drop a team of OSS advisors into a remote part of Austria, where members of CASSIA would serve as a reception committee. OSS was eager to avoid the disaster of previous missions into Austria, wherein parachuted officers and agents had been sent in "blind," without advance notification to cooperative resistance elements that could securely receive them, and had been quickly wrapped up. According to OSS's plan, these advisors would assist the Austrians in organizing sabotage and other armed resistance units.[8]

Schwarz's efforts to facilitate the passage of the radio and the money were a gift to German intelligence. The DOGWOOD agents whom he selected, JASMINE and JACARANDA, were also accomplished double agents, reporting to the Abwehr and probably to other German security services.[9] JASMINE was Hungarian Army Lieutenant Colonel and Military Attaché Otto Hatz (claimed birth name "de Hatzsegy"[10] or "von Hatz"[11]—to suggest noble ancestry), who OSS Headquarters suspected was under hostile control; and JACARANDA was Hungarian Lothar Kövess[12] (sometimes rendered Luther Kovess),[13] a down-on-his-luck petty aristocrat and naval officer of the defunct Habsburg Empire, who was a personal friend of both Schwarz and Hatz and whose past pro–Nazi sympathies had apparently been forgotten.[14]

As for OSS Headquarters' suspicions that Hatz was a double agent, a trusted British source had acquired from a known German agent a report on a secret OSS operation to which Hatz had privileged access. It was clear to the British and to OSS HQS—but not to OSS-Istanbul—that only Hatz could have leaked the information.[15]

One might well ask why DOGWOOD hosted so many Hungarian agents; after all, while Hungary had sided with the Axis in 1941, it was not at the center of German policies and plans. The answer is twofold: Schwarz had developed close friendships with some Hungarians and, as personal favors, he brought them into DOGWOOD[16]; and Coleman was eager to develop more lines of access into Hungary and thus gave Schwarz a very free hand in recruiting such sources.

Coleman's enthusiasm about Hungary was rooted in his general desire to expand DOGWOOD's access into new areas and was amplified by dunning influence from Washington. In 1943, as the tide of the war was changing, the U.S. Joint Chiefs of Staff decided to court secretly an affiliate state of the Axis (i.e., Romania, Bulgaria, or Hungary), in hopes that the selected country could be persuaded to side with the Allied cause. In response to this directive, OSS-Istanbul suggested pursuit of Hungary and later received permission from Washington to explore options for developing access to key Hungarian officials.[17]

OSS-Istanbul immediately began tasking its Hungarian sources for intelligence on the current state of affairs in Hungary and for the names of Hungarian officials who might be receptive to a discreet approach from the Allies. For his part in this show Coleman turned to two Hungarian sub-sources whom Schwarz had personally endorsed: Hatz and one of Hatz's stringers, András György, whom OSS had codenamed TRILLIUM, after a flowering plant of the lily family.[18]

In Hatz Coleman had made an extremely poor choice. As a military attaché he was, ipso facto, a Hungarian intelligence officer whose loyalties OSS had not thoroughly sorted out. Even if Coleman and Schwarz had more fully understood Hatz's commitments to and within Hungary, which, as it turned out, were with the pro–Axis faction, they still lacked the counterintelligence skills and discipline to discover—or even merely to suspect—that Hatz was a dyed-in-the-wool German double agent. And any such suspicions of or conclusions about Hatz would have consequently cast doubt on György, for as with the master, so too usually with the servant.

In the case of György, Coleman had every reason to be doubtful and no cause to be trustful. György, who like Laufer was of Jewish ancestry but who had converted to Catholicism, was a particularly slippery character. He was an accomplished smuggler who specialized in moving currency, gold, diamonds and Persian carpets, and changed names as almost as often as he changed suits, alternating between such aliases and nominal variations as Andor Gross (or Groß), Bandi (or Bandy) Grosz, Andreas Grosz, Antal Grosz, András Grainer, and Andrea (or André) Gyorgy.[19]

György traded allegiances with similar frequency, sometimes serving himself, other times the Hungarians, and still other times the Germans. He had been a felon since his early twenties, when he ran an undefined illicit trade from a coffeehouse in Budapest, which culminated in his arrest in 1941 and in his subsequent decision to work for the Abwehr to avoid an 18-month jail term. After doing the Germans' bidding in Switzerland and Bulgaria, György returned to Budapest in August 1942 to find the authorities still keen to lock him up, so without telling the Abwehr he volunteered to Hungarian military intelligence, which apparently made his prison sentence disappear.[20] British code-breaking operations revealed that György was working simultaneously for the Germans, Hungarians, British, and Americans, but it appears that the OSS dismissed this hard evidence in favor of Schwarz's opinion of his friend György, whom he described as committed to the Allied cause.[21]

But despite Hatz's professional background and OSS Headquarters' concerns about him, and despite György's dubious past and equally dubious present, Coleman persisted in relying heavily on these two men. For Coleman's clumsy efforts Hatz and György were able to play a role in advising the Germans about pro–Allied sentiments in the Hungarian government, which in part prompted Hitler in the spring of 1944 to occupy the country and to take over its governance.[22]

Then, not satisfied with selling out their own country, which in the final year of the war suffered extensive damage and infamously played a greater part in the Holocaust, Hatz and György burrowed ever more deeply into the DOGWOOD network. In the permissive operational environment that Schwarz and Coleman had created, the two Hungarians easily strayed into areas of the network that should have been protected by unassailable compartments. In the official postwar history of OSS, the U.S. War Department neatly summarized the steps leading to German penetration of DOGWOOD: "[A] new Hungarian Military Attache [Hatz] arrived in Istanbul in November [1943] and contacted OSS through 'Dogwood.' The Attache, the Hungarian double-agent, and other Hungarians [i.e., Kövess and György] served as couriers.... As suspected, the operation turned out to be an attempt to infiltrate OSS.... [T]he new Hungarian Attache in Istanbul was, privately, also in Gestapo pay."[23]

However, while some studies have implicated György in CASSIA's downfall, his role—if any—in this regard has not been well defined, although he certainly betrayed to the Germans those parts of DOGWOOD to which he had access. But György's help in compromising CASSIA was hardly needed; Laufer, Hatz, and Kövess had covered all of the angles.[24]

Kövess's role in the debacle served as a further condemnation of OSS-Istanbul's shoddy security practices. When he was put on OSS's payroll, Kövess was ostensibly working as the Istanbul representative for Danube Shipping, a flimsy front used by the Abwehr.[25] The company's thin camouflage would have dissolved under the slightest counterintelligence scrutiny. But Schwarz put no such attention on Kövess or on Danube Shipping, and neither Coleman nor MacFarland asked any questions or raised any objections. In fact, Schwarz stated for the record that Kövess was loyal to the Allies and "an inveterate enemy of Nazi Germany."[26] And so, with little effort, letting OSS and its star agent do all of the work, the Germans dropped yet another spy into DOGWOOD.

Without a thought to operational security or agent suitability, and instead focusing on who could readily travel to and from Hungary, Schwarz instructed Hatz to smuggle two radio sets into Budapest and to pass them to Kövess. For his part, Kövess was told to issue one set to Laufer, presumably for use by the Czech underground, and the other—along with a packet of money—to an Austrian agent, Messner.[27] In other words, courtesy of Schwarz's and OSS's ineptitude, the Germans had spies insinuated into every stage of this sensitive operation. As the pieces of the puzzle were still coming together, Laufer probably stepped in and, with his excellent visibility into CASSIA, clarified the whole arrangement for and highlighted its vulnerable spots to his German masters, allowing them to begin planning a counter-operation.

But one person remained wary of the whole affair. Before committing to OSS-Istanbul's plan, Messner decided to travel to Switzerland for a second meeting with Allen Dulles. Issakides accompanied him. During the ensuing discussion with Dulles, which took place during the weekend of 11/12 March 1944, Messner described what he knew about OSS-Istanbul's plan to deliver the radio and money to him in Budapest.[28] Almost certainly Messner was unaware of the number of other unrelated DOGWOOD agents—Hatz, Kövess, and Laufer—who were playing key roles in the operation; in his defense, Dulles probably didn't know about these agents, either. In the end, Messner solicited, and received, Dulles's endorsement of the Budapest operation.[29]

At this same meeting, Messner advised Dulles that Soviet influence was growing in parts of the Austrian resistance, and he entreated OSS to initiate an Allied publicity campaign, delivered through commercial radio broadcasts, to diminish the Soviet monopoly on propaganda in the country. According to OSS's official history, Messner reported that "fifteen to twenty experienced Communist agents ... were being parachuted every month into Austrian territory."[30] Messner had decided to advise Dulles on this point because OSS-Istanbul had turned a deaf ear to CASSIA's pleas. In fact, one month earlier MacFarland had advised OSS Headquarters that "through its communistic members, [CASSIA] is already in touch with the USSR, and we [OSS-Istanbul] have encouraged them in this endeavor."[31] Dulles heard Messner out on this issue and dutifully reported the details to OSS Headquarters.

Their business with Dulles concluded, Messner and Issakides returned to Vienna, and about two weeks later Messner drove his car[32] to Budapest, ostensibly on a business trip.[33] But as events played out, Messner's instinctive worries about OSS-Istanbul's plan, which drove him to seek out Dulles's opinion, were justified—and then some.

Back in Vienna, the Gestapo was busy. It picked up Wyhnal on 18 March 1944.[34] Then, on Tuesday, 28 March 1944,[35] after morning mass at the Gersthof Parish Church, two men in leather coats flanked Maier and pronounced, "In the name of the Führer, we arrest you."[36] He was bundled into a waiting car and brought to Gestapo Headquarters.

It was a scene from a Hollywood B movie: The patently symbolic setting; the Gestapo thugs with their banal wardrobe; their laughably predictable lines. But this was no fiction wherein in the handsome protagonist suffers eye-widening setbacks only to prevail heroically in the end. This was a sinister reality with painful, and very likely mortal, consequences. For Maier, the appearance of an idling car at the curb and grim-faced men in shiny black jackets was tantamount to a death sentence. He was about to learn that some nightmares persist into waking hours.

Maier fully comprehended the great peril of such things, particularly of the Reich's hackneyed slogans. The line "IM NAMEN DES DEUTSCHEN VOLKES!" was splattered across the tops of Nazi court documents and Gestapo reports. "IN THE NAME OF THE GERMAN PEOPLE!"—the upper-case letters and exclamation point were a fanatical preface to whatever demented pronouncement followed. The phrase was emblematic of—as was "In the name of the Führer"—a deficiency of reason and humanity, and an abundance of cruelty. To be its object was to descend into Kafka's *Castle*, a literary horror made real by the Nazis, and one had little chance ever to leave, but to be carried out, usually in two pieces, head pared from body.

On 29 March, unaware of the Gestapo's foul work back home, Messner and his Semperit personal secretary, probably Hilde Palme,[37] arrived in Budapest and wended their way to the appointed rendezvous, where the designated intermediary (Kövess) would pass them the radio and money.[38] In a hotel room, probably in the presence of the traitorous Kövess, Messner was ambushed and arrested by the Gestapo, and then hauled back to Gestapo-Vienna Headquarters at Morzinplatz.[39] (In its official history of OSS, the U.S. War Department recorded that the Gestapo arrested Messner in Budapest on 21 March,[40] but this date is at variance with other sources, to include Gestapo reports.)

At about the same time in Vienna, with Laufer's assistance, using established CASSIA protocols, the Gestapo sent a false message to Barbara Issakides, instructing her to retrieve a bundle of Reichmarks at an accommodation address and to deliver the money to Maier.[41] In spy jargon, an accommodation address, alternately called a safe address, is a location—often a mail drop, such as a poste restante, but sometimes a house or apartment—that is unaffiliated with any of the parties involved in an intelligence operation and that is used by an agent and his or her handler(s) to send and receive messages and other items.

In Issakides's case, the address was the apartment of Margarethe "Grete" Rotter, who had been secretly cooperating with the Abwehr office

Gestapo booking photographs of Franz Josef Messner, March 1944 (courtesy of DÖW).

in Vienna and who was one of Laufer's trusted contacts. (By this time Hitler had disbanded the Abwehr, so the Gestapo or the SD—or perhaps both—had assumed handling responsibility for Rotter.) But when Issakides showed up at Rotter's flat on 31 March she found no package stuffed with cash. Instead, two Gestapo officers were waiting for her, and on the spot they arrested her and took her to Morzinplatz.[42]

Next to fall were Legradi on 3 April and Sokal on 4 April.[43] Klepell was arrested on 24 April, and Ritsch on 11 May. Fulterer was hauled in around the same time of Ritsch's arrest. Vienna court documents record that von Pausinger began his incarceration at the Liesl prison on 1 June 1944, suggesting that the Gestapo arrested him on or shortly before that date.[44]

The Gestapo had outdone itself on the CASSIA case but knew that one or two pieces of the puzzle were still missing. For example, from Romen's unsubstantiated charges, Laufer's methodical treachery, and the initial interrogations of CASSIA members, the Gestapo had discovered Rüdiger's alleged involvement in the conspiracy. But it didn't act immediately on these suspicions, probably because Rüdiger's loyalties remained uncertain, and since any operation against him on Istanbul's streets would draw the attention of the Turks, who in 1944 were beginning to lean slightly toward the Allies and to monitor more closely German intelligence work in Turkey.

Part of the Gestapo's ambivalence likely stemmed from Rüdiger's history of service to the Reich. In fact, it was a matter of record that he was in some way associated with the Abwehr office in Istanbul. Back on 7 February 1944, SD-Istanbul chief *SS-Obersturmbannführer* (Lieutenant Colonel) Bruno Wolff had even mentioned Rüdiger in a joint SD-Gestapo counterintelligence report, noting that he—among a list of others—was either a member of or was closely connected to the Abwehr office in Istanbul.[45]

Wolff's report presaged an event that cast even greater doubt on Rüdiger. In late February 1944 two Istanbul-based undercover Abwehr officers, Austrians Wilhelm Hamburger and Karl Alois von Kleczowski, along with von Kleczowski's wife Stella, defected to the Allies. Their names had also appeared in the SD-Gestapo document.[46]

In the end, it seems, the Gestapo had theories but no conclusions. Rüdiger might be a loyal subject of the Third Reich; his contact with the Abwehr might have been merely routine and perfunctory; he may have collaborated with traitors like Hamburger and the von Kleczowskis; or he might have used his access to the Abwehr only to further CASSIA's interests.

The Gestapo may have been groping for answers, wondering if Rüdiger was aligned with the Allies or with the Axis (or maybe with no one but himself), but to his CASSIA confederates, particularly to Messner, Rüdiger's loyalty had always been readily apparent. For CASSIA, the explanation behind Rüdiger's Abwehr links was simple: He was the local Semperit representative and as such had to portray himself as being loyal to the Reich, and a key component of that portrayal was maintaining cordial relations with Istanbul-based German intelligence officers. In fact, it would have only been alerting if he had avoided such contact.

The Gestapo realized that there was only one way to get to the bottom of Rüdiger's presumptive role in CASSIA. It had to lure him onto turf that Germany controlled, to capture him, and to interrogate him, but Rüdiger would be wary of any unexpected offers, so the Gestapo had to employ a convincing guise. Who better to pull off the operation than the man who personified duplicity—double agent František Laufer.

In April 1944, only a few weeks after Operation MARGARETHE, Germany's occupation of Hungary that Hatz and György had helped to realize,[47] Laufer attempted to entice Rüdiger to Budapest on contrived CASSIA business. Unaware that in late March a nearly identical operation had netted his boss, cagey Rüdiger nonetheless heeded Messner's previous warning to stay beyond the Nazis' reach, casually demurred on Laufer's invitation, remained in Istanbul, and thus narrowly avoided the fate that had recently befallen many of his friends.[48]

Rüdiger was still at large, but the Gestapo had every reason to celebrate its success. In fewer than six months, it had dismantled OSS's most successful intelligence-gathering operation in Austria.

18

Intelligence Esoterica—Analysis of the Order of Arrests

One might well ask why Caldonazzi and Hofer were taken first. The likely answer is that the Gestapo viewed their criminal cases as easy to prove, while the others—particularly those of Maier and Messner—were complicated espionage cases, involving rumored clandestine contacts, the alleged practice of nebulous tradecraft techniques, and questionable but justifiable international travel. Such shadowy cases must be built with care, over time, and evidence will come in myriad odd forms, to include counterintelligence source reporting, suspicious snippets of intercepted telephone calls, and surveillance photographs and logs. Acting too soon and too loudly on espionage cases can queer the deal: Important players may go to ground, at home or abroad, or may defect. Many espionage cases have sputtered to a stop when the culprits have simply vanished.

But Caldonazzi's activities were different. He and his fellows drafted and distributed anti–Nazi fliers and tracts, fraternized with foreign prisoners of war, and helped numerous conscripts to feign illness. These operations greatly exposed Caldonazzi and his closest co-conspirators—most notably (from the Gestapo's perspective) police sergeant Hofer. With this exposure came danger.

Romen's snitching, Laufer's reporting, and Gestapo informants' whispers led to a quick identification of Caldonazzi and Hofer, and in turn to an open-and-shut case against them. The Gestapo had collected unambiguous evidence on their activities, which produced equally solid charges, which in turn gave prosecutors—such as they were in the Reich—a very strong criminal case.

Maier's arrest was inevitable. He was at the center of CASSIA. Laufer had implicated him as having played a key role in virtually all of the group's activities. Those arrested before him—Caldonazzi, Hofer, and Wyhnal—had likely coughed up his name and further evidence of his culpability, along with a lot of blood, during their interrogation sessions. But the Gestapo had to time carefully Maier's arrest—too early, and Messner and Issakides would have been spooked; too late, perhaps a few days after Messner was taken, and Maier would have heard the bad news about his friend and gone into hiding. It was so much easier to descend upon the unsuspecting priest in the church after mass. In this respect, policemen—even those in the employ of the Gestapo—are no different from anyone else: Why make things more difficult than they need be?

But how to get the other principal actors, Messner and Issakides? Police forces like to catch criminals in the act, and the Gestapo was no different. And so it relied on a time-tested strategy: the sting operation. With Laufer as stage manager, and with Kövess and Hatz as important supporting actors, the Gestapo lured Messner and Issakides—the unwitting male and female leads—to specific spikes,[1] where they were cued to commit offences and were promptly ensnared.

Then, with so many CASSIA members under interrogation, the Gestapo didn't have long to wait until other names surfaced: Legradi, Sokal, Klepell, Ritsch, Fulterer, and von Pausinger. The Gestapo realized that some minnows might have slipped through the net, but was confident—and correctly so—that, with the exception of Rüdiger, all of the big fish had been landed.

19

The Hotel and the Prison

Two recurring characters in this story never lived: the Hotel Métropole and the Liesl prison. They may have been inanimate—mere structures of concrete, steel, brick, stone, and wood—but still they lingered in the minds of the story's heroes, who perceived them as dark, stalking presences.

And for good reason. It was in the hotel and the prison where the core members of CASSIA, who wobbled on a razor's edge of Nazi caprice, would be kept alive until the appointed time of their murders or would be allowed to live to see the war's end. It was as if those very buildings, whose fetching architecture outside contrasted with the heinous work inside, would play a crucial role in deciding the OSS spies' fate.

Surviving the ordeal would not necessarily bring reward. One might leave forever broken, dehumanized and crippled, perhaps no less captive on the street than back in the cell. Or one might depart intact, or at least capable of recuperation, permanently released from the bonds of injustice, reunited with loved ones, and returned to a world in which men and women are allowed to think, speak, and act freely. In such extreme circumstances, one's potential resilience was far from predictable. Strapping men and scrappy women found that their vitality gave them no advantage over the rawboned and reserved; under the fickle heel of the Nazi jackboot, the chances of survival for the delicate were equal to those of the durable.

At the risk of suggesting that buildings and locations might be capable of sentience, and perhaps at the greater risk of using prose that carries a purple hue, it should still be said that some people who visit these locations today might sense that they are standing on hallowed ground. Could places that once hosted untold misery and death still echo with sadness, still bestow a profound melancholy on sightseers and passersby?

During the war, these buildings' offices, interrogation rooms, and cells heard the screams, sobs, pleas, and death rattles of thousands of men and women whose only crimes had been to distinguish right from wrong, and good from bad. But "men and women" hardly capture the range of humanity that shuffled across hard floors in the company of harder men. Those terms suggest that only able and aware adults were subjected to the whims of the Reich's legal and penal systems. But in truth, some victims were adolescents, others were elderly pensioners, still others were of various ages but infirm. Tyranny discerns not between those in whom it suspects dissent.

So, one might ask, who were these despicable characters? What did they look like? What did they do before the war? Had they always been unsavory, or did the war change them, as it did so many others? Were they rehabilitated after the war?

The Métropole was the more peculiar of the two. It was also the more infamous, and as such will receive herein a thorough going-over.

Sited at Morzinplatz 4 in Vienna's 1st District on a plot that ran along the Danube Canal, the Métropole had been a respectable upscale hotel for 65 years before the war. Among the rich and famous who crossed its threshold in those days was Samuel Clemens, better known as Mark Twain, who stayed there from September 1897 to May 1899.[1]

Eager to gain publicity by accommodating the famous author, the hotel manager offered Twain a discount for a large suite: U.S.$460 per month, which was still steep—the rate in 2016 would exceed $12,000—but apparently less than the list price. For his money Twain and his family got full board, a living room, a music room for his daughter Jean, a study, and four bedrooms. Curiously absent from this wealth of floor space was a bathroom. Instead, for an extra fee, Twain and his family were allowed to use the common facilities, some 150 feet down the hallway. Twain lamented in good humor that the hotel management did not permit him use of a bicycle for the journey.[2]

Around the time that Twain rented his seven-room suite, an English-language advertisement appeared in a newspaper, describing the Métropole as a "First-Class" concern and as being the "Best-Situated" hotel in Vienna. It boasted of "300 well-furnished Bedrooms and Sitting-Rooms," and a reading room stocked with international newspapers. Near the bottom of notice, for customers such as Twain who preferred to nest for a few weeks or months, was written "**Arrangements** can be made for a protracted stay at **moderate prices**." L. Speiser was listed as the hotel manager—perhaps the very man with whom Twain had negotiated his deal, though the writer's price, which excluded access to indoor plumbing, seems upon closer inspection to have been rather immoderate.

To give the well-appointed lady her full due, a German-language newspaper advertisement, printed some 13 years after Twain checked in, elaborated that 30 of the Métropole's 300 suites and studios had private toilets. Either none of these rooms was available or suitable for the American wordsmith, or these upgrades had been added between 1899 and 1912. The German blurb noted a few other amenities not mentioned in the English posting: a post office, women's lounge, hair salon, ballroom, clubroom, and conference rooms.

In short, patrons wanted for nothing at the Métropole. For its time it was among the most comfortable of Europe. Its rooms were lavishly decorated and furnished, its exterior was grand, and its location was exclusive. One must assume that some of the formerly well-to-do prisoners—to include Messner—must have frequented the hotel in much better times, and the bitter irony of their later circumstances must have dealt them a shattering blow.

Designed by Austrian architects Carl Schumann and Ludwig Tischler, the Métropole was built between 1871 and 1873 to commemorate the Vienna World Exposition 1873 (*Weltausstellung 1873 Wien*).[3] By American reckoning, the building had five floors—a ground floor that included shops (a branch of Länderbank was located at the front corner closest to the canal), four main guest floors, and what appeared to have been a smaller penthouse that rose above the roof tiles at the structure's midpoint.

The front entrance was covered with a portico, which was supported by four Tuscan columns. Above the portico, between the second and third floors (third and fourth in the United States), ten Corinthian columns—four sets of doubles and two singles—lined the façade. Between them ran low balustrades. On top of the single columns stood Greek-style stone sculptures, a caryatid (female) on one and an atlas (male) on the other. Below and to the left of the caryatid's feet and to the right of the atlas's, METROPOLE was engraved. Centered one floor above the two figures at the roofline was a large clock, set in a shrine-style frame. A glass roof covered the hotel's inner courtyard, allowing patrons to dine, to take coffee, to smoke, and to lounge in all seasons.[4]

This was the magnificent building that the Gestapo confiscated in 1938 shortly after the Anschluss and declared its headquarters for the duration of the war. At the height of the hotel's operations under "new management," some 900 Gestapo, SS, and SD officers worked in the

Gestapo Headquarters, Vienna, formerly the Hotel Métropole (from German *Wikipedia* article "Hotel Métropole").

Métropole—the nerve center of the Reich's largest security apparatus outside Germany proper.[5] One may assume that the most senior officers laid claim to the 30 rooms with private baths.

During the next seven years, approximately 10,000 prisoners were dragged into the hotel's back entrance on Salztorgasse and into holding cells. Most of these inmates were interrogated and tortured, and some of them died under such duress or committed suicide to escape it. Many prisoners—particularly Jews, Romani (often called Gypsies in the United States), the mentally and physically disabled, and other so-called enemies of the state—were deported by rail to the Reich's vast network of concentration camps, from which most of them never returned.[6]

An American prisoner of the Gestapo gave an account of the hotel's interior layout, which illustrates how the Nazis had effectively sucked the grandeur out of the old hotel, and how its inmates were housed and treated:

> On the mezzanine floor were twelve cells, six on each side of the building with their windows cemented up to within a foot of the top and with bars well embedded. These

> "windows" opened on an inner court but one could not tell day from night because they were painted over and a light burned in the cell 24 hours a day. The cells were soundproof rooms about 12 feet long by 7 feet wide with typical cell and door about 4 feet in from the outer door, thus limiting the actual "living space" to 8 by 7 feet. The outer door had a peephole so that occupants could be observed unknowingly.... One was permitted to go to the toilet only at three specified times daily when there were two guards on duty and no prisoner ever saw any of the others. One guard paced the hall on which the cells faced and "observed" at least twice a minute. The hall itself was also closed off with bars and door.[7]

In terms of lavatory access, Mark Twain could have commiserated with the wartime "guests" of the Métropole.

The Métropole's celebrated kitchen may have still produced sumptuous treats for the Gestapo, but the prisoners dined on very different fare: "[B]reakfast ... consisted of hot water (very diluted unsweetened ersatz coffee) and a thin slice of black bread.... Lunch consisted of very weak erpsin (beet) soup (no meat-broth, bone or other vegetable), about four tablespoons of vegetable stew such as erpsin, carrots or potatoes, and one thin slice of bread. For supper, one had the same stew and similar slice of bread. For Saturday supper, a small cube of cheese was substituted for the stew and for Sunday a small slice of wurst the size of a silver dollar was substituted."[8]

The narrator's mention of "erpsin" soup and stew may be a reference to *Erbsen*, which is German for peas. Pea soup—*Erbsensuppe*—is a common dish in Germany and Austria. Beets, which the American prisoner hypothesized were the basis of his soup, are *Rüben* in German.

At times the prisoners endured additional restraints and were denied even those meager rations: "On the orders of the Gestapo, certain prisoners were chained backwards to the bars in the cell with their toes barely touching the floor, others were permitted no 'food' for several days while others had their wrists chained together at night, etc. During air raids, all cell prisoners had their wrists chained and remained in their cells while the Gestapo personnel went in the basement air raid shelter."[9]

After the Nazis had sullied the good name of the Métropole, the hotel made a couple of guest appearances in popular literature and film, once during the war and once after it. In exiled Austrian author Stefan Zweig's final work of fiction, the 1941 novella *The Royal Game* (also published as *Chess Story*), the narrator, who had been psychologically scarred during his Gestapo captivity, described where he had been held: "You will recall that our Chancellor, and also Baron Rothschild, from whose family they hoped to extort millions, were not planted behind barbed wire in a prison camp but, ostensibly privileged, were lodged in individual rooms in a hotel, the Metropole, which happened to be the Gestapo headquarters. The same distinction was bestowed on my insignificant self."[10]

The "Chancellor" was Kurt Schuschnigg (1897–1977), who had become Austria's leader upon Dollfuss's assassination in 1934, and in whose administration Rüdiger's father-in-law, Otto Ender, had served. Schuschnigg was deposed after the Anschluss, arrested, imprisoned in the Métropole, and later deported to concentration camps in Germany.

"Baron Rothschild" was Ludwig Nathaniel Freiherr von Rothschild (1882–1955), a member of the Jewish family that had founded the Creditanstalt banking dynasty in Vienna. The Nazis confiscated much of the vast fortune of the Austrian Rothschilds, to include its several Viennese mansions, which were chockablock with great works of art, antique furniture, antiquarian books, and other valuables. Ludwig was later released—presumably ransomed, that is—from Gestapo custody and allowed to join his relatives in the West. After the war, the Austrian Rothschilds received little recompense for their staggering losses of property.

The hotel's final appearance was as an extra in the 1949 British noir film *The Third Man*, which here serves to foreshadow the fate of the Métropole at war's end. In one scene, Holly Martins (played by Joseph Cotten) calls at the house of Baron Kurtz (Ernst Deutsch), a Viennese acquaintance of Harry Lime (Orson Welles), whom Martins, one of Lime's childhood friends, is trying to track down. Kurtz's house fronts Morzinplatz and in the background one can see a few workers sorting through a huge pile of rubble, which seems to crest at some 15–20 feet (4.5–6 meters). Those ruins are all that remained of the bombed-out Hotel Métropole when the film was shot.

The Gestapo housed many prisoners at the Liesl prison, for its headquarters on Morzinplatz had a limited number of holding cells, which were largely designated for "special" prisoners of high priority. During their initial interrogations, the CASSIA members probably stayed at the Métropole, but as the months passed and new important arrests were made, they were shifted to the Liesl.

The Liesl was likewise sited on the Danube Canal at Rossauer Lände 9, a three-minute drive north of the Métropole. One could have walked the route at a comfortable pace in under 15 minutes, but prisoners were transported under heavy guard in green prison vans that the Viennese had nicknamed "The Green Henrys."[11] This moniker was not only a simple reference to the vans' color, but was also a literary allusion: *Der grüne Heinrich* ("The Green Henry") was a 19th century German novel by Gottfried

Keller. The story followed its protagonist's life from a youthful nonconformity—marked by mischievousness, idleness, and keen interest in art—to a civil servant's staid and stable conventionality.

When a new prisoner arrived at the Liesl, he or she was encouraged to learn the lyrics of "The Song of the Green Van" and to sing it often with fellow inmates, in an effort to buoy and maintain everyone's spirits:

> One harmless word, one little song
> And the green van'll come along,
> It'll take you away, you don't have to pay
> First stop Rossauer Lände.
> They swipe your matches, fags, and pen,
> And take away your clothes, and then
> It's into the cell you go.[12]

Built in the early 20th century as a police-administered prison, the off-white Liesl was mostly indistinguishable from nearby apartment buildings, save for a few of its architectural flourishes, to include faux battlements and a 125-foot (38-meter) tower on one corner. The complex featured offices for prison administrators, cells for 300 prisoners, a prison yard, and barracks for guards and police officers. Unlike rooms in the Métropole, each cell in the Liesl had a toilet; the inmates at the Liesl weren't limited to three lavatory trips a day as they were at the hotel. During the war, however, cells that were designed to accommodate four inmates held as many as ten.[13]

The Liesl's cellblock was built around a large central stairwell—nicknamed *Der Lauf*, The Run—in which flights of steel stairs ran between steel landings. The cells that fronted The Run were prime real estate, since the stairwell was the focus of the cellblock's activities. Out on the far end of a wing, a prisoner began to feel isolated and forgotten, and to suspect that he or she was being deprived of the fresh news and full rations that the prisoners allegedly enjoyed on The Run.[14]

Food was served to Liesl prisoners from large tubs, which were carried up The Run and placed on trollies, which in turn were rolled out along each floor. A trustee—probably under the watchful eyes of a guard—would dump a ladleful of "watery stew" onto each prisoner's tin plate. This paltry provender was supplemented some evenings with bread and a piece of sausage or cheese. In the morning inmates received a cup of ersatz coffee or tea and a piece of bread. This was hardly enough food to sustain life, let alone good health, but still, not all of the bread found its way into stomachs: Some of it was molded into chess pieces and put into play on expedient boards, to pass the time and to occupy troubled minds.[15]

The "Liesl" prison at Rossauer Lände 9 (from German *Wikipedia* article "Polizeigebäude Rossauer Lände").

Games were not the only diversion in the Liesl. Older inmates had worked out an intricate system of communication based on a type of Morse code. Messages were tapped out on cell walls and were then relayed, cell-by-cell and floor-by-floor, to the intended recipient. Twelve hours might pass before a message arrived at its destination on the far side of the prison.[16]

Liesl guards roused the inmates at six o'clock every morning. The prisoners stowed their hinged wood-plank beds and for the rest of the day lounged on the cells' benches. Each cell had a barred window with frosted glass on its lower half and clear glass on its upper half, through which a covetous glimpse of the sky might be had. On occasion prisoners were allowed to open the upper section of the window for fresh air. The lights dimmed at eight o'clock in the evening, signaling the prisoners to lower their plank beds and to lie down for the night.[17]

For several months the hotel and the prison hosted the dozen CASSIA members whom the Gestapo had apprehended. For half of them, the hotel and the prison numbered among their lives' final waypoints. The condemned would have been invaluable to Austria in her difficult postwar years, not only for their intelligence and expertise, but also for their integrity, which would have shone as a steady beacon in those gloomy and disorienting times.

Had those six lived, their signal experiences may have evoked and defined their compatriots' conscience. They may have reminded their fellow Austrians—some who were all too ready to embrace a fabricated and fatuous victimhood (which suggested, incredibly, that Austria was among the first to fall to Hitler) and others who affected amnesia about the war—that only the truly aggrieved may choose to forgive and forget. Those who are guilty, whether by offense or by association, must never forget. Perhaps, when the bearers of conscience have been killed, the sincere study of history might edify remembrance.

20

The Interrogations

Gestapo-Vienna was known for its cruel interrogations. At all hours of the day and night, its officers would pull men and women from their cells in the Liesl prison and would subject them to both officially sanctioned and proprietary methods. The exact nature of the interrogations that the CASSIA members endured is mostly unknown but, based on the charges of high treason against them, it is likely that the Gestapo subjected them at least to its standard repertoire of brutality.

There is some circumstantial evidence to support this assertion. In his Gestapo booking photographs, taken before official interrogations began, Maier appeared to have bruises and swelling on the left side of his jaw. Also, a line from one of Caldonazzi's jailhouse letters, which somehow slipped by the censor, suggested that, in addition to its more violent methods, the Gestapo used exhaustion and extortion: "I was threatened during my second twelve-hour interrogation that, if I continued my denials, [the Gestapo] would arrest my bride, parents, and others."[1]

From analysis of surviving interrogation reports, particularly those of Maier, who the Gestapo had quickly determined was at the heart of the conspiracy, it is clear that, at first, CASSIA members revealed very little, sprinkling bits of truth among larger quantities of misleading information. Over time, though, as the duress against their bodies and minds increased and as their defenses began to crumble, the reports became more detailed and accurate until, in the end, they had divulged most of the group's activities.[2]

There is no evidence that the group's members implicated any their relatives or betrayed any of their sub-sources or supporters. For example, Caldonazzi never disclosed the assistance that his father lent CASSIA in the Tyrol, and the Gestapo never sought to detain Messner's wife, Franka.

And as described earlier in this narrative, Maier suggested that his uncle, Oskar, was unaware of his true reasons for wanting to meet Theodor Legradi, thereby both indemnifying Oskar and protecting the man responsible for the introduction, former Vienna mayor Karl Seitz.

Legradi and Sokal never betrayed the members of their CASSIA cell, to include Eva Pawlin, whose communist-functionary husband had previously been arrested, interrogated, and then executed for his resistance work. As for CASSIA's prominent sub-sources and supporters, Stümpfl, Hurdes, Ender, Gratz, and Joham all lived beyond the war's end and some to ripe old ages. For the likes of Hurdes, Gratz, and Ender, who had already seen the inside of concentration camps for different reasons, conspiracy with CASSIA would have been the final nail in their coffins, and for a ranking Wehrmacht officer such as Stümpfl, high treason would have summarily demanded a death sentence.

Although Maier was able to prevent any such collateral damage, the Gestapo's interrogations of him bore particularly damning evidence against some of the other members of CASSIA. As the focal point for CASSIA's sections, which included Caldonazzi's crew and the Sokal-Legradi cell, Maier had the most comprehensive understanding—greater than that of even Messner—of the group's varied membership and activities. The most incriminating evidence surfaced when Maier confessed under torture that Messner, following an unsuccessful attempt by Sokal, had established clandestine contact between CASSIA and the Allies.[3]

Then, in an interrogation report dated 7 April 1944, Maier admitted that, during a trip to Turkey, Messner had met with "American General Mac Farlane" and on behalf of the group had entered into a clandestine relationship with the United States. But CASSIA principals confessed only to contact with Istanbul-based U.S. officials; as for Switzerland, they claimed to have met Austrian exiles, most notably attorneys Kurt Grimm and Hans Hollitscher, and Catholic theologian Otto Karrer, but avoided any mention of Dulles and his staff.[4]

Unaware that Messner had already been arrested, Maier also revealed that Messner had traveled to Budapest to receive 100,000 Reichmarks from the United States to fund CASSIA's operations. At the end of this report, in a last-ditch effort not to implicate any other CASSIA members, Maier stated, "If Isakides [sic] played any role in this matter, I do not know." Later, when the Gestapo tried again to implicate Issakides, Maier responded with an even clearer indemnification: "Miss Barbara Issakides was not made aware of my political activities … [or of the fact that] these activities were financed by … Dr. Messner."[5] It is very possible that these statements, which Messner corroborated, combined with a lack of hard evidence other than her "favor" for Maier (the retrieval of a package at Grete Rotter's flat), saved Issakides's life.

By 25 April 1945, Maier had provided some of the group members' names, to include Caldonazzi, Hofer, and Klepell, but was still making an effort to hold back some details. He steadfastly continued to avoid incriminating Issakides and, instead of giving up Wyhnal and Ritsch, he implicated a fictitious "Dr. Wich or Witsch." Two days later, however, probably confronted with the other arrested men's names and confessions, and almost certainly under torture, he admitted to Ritsch's involvement in CASSIA.[6]

But not until 10 June 1944 does Dr. Josef Wyhnal's name surface. In this report Maier stated, "In January 1944 Wyhnal advised that there was a prison camp in Döllersheim that held 4,000 French soldiers, mostly officers. Wyhnal wanted to contact these French officers, so that, in the event of a breakdown of discipline [in the camp], which would result in its Eastern [European] workers going on a rampage, the French could be used as an additional force to reestablish order."[7]

Döllersheim, a village in Lower Austria approximately 70 miles—some 113 kilometers—northwest of Vienna, was cleared of its residents after the 1938 Anschluss and thereafter was used as training grounds by the Wehrmacht. In 1940, a prisoner-of-war camp for officers, Oflag XVII-A, was established in the village's vicinity. Most of the camp's prisoners were French, although a few hundred were Polish.[8] Döllersheim and another nearby village, Edelsbach, remain ghost towns to this day.

Maier's admission was, of course, nonsense. The Gestapo likely presented him with other confessions about Dr. Wyhnal's contact with French prisoners, a very serious act of treason, but clever Maier attempted to turn that revelation on its head, to suggest that Dr. Wyhnal was really acting in the Wehrmacht's interest to mitigate the effects of a supposedly looming prison riot. The Gestapo interrogators persisted in this line of questioning, elaborating on their suspicions, but with finality Maier responded, "I am not aware of Wyhnal's intentions to help French prisoners to escape and, in order to help them, to give them maps."[9] Dr. Wyhnal had, of course, told Maier in great detail about his plans to help the prisoners.

Some analyses of the interrogation reports of Maier and Messner suggest that, at first, Maier may have attempted to shift most of the culpability for CASSIA's activities onto Messner, working under the assumption that his second passport from Brazil might reduce or even prompt the rescinding of any criminal sentence.[10] But the Gestapo used Maier's finger-pointing to provoke a response from Messner. Messner was confronted with a sheaf of Maier's typed and signed disclosures, which strongly implicated Messner; Messner read all of the documents but refused to confirm any of their claims.[11]

Later, in a secret jailhouse note (to an unidentified recipient) that the Gestapo intercepted in late May 1944, Messner vented about Maier (as one might expect), calling him a "swine" and countering that, if anyone was to blame for the group's alleged offenses, Maier was more culpable than anyone else.[12] Over time, however, despite the great pressure and pain these two men were experiencing, both Maier and Messner figured out the Gestapo's little game—using one man's exaggerated testimony to goad a reaction from the other—and Messner quickly recanted and Maier withdrew all of his accusations.[13]

As examples of what Maier, Messner, and the other CASSIA members were enduring in these sessions, the following eyewitness testimonies describe the scope of interrogation and torture techniques that Gestapo-Vienna routinely used on its prisoners. In one instance, a written account was smuggled out of the Liesl prison before its author was executed; others were given orally after the war by some of the very few survivors of Gestapo captivity.

Gestapo-Vienna often drew liberally from the inventory of approved questioning techniques called *Verschärfte Vernehmungen*, which literally means "sharpened interrogations" but which may be best translated as "intensified interrogations." These methods included exposing subjects to extreme cold, tightly binding subjects in contorted positions and sometimes hanging them in such a way that their own bodyweight produced acute pain (and often injury), and depriving subjects of sleep.[14]

But the Gestapo did not limit itself to these codified methods. Its officers frequently used other exceptionally violent techniques. Sometimes the Gestapo moved beyond the *Verschärfte Vernehmungen* to heighten a prisoner's duress during a formal interrogation session, and at other times only to torture a victim, satisfying some sadistic desire, with no apparent interest in prompting a confession.

One prisoner described how Gestapo officers removed his broad Wehrmacht belt, adorned with a heavy buckle, and beat him mercilessly with it, knocking out some of his teeth and rendering him bloody and semi-conscious. He was thrown back in his Liesl cell, where some of his fellow prisoners could gape at his sorry state, before the Gestapo again fetched him for more of the same.[15]

Another young prisoner recounted that he was strung up by his hands and severely beaten. Meanwhile, next to him, one of his alleged co-conspirators, a man who had only one impaired kidney, endured sessions of having water poured over his face, to simulate drowning, while the man's mother was forced to watch the ordeal through a peephole into the interrogation room. The Gestapo's idea was if the young man did not confess under water torture, perhaps his mother would reveal his secrets to stop the interrogation.[16]

In another session, a Gestapo officer restrained a female resistance member with chains and then pummeled her, as if she were a punching bag. After he grew tired, the officer picked up a pizzle—a vile flogging device, made from a bull's penis, that looks like a thick, truncated bullwhip of twisted rawhide—and lashed her with it until her "body was full of bloody welts and [her] skin was hanging in shreds."[17]

The day after this savage flogging, the same Gestapo officer stripped her down to her undergarments, exposing her horribly bruised and lacerated body. He then bound her hands and feet, and pushed her into a bathtub filled with cold water. Again and again he dunked her head, and at the very moment she was certain that she would drown, the officer would allow her head to breach but would direct a jet of water at her face as she gasped for air. All the while, the officer narrated to a group of several young Gestapo officers who were observing the session, explaining each technique and its relative effectiveness for making prisoners talk.[18]

Another female resistance member, who along with her parents was accused of aiding a Soviet agent dropped by parachute into Austria, was flogged repeatedly. After binding her hands tightly in front of her, the Gestapo officer in charge would whip her with a walking stick until he became fatigued, and then would pass the cane to a young Gestapo officer who would continue the beating. After a short time of watching his subordinate, the senior Gestapo officer would criticize his technique and demand the return of the walking stick. He would then resume the lashing with enthusiasm and vigor, to demonstrate how it was best done. Each time the young resistance member fainted from this abuse, the senior Gestapo officer would shout at her, ordering her to get off the floor. Once when she was lying down, he kicked her in the stomach several times.[19]

On occasion, this same Gestapo officer would chain her hands behind her back and pull her arms up until she felt that her joints would dislocate. Once she was in this excruciating position, the officer would viciously slap her, stopping only to pull the chain farther upward. Meanwhile he constantly mocked her, asking her rhetorically if she still hadn't come up with the answers that he wanted and if she still didn't just want to confess everything.[20]

After one particularly cruel session, the battered resistance member was dragged to her cell at the Liesl, but after only 20 minutes was brought back to Gestapo Headquarters at Morzinplatz. It had already been a horrible day and she was nearing her breaking point. Escorted by a young officer, as she approached the fourth floor landing in the Headquarters building, the old Hotel Métropole, the young woman flung herself over the guardrail and plummeted down the stairwell—better to commit suicide than to face another interrogation and to risk divulging her colleagues' names. She was severely injured but, after extensive treatment at Vienna General Hospital, she not only survived the fall and her nightmarish experiences at the Hotel Métropole, but also the war.[21]

The members of CASSIA were experiencing similar treatment, or possibly worse. One of them, though, found a way to stop the misery. After three months in detention, Helene Sokal suffered an acute stomach disorder; in a postwar manuscript, Sokal claimed that she had actually feigned appendicitis. The Gestapo transferred her from the Liesl to Vienna General Hospital for treatment, and on 5 July 1944, only a few days after undergoing surgery, taking advantage of the facility's lighter security, she escaped.[22]

Sokal then went underground in Vienna, where, as she would write years later, she lived like a "submarine," descending into the homes of friends and sympathizers, and only surfacing to change locations for the sake of her and her hosts' security. Beneath the stormy waves of Vienna she remained for nine months until the beginning of the Soviet offensive against Vienna in early April 1945, when she emerged to lend a hand, once again, to the anti–Nazi resistance.[23]

21

The Executions

On 27 October 1944, the Third Reich presented its evidence at the show trial of ten CASSIA members: Maier, Messner, Legradi, Caldonazzi, Hofer, Klepell, Wyhnal, Ritsch, von Pausinger, and Fulterer. The prosecution began following a script that would lead to a fixed denouement.

Curiously absent from the list of defendants was Issakides. She was neither charged with her coconspirators nor called as a witness.[1] One account noted that Issakides was, in fact, present at the trial, perhaps held as a prospective witness,[2] but that the past six months of harsh interrogations—in her case without violent torture, possibly due to her fame as a pianist—had left her in a state of total exhaustion.[3] Also missing of course was Sokal, who was still on the lam; the Reich had decided against trying her in absentia. The Gestapo, still stinging from her escape, may have equivocated that her recapture was imminent and that in time she would stand trial in person for her crimes.

Around this same time, Gustav Rüdiger learned of his colleagues' fate. He breathed a deep sigh of relief that he had not fallen victim to Laufer's ploy. But it was just a matter of time, he knew, before the Gestapo threw caution to the geopolitical wind, plucked him from the streets of Istanbul, and smuggled him back to Vienna for a similarly farcical trial. Or perhaps the Gestapo or the SD would simply dispense with procedure and assassinate him. Ever practical, Rüdiger packed a bag and defected to the OSS.[4] He was relocated to Cairo until it was safe for him to return to Istanbul.[5]

On 28 October 1944, only one day after the trial began, the People's Tribunal (*Volksgerichtshof*), the dreaded Nazi court that handled cases involving charges of treason and of "undermining military strength,"[6] announced its verdicts. Maier, Messner, Caldonazzi, Hofer, Klepell, Wyhnal, Ritsch, and von Pausinger were found guilty of "conspiracy to commit high treason" and a host of other offences and were sentenced to death. Legradi was also found guilty of conspiring to commit high treason and, possibly due to his age (64), was given a prison sentence. Fulterer was acquitted.[7] For six of the condemned, the last vestiges of hope had now slipped below the far horizon, but two of them still had a few tricks up their sleeves.

In its final judgment, the Tribunal enumerated its assignations of guilt: Joining a separatist movement (Maier, Messner, Caldonazzi, Hofer, Klepell, Ritsch, Messner, von Pausinger); Aiding the enemies of the Reich (Maier, Messner, Caldonazzi, Hofer, Klepell, Ritsch, Messner, von Pausinger, Wyhnal); Producing and distributing antigovernment leaflets (Ritsch, von Pausinger); Contacting the Reich's enemies abroad and disclosing details on locations of targets for aerial raids (Maier, Messner); Assisting French prisoners of war and a German soldier in their efforts to escape the Reich to Allied countries (Wyhnal, Hofer, Klepell, Ritsch); Procuring and administering fever- and infection-causing substances to police officers and soldiers to render them unfit for active duty (Wyhnal, Hofer, Caldonazzi).[8]

The Tribunal added, "[The condemned men's] claims [even in death] to any rights or honors [given by the state] are forever revoked; the accused Legradi is sentenced to ten years in prison, and all of his rights and honors are revoked for life. The accused Legradi's 6 months of time served in custody are recognized and credited to his total sentence. The assets of the accused Messner are seized."[9] That final statement meant that Messner's wife, Franka, was evicted from the couple's handsome villa at Hasenauerstrasse 61, and that the Gestapo appropriated it. Never again would Messner stand on the front balcony, the verdant tranquility of Türkenschanzpark spread out before him, as the bells of Maier's church tolled in the distance.

In the months that followed the verdict, there were calls for clemency, but all fell on deaf ears. Catholic Cardinal Theodor Innitzer (1875–1955), the Archbishop of Vienna, whose pan-German proclivities had led him to embrace the Anschluss (a choice he later regretted), sent an appeal to Berlin, which simply ignored it.[10] Meanwhile, Brazil attempted to intervene in Messner's case—at least in part secretly prompted by OSS-Bern—noting that he was a naturalized citizen of the country.[11] These efforts lent some ex-post-facto validity to Maier's strategy during his interrogations, when he had attempted to shift some blame onto Messner in hopes that Brazil might entreat the Germans for leniency. Although some parties in Germany seemed amenable to these overtures, the Reich Judiciary paid them no heed. In the end, Brazil's efforts were thwarted and Nazi "justice" prevailed.[12]

The Tribunal found Caldonazzi's fingerprints on some of CASSIA's subversive activities. The court noted that one of his most reprehensible acts had been to provide fever-inducing substances to soldiers who had been facing military fitness examinations. Caldonazzi's crimes of high treason and "undermining military strength" aligned perfectly with the Tribunal's responsibilities. As such, he would be the first member of CASSIA to pay for his misdeeds.[13]

In the final weeks of his life, Caldonazzi committed his thoughts to a letter for his family:

> My days and hours are now numbered, but I would lay down my life again for our homeland, though I know that the cost [of my actions] would be many a bitter tear from my Hedi and Hertha. [Hedi Kapeller was Caldonazzi's bride, and Hertha, sometimes spelled Herta, was his sister.] You know, I was always an opponent of the war, always an enemy of mindless Prussian militarism.... Hedi, You need never be ashamed of my death, even if today it is considered dishonorable. The future will cast my death in a different light.... Do not be too sad if I pass: We die not as criminals, but as Austrians who loved their homeland and who were opponents of this war, this slaughter of peoples. We wanted to save our home from the sad destruction that is being experienced [elsewhere] in the Reich.... During this year, 1944, I have learned of the brutality and callousness of people, which make it possible for me to depart easily from the earth. The spitefulness of people, as well as the hunger and the cold [that we suffer], allow us easily to bid farewell to the world.... Father, it is God's decision that I lay down my life for a good cause: Better to die this way than to go against my convictions and to die for Hitler as a soldier. Your Walter.[14]

Protestant Pastor Hans Rieger (1892–1980), who provided religious support and counseling to death-row prisoners, revealed the plight of most jailhouse correspondence: "The condemned write their farewell letters in the morning [before their executions].... [M]any farewell letters never reached their intended recipients.... [T]heir last words ... were not sent to their relatives but were confiscated by the Gestapo."[15] So the indignities that the prisoners suffered in their final days followed them into death. The Gestapo even denied their parting words of affection, hope, contrition, or regret to loved ones.

On the evening of 9 January 1945, Caldonazzi was escorted from his cell to the Vienna Regional Court, where death sentences were carried out.[16] Pastor Rieger described the typical scene: The guards removed the condemned prisoners' wooden slippers so that they "must slip from life wearing only their socks. Hands and feet shackled together, [the condemned] stand before their judges. The prosecutor reads each sentence ... [and] the prisoners are asked, 'Did you understand the verdict?'"[17]

After these formalities, Caldonazzi was led through a large door to the execution chamber, where the court's guillotine stood. It was not a reengineered clinical device, as one might expect from the villainous scientists of the Third Reich, but a grotesque medieval apparatus. It was built from heavy timber and comprised a long bench that terminated at a pillory for the victim's neck. Above the pillory hung a heavy angled blade that, when released, dropped down the grooves of an upright frame and decapitated the victim.[18] Purposefully absent here were the death camps' efficiencies; the guillotine was used not only to kill but also to make a primal and very patient point—its slow, steady jetsam of severed heads and blood splatter dissuaded those who might consider crossing the Nazis.

On the scaffold, leaning slightly to favor his good leg, Caldonazzi spoke before the attendants ushered him onto the bench: "Heavenly Father, please do not count the actions of my executioners as sin. Lord, forgive them, for they know not what they do. Nearer my God to Thee. Long live Christ the King. These are my last thoughts. Farewell, all my loved ones."[19] Caldonazzi was the first CASSIA member to fall, but he would not be the last.

Less than a week after Caldonazzi was murdered, the Gestapo arrested 21-year-old Frederiksen under suspicion of his being an Allied agent. His incarceration meant that OSS no longer had any viable sources in Vienna who could ascertain the fates of the apprehended CASSIA members and who could reestablish contact with those who had evaded arrest. During his time in the Métropole and Liesl, Frederiksen may well have heard scuttlebutt on the meting out of the CASSIA members' sentences.

In its verdict against Maier, the Tribunal had described how the priest stood at dead center of the conspiracy, arranging for contact with the enemy, recruiting members to his cause, planning for an overthrow of the Nazi government:

> [T]he accused Maier believed that he was able to foresee clearly the defeat of Germany in the present war. He frequently had animated meetings with the divorced wife of an émigré Jewish Viennese lawyer, Mrs. Sokal-Myrna [sic].... Over time they decided to attempt contact with the Western Powers in an effort to establish regular communications with them. Maier wanted the enemy to know that already in the country formerly known as Austria an anti-Nazi resistance movement existed and that the enemy could expect help from this movement if the need arose. So when the Sokal traveled to Switzerland in 1942—it remains a mystery how she succeeded in obtaining travel authorization, given her questionable political antecedents and her prior marriage to an emigrant Jew—she brought a message to a former Jesuit priest

> living in Lucerne, Dr. [Otto] Karrer, who Maier knew shared certain beliefs with him.... Sokal learned [Maier's] message by heart and passed it orally to Dr. Karrer, who promised to forward it to the British Ambassador in Bern.... The accused Maier soon gathered around him a number of people who agreed with his political views and who, like him, had decided to contribute to the re-establishment of an independent Austrian state. They wanted this "new" Austria to have a monarchist form of government, and for its territory to include not only the current states, but also South Tyrol and Bavaria.[20]

There would be no reprieve for such a complete betrayal of the Reich.

Active as always, "Hans Steam" Maier spent his time in prison learning English and French. In his final days, Maier wrote to Alfred Missong, who worked for the law firm that had "represented" him during the show trial: "I die happy. I am now well prepared for death. What I did, I cannot regret. I did it for Austria."[21]

On 22 March 1945, the final day that the Vienna Regional Court carried out executions before the Soviet Red Army launched its early April offensive against the city, Curate Maier was led from his cell to the scaffold.[22] Moments before he was guillotined, Maier called out, "Long live Christ the King! Long live Austria!"[23] Thus were the last words of a steadfast man, a man who refused to deny his God and his hope for the rebirth of an independent Austria. The blade fell at 6:40 p.m.,[24] ending a life of kindness, intelligence, devotion, and courage.

Later the same day Klepell followed Maier to the execution chamber. He stood and listened to a recitation of his crimes. Special emphasis was laid on his having consorted with the enemy. He had, among his other misdeeds, "tried to assist French prisoners of war and a German soldier in fleeing the Reich."[25] His last moments were captured by Pastor Rieger: "A few minutes later, Kleppel [sic] began walking his final course. By his side, I accompanied him along the poorly lit corridor.... We stood before the infamous black door. When it swings open, the rest is the work of less than a minute. And in this, the last moments of his life, Kleppel turned to me and said, 'Pastor, please go to my parents tomorrow, so that they may have a good night and sleep peacefully.' The door opened and was quickly closed behind us.... [Klepell and his associates] were sentenced to death for high treason; the verdict is now being enforced."[26] Klepell was also guillotined on that fateful Thursday evening.[27]

In addition to the verdict of high treason against him, Dr. Wyhnal was also found guilty of "assisting French prisoners of war" in their efforts to escape the Reich and of "administering fever- and infection-inducing substances to members of the armed forces and police, thereby rendering them at least temporarily unfit for the war effort."[28] On 22 March 1945, the same day that Maier and Klepell were murdered, Dr. Wyhnal, a man who had dedicated his life to easing the suffering of others, was guillotined at the Regional Court of Vienna.[29]

Among his other offences, Hofer was found guilty of providing fever-inducing substances to his fellow policemen and to soldiers. In middle April 1945, after more than a year of brutal incarceration, Hofer was force-marched with other condemned prisoners from Vienna to Stein an der Donau, a quaint riverside village in Lower Austria, about 48 miles—some 78 kilometers—northwest up the Danube from Vienna. Despite the beautiful backdrop, with church spires and tile roofs and blossoming trees huddled along the gentle meanders of the Danube, Hofer's was no fairytale ending. This idyll stood in stark contrast to the ugliness that little men in *feldgrau* were preparing to unleash. Here, on 15 April 1945, Hofer was shot and killed with 43 other prisoners.[30]

The judgment against Legradi implicated him in CASSIA's attempts to contact the Allies in Switzerland, but suggested that his involvement was reluctant. To wit, the judgment asserted that in September 1943 Maier decided to send another message to the Allies in Switzerland and that to this end he asked for help from Legradi, who already was planning a

Vienna Regional Court (now called the Vienna Regional Criminal Court), where four CASSIA members were guillotined in 1945 (taken by the author, 2016).

business trip, probably to Wander headquarters in Bern. But Legradi demurred, saying that the task was too dangerous. So Maier turned to Sokal, who had a relationship with Legradi, and implored her to persuade Legradi to cooperate.[31] (The judgment later noted in lurid terms that Sokal was in a sexual relationship with the much older Legradi.[32])

Apparently Legradi buckled under Sokal's wiles. He traveled to Switzerland on business (possibly with Sokal) and once there wrote Maier's short message on a piece of paper and sent it (probably by courier or post) to Catholic theologian Dr. Otto Karrer. The message was fairly bland and was not, as Legradi contended, particularly dangerous; it merely stated Austria's willingness to exercise her right of self-determination and asked for assistance to realize that goal.[33] In reality the truly risky message had been delivered a month earlier when Messner and Issakides had met Kurt Grimm in Zurich and had passed intelligence on the Peenemünde V-weapons facility that had contributed to the vast nighttime British bombing mission of 17/18 August 1943.

In addition to Legradi's portrayal of himself as an unwilling spy, the Gestapo's—and hence the Tribunal's—confusion about exactly what he had done and when he had done it might have also contributed to weakening the case against him. Analysis of Maier's interrogation reports reveals that he was responsible for much of this uncertainty.

According to an early report, Maier—who was at the time still resisting and misdirecting his questioners—claimed that Legradi's trip to Switzerland in 1943 allowed CASSIA to deliver its first message to Otto Karrer, and that Legradi had arranged to meet again with Karrer to solicit any response from the Allies. However, Sokal had passed the group's first message to Karrer in 1942 and by September 1943 CASSIA had already established contact with the Allies through Grimm, whom CASSIA emissaries had already met multiple times and whose role Maier was therefore likely trying to minimize. Maier further claimed that Legradi's wife then fell seriously ill, and he was unable to make a second trip to Switzerland.[34]

Based on these discrepancies, the Gestapo and the court probably realized that they had ventured into uncertain territory with regard to Legradi's activities in CASSIA, for during the sentencing phase of the show trial, the court's "Senate" cited provisions in the applicable criminal code that allowed "for mitigation of the penalty for defendants" who are accused of such crimes, and announced its decision "to make use of these provisions, while ensuring that [Legradi] will still face a suitable punishment." (Special Senates were attached to the Higher Regional Courts and played a key role in the sentencing of convicted defendants.[35]) The "suitable punishment" was, of course, the previously mentioned 10-year prison sentence, along with removal of all state-provided rights and privileges. However, in an unusual instance of mercy (or perhaps pity), the Senate decided to allow Legradi to retain his estate, ruling against the prosecutor's recommendation that the Reich should confiscate all of his assets. In its conclusion on Legradi's case, the Tribunal and the Senate noted that "Legradi, as the director of an industrial enterprise, did not hesitate to abuse the privileges that enabled him to travel abroad, and in so doing he committed a serious breach of [the Reich's] trust."[36]

Beyond uncertainties about his role in CASSIA, Legradi's age and health may have also influenced his sentence. He was thin and drawn, and had a sallow complexion and baggy eyes. The court may well have viewed ten years in prison as tantamount to a death sentence for him. Implying that Legradi may not have enjoyed robust health, the judgment added lewdly that Sokal must have exercised care in her ministrations to a man of Legradi's advanced age.[37]

In its verdict against Ritsch, the Tribunal emphasized that he had committed a most grievous crime by "helping French prisoners of war" and that he had also conspired with von Pausinger to create and distribute anti–Nazi and antiwar handbills.[38] During the proceedings, CASSIA's defense attorney argued—possibly with von Pausinger's coaching—that at the time of the alleged crimes Ritsch and von Pausinger had lacked the mental capacity to understand the gravity of their actions. In short, the lawyer was using the insanity defense, a legal Hail Mary pass; he was asserting, incredibly, that these two intelligent men had not been—and presumably were still not—in their right mind. The attorney's entreaty must have been artful. Although the Senate remained doubtful about the authenticity of his claims, in the end it decided to send von Pausinger and Ritsch to Berlin, where their case would receive further consideration.[39]

During the trial, Fulterer was charged with complicity in the drafting of anti–Nazi and antiwar handbills: "Fulterer, having knowledge of the objectives of the co-defendant Ritsch, who has been found guilty of high treason, provided a typewriter for Ritsch's illicit use."[40] The court, despite its strong suspicions of Fulterer's collusion in CASSIA activities, was unable to prove that he understood fully Ritsch's intentions and thus found insufficient grounds for a guilty verdict against him. He was allowed to go free.[41]

The Nazis weren't sure what to do with Messner. After all, as the leader of a strategic industrial concern, he had been above suspicion, and senior Nazi officials had shared all manner of confidences with him. Some researchers have considered the possibility that Messner might have even held Nazi Party membership, which given his position would have been understandable and given his clandestine agenda would have been advantageous.[42] But after months of investigation by the German security services, the Tribunal had only this to say on the subject: "Messner has, insofar as can be determined, no confirmed political affiliation."[43] It seems that Messner was able to hold a key job in the Third Reich while avoiding a formal commitment to the Nazi party and its twisted ideology. Only a very shrewd operator could have pulled off such a feat.

And then there was the question of Messner's citizenship. Was he an Austrian or, as a naturalized Brazilian and as that country's former honorary consul to Austria, was he a foreigner?[44] Muddying the waters even further, Brazil approached the Third Reich with a proposal to exchange Messner for a German prisoner being held in Brazil.[45] During this time of indecision and debate, the Nazis locked Messner in the Liesl, and the Gestapo brought him out for occasional questioning, which apparently yielded nothing consequential.

Then, in early November 1944, Evelyn Wagner, a member of the CASSIA cell at Semperit, devised a plan to free Messner. She recruited three Wehrmacht deserters and an active-duty soldier named Bruno Schmitz to execute the operation, which apparently involved either springing Messner from his cell or ambushing the guards who regularly transported him between Vienna's penal and judicial facilities. When the four men were poised to act, a routine police patrol stumbled across them and detained them, probably for loitering or acting suspiciously in the vicinity of the Vienna Regional Court, where Messner was then being temporarily held. Under interrogation, they confessed the details of the plan and revealed Wagner's foundational role in it, and on 11 November 1944 two Gestapo officers went to Semperit and arrested her. She spent the rest of the war in prison.[46] The fates of the Wehrmacht deserters and Schmitz are unknown, but one must assume that their punishment was very unpleasant at best and lethal at worst.

Later in November, possibly in retaliation for Wagner's foiled rescue attempt, Messner was transferred to Mauthausen concentration camp,[47] located approximately 100 miles—160 kilometers—west of Vienna, just east of the city of Linz. Once there, he socialized with a few old acquaintances, to include Felix Hurdes, the nationalist Austrian politician whom in the late 1930s Maier had recruited into his anti–Nazi network, and Lois

Weinberger (1902–1961), an Austrian politician who had been imprisoned for his resistance activities.[48] Little else is known about what happened to Messner at the camp. He probably pulled some time on work gangs and otherwise focused on keeping his head down, to avoid the sadistic attentions of the SS guards.

In January 1945, Messner was suddenly dragged back to Vienna.[49] Perhaps Brazil's interventions had prompted the Reich to reconsider his case, or maybe the authorities planned to guillotine him with the other CASSIA members. Messner must have watched in horror as his brothers in arms—Caldonazzi, Maier, Dr. Wyhnal, and Klepell—were taken one by one to the Vienna Regional Court, never to return. Messner probably thought that he would be next, but for some reason his execution was forestalled.[50]

During this time, an American prisoner of war had a few indirect brushes with Messner. The POW was none other than an OSS officer—U.S. Navy Lieutenant Jack Taylor, who had been captured on a dangerous mission behind enemy lines. His unique observations offer some insight into what Messner may have endured between January and April 1945.

Taylor and his three-man team of Wehrmacht "deserter-volunteers" had parachuted into Austria late on the night of 13 October 1944—a Friday, to prove that sometimes superstitions should be heeded. Their slapdash mission, launched from southern Italy, was codenamed DUPONT. After losing their radio during the blind drop but still managing to log some minor successes at intelligence gathering, Taylor and his men were betrayed by an informer and arrested on 30 November 1944. The four men spent some three months at the Métropole and in the Liesl (Taylor was also held at a third facility for just shy of one month), and then more than one month at Mauthausen concentration camp—all around the same time that Messner was being held at these same locations.[51]

In fact, either at the Liesl or in a Gestapo Headquarters holding cell, for a few days Messner was confined with a member of Taylor's infiltration team. Messner told the man that his arrest had been the result of his involvement "with inept OSS agents in Istanbul."[52] So came confirmation that Messner understood fully who was to blame for the muddle that had doomed him and his colleagues.

Around the first of March 1945, after an Allied air raid damaged part of the Hotel Métropole, to include the offices of *Kriminalrat* (Major) Johann Sanitzer (1904–1957), a senior—and quite notorious—Gestapo detective in charge of apprehended foreign infiltration agents, the Gestapo temporarily shifted some of its operations to Messner's appropriated villa.

Taylor, who was in very poor health at the time, was also sent to the villa, along with some other unidentified "special" prisoners.[53] There, the Gestapo held Soviet and British agents who had been dropped by parachute into Austria and subsequently apprehended—and controlled these agents' radio transmissions back to their handling agencies, providing all manner of disinformation.[54]

In a postwar debriefing, Taylor acknowledged that he was aware of the sad history of his new dungeon: "This villa was formerly owned by Herr Messner, head of the Saperfit [sic] Rubber Co. (Austrian-American Rubber Co.) and had been confiscated from him while he was a Gestapo prisoner."[55]

Taylor's time at the villa was an improvement over his deplorable circumstances at Gestapo Headquarters, where his injuries (suffered at the time of his arrest) and acute dysentery (contracted in lockup) had gone untreated. But this respite was to last only a scant month. At the end of March 1945, with the Red Army bearing down on Vienna, the Gestapo transferred several prisoners, to include Taylor, to Mauthausen.[56]

On the train en route, one prisoner, who had previously served sentences in both camps, warned Taylor that Mauthausen "was definitely worse than Dachau." These disturbing words doused any glimmer of hope that Taylor had. "We could see, on the hill," he lamented, "the lights of the most terrible Lager in all Germany, which was to become our last home until execution."[57] By "Lager" Taylor meant *Konzentrationslager*—concentration camp. A couple of days later, on 2 or 3 April, the Gestapo also sent Messner to Mauthausen.[58]

In a scene that was likely repeated for Messner, Taylor described his reception at Mauthausen on 1 April, Easter Sunday, where he and the other prisoners assumed they would toil in the granite quarry until they died from disease or exhaustion, or where they would be summarily executed: "We arrived at a group of buildings just outside the main entrance and were turned over to the Mauthausen SS who didn't waste any time intimidating us. SS Unterscharfuhrer Hans Prellberg was particularly brutal as he slapped, punched, kicked and beat most of us over the head with a cane belonging to a crippled Slovak in our group.... We were marched through the main gate and lined up outside the shower room where we were individually questioned, slapped, slugged, and beaten with a stick by three SS men in relays for approximately three hours; in addition, some were spat upon."[59]

A prominent feature of the camp was its gas chamber, which was located in a larger structure called the Death House where all executions—

by firearms, the noose, and poison gas—were carried out. Another ghastly facility, the crematorium, was still under construction, and Taylor was assigned to one of the labor gangs tasked with finishing it.[60] At this late stage in the war, with Germany's defeat imminent, the SS officials in charge of Mauthausen were eager to kill as many prisoners as possible, since they were all witnesses to the atrocities that had occurred there, and to incinerate their bodies, thereby leaving behind no evidence of the murders.

Taylor described the interior of the gas chamber in great detail and explained how the SS used it:

> The normal methods of executions were gassing, shooting and hanging which were all carried out in the Death House.... The gas chamber was approximately 15 feet square and fitted as a shower room with tile wainscoting and overhead shower nozzles. The victims were told that they were going to take a shower; all were undressed in the back courtyard and led into the chamber; the heavy air-tight door was slammed and locked and the gas introduced through the shower nozzles. Normal operation was twice daily at 9 AM and 5 PM, 120 victims at each time. Once 220 were packed in and the SS fought each other to look through the small plate glass window in the door and watch them struggle in their agony. They were thrilled with this mass spectacle. Frau Ziereis, the Commandant's wife, came once to see the sight.
>
> The gas used was Cyclone B [Zyklon B[61]] cyanide a granular powder, contained in pint-sized cans and the same used for [dis]infection of clothing. In a small room, adjacent to the gas chamber, was a steel box connected immediately to a blower, which was in turn connected to the shower system. While wearing a gas mask, the operator bashed in the ends of two cans of powder (one can will kill 100 people) with a hammer and after placing them in the box, clamped the lid on hermetically tight and started the blower. (In winter, when the gas would not evaporate fast enough from the powder, steam was introduced into the box from the other end.) After two hours, the intake blower was stopped and the larger exhaust blower was turned on for about two hours. Wearing gas masks, the prisoner operators removed the bodies to the cold room (capacity 500) where they were stacked like cord wood awaiting cremation.
>
> SS Standartenfuhrer Siereis (Ziereis), Commandant of Mauthausen, personally executed 300 to 400 men [in various ways].[62]

As Messner began his third week at Mauthausen, perhaps he clung to some small hope of surviving this ordeal. The former industrialist was a well-known figure around the camp, but now his silvery white hair was unkempt and dirty, his once powerful frame was wasted and bent, and his confident gait was reduced to a shuffle. The Brazilian government managed to send him a care package, whose contents he shared with some of his fellows.[63] To Messner the package was a signal that someone outside the barbed wire knew that he was still alive. Maybe even Franka knew. And maybe, just maybe, those people were doing their best to have his death sentence commuted.

At one point, as proof the war's end was near, USAAF P-38 fighters, their dual turbocharged engines growling at full throttle, flashed over the camp at extremely low altitude. No one could mistake the distinctive twin-boom configuration of the lethal "fork-tailed devils" (*Die Gabelschwanz-Teufeln*) and the white stars stenciled on their fuselages and wings. The camp guards impotently blasted their machineguns at the breathtaking display of speed and firepower, but all of them must have known that Germany was defeated.[64] The surrender would come later, but only to formalize what already was.

All of them must have known, that is, except the lunatic in charge. For Mauthausen camp commander *SS-Standartenführer* (Colonel) Franz Ziereis, it was still business as usual. And business on 23 April 1945 was no different from that on the horrific days before, and would be no different from that on the few remaining wartime days that followed. On this particular day, though, Ziereis would personally see to the extermination of one of the Reich's worst enemies, a man who for years had pretended to be a stalwart but who all along had actually been turncoat.

SS-Oberscharführer (Senior Squad Leader) Josef Niedermayer, who was in charge of the Mauthausen block where Messner was held, later described the events of that afternoon: "On 23 April 1945 at 1500 hours, Commander *SS-Standartenführer* Franz Ziereis personally came to the bunker and ordered me to take forty prisoners, among them Dr. Franz Messner, to the gas chamber. While leaving his cell, Messner wanted to tell me something, but the commander's presence prevented that. None of the prisoners was beaten. The commander himself initiated the flow of poison gas. The gassing worked quickly, since only five minutes later I was told to open the doors and to switch on the ventilators. That same night, 23/24 April 1945, the corpses of the gassed individuals were incinerated in the crematory of the Mauthausen concentration camp."[65]

Messner died never knowing just how close he had come to living. On 5 May 1945, 12 days after he was murdered, a reconnaissance unit from the U.S. 11th Armored Division stumbled across Mauthausen and liberated it from the remaining guards.[66] Much to their surprise, the battle-hardened dogfaces of the 11th, tested in combat from France through the Belgian Bulge to Germany and now to Austria, found a U.S. Navy man, beached higher and drier than any of them could have imagined. On that day, Lieutenant Jack Taylor took his first step on a long journey home.[67]

22

The Opposition

After suffering through the preceding descriptions of the interrogations, torture, show trial, and executions of several CASSIA members, one might feel compelled to ask how captured spies were treated in the United States during the Second World War. Were they abused and subjected to farcical court proceedings? Were they condemned and executed? If so, how were they killed? Two high-profile cases may serve as relevant examples.

The first concerned the German agents of Operation PASTORIUS. In middle June 1942 two four-man teams were inserted by submarine into the United States. One landed on a beach near Amagansett, Long Island, and the other on a beach just south of Jacksonville, Florida. The eight men were carrying a hefty supply of explosive ordnance and had been trained at an Abwehr sabotage school to destroy a variety of U.S. defense-industry targets. The Abwehr wanted not only to disrupt U.S. military production but also to terrorize the American public, sowing fear and paranoia with each attack. In addition to their demolition matériel, the agents were carrying U.S.$175,000 in cash—some $2.5 million in 2016 buying power. The Abwehr had selected the team members for their ability to blend into American society. All of them had lived in the United States, and two were naturalized U.S. citizens.[1]

But after the insertions, the enthusiasm of a team leader, George Dasch, quickly flagged and he confided his doubts in Ernest Burger, one of the teams' naturalized U.S. citizens who had pulled a one-year stint in the U.S. Army in the late 1920s. Dasch and Burger agreed to betray the mission to the U.S. authorities, and by late June all eight men were in FBI custody.[2]

On Wednesday, 8 July 1942, a U.S. military commission began a trial of the Abwehr agents and 28 days later, on 4 August, pronounced that all eight men were guilty. The most serious charges involved the conduct of espionage and violation of accepted rules of war through conspiracy to conduct sabotage. All of the saboteur-aspirants were sentenced to death.[3]

President Roosevelt commuted the sentences of informers Dasch and Burger. Dasch got 30 years in prison and Burger life. The six other Abwehr agents were executed by electric chair on 8 August 1942.[4]

In 1948, U.S. President Truman granted executive clemency to Dasch and Burger on the condition that they would be summarily deported from the United States. Both men were then taken to Germany and were released.[5]

So where do the comparisons begin and end between the arrested CASSIA members and the agents of Operation PASTORIUS? The Austrians were civilians and enlisted military personnel who were found guilty of conducting classic espionage against the Reich, of subverting the morale of soldiers and policemen, of spreading anti–Hitler and antiwar propaganda, and of fraternizing with foreign prisoners of war. The Abwehr operatives had infiltrated the United States on a secret sabotage mission for Germany and were in possession of explosive ordnance and a great sum of money to accomplish their objectives.

CASSIA was betrayed from without, and PASTORIUS from within. Twelve CASSIA suspects were arrested, and all eight PASTORIUS agents were arrested. The CASSIA trial lasted two days; it began on 27 October 1944 and at the end of the next day the verdicts were announced.[6] The PASTORIUS military trial was about 25 days long and the verdicts were announced after deliberations on the 28th day. Six CASSIA members were executed—four by guillotine, one by firing squad, and one by poison gas. Six of the Abwehr men were executed by electric chair.[7]

Some researchers have pointed out that, in the early days of the war, the American public had demanded swift and severe treatment of the saboteurs, but some two years later, the collective mood had softened. To wit, in late 1944 two German agents, William Colepaugh and Erich Gimpel, were inserted from U-boats on the coast of Maine and were quickly apprehended by the FBI.[8] Of the incident, one writer noted, "These agents benefited from the calmer state of public nerves in the later years of the war and received prison sentences rather than the death penalty."[9]

In Austria, however, the trajectory of sentiments, both in the government and among the public, was reversed. As the war became more desperate for the Reich, its judicial system, which already had a long history of perversion and cruelty, became even more volatile and dangerous, and perhaps a substantial portion of the citizenry—who were at that point experiencing the horrors of the war firsthand—supported such extreme reactions.

These two cases may be too different and their subversive activities—both the perpetrated and the intended—too disparate for a meaningful comparison. Perhaps a more fitting example would involve a large German network that conducted classic espionage against the United States. Enter the infamous Duquesne Spy Ring.

At the center of this drama stood William Sebold, a native of Germany who had become a naturalized U.S. citizen in 1936. In 1939 Sebold returned to Germany to visit his mother and was approached by and eventually recruited by the Abwehr. Sebold would later claim that he felt compelled to cooperate because he feared reprisals against his family who still lived in Germany.[10]

Sebold had earlier lost his U.S. passport and with Abwehr's blessing he went to the U.S. Consulate in Cologne to apply for a replacement. Once he was safely inside the American facility Sebold confessed to U.S. officials that the Abwehr had enlisted his services as a prospective spy. He claimed that he wanted to cooperate with the FBI when he went back to the United States.[11]

Sebold then returned to the Abwehr fold and began preparing for his espionage mission. He was taught how to encode and decode messages and how to take and process microphotographs. At the end of his training, Sebold received instructions for making contact with German agents in the United States and was provided sensitive materials to pass to them. He was assigned the alias "Harry Sawyer" and was dispatched to New York City via Genoa, Italy. Apparently Sebold had secretly conveyed all of these details to the U.S. Consulate in Cologne, which in turn had relayed the information to the FBI.[12]

When Sebold arrived in New York in February 1940 the FBI was there to meet him. FBI special agents helped Sebold establish his residency in New York as Harry Sawyer and to set up a cover office from which Sawyer ostensibly ran a diesel-engineering consultancy. At this office Sebold would meet with other German agents, some of whom the FBI would secretly observe and film.[13]

Later in February Sebold initiated contact by letter with the Abwehr's top agent in New York, Frederick "Fritz" Duquesne, who ran a business called "Air Terminals Company" in the city. Duquesne, a native of South Africa, harbored a deep hatred of the British dating back to his experiences in the Second Boer War and the First World War. Their first meeting occurred in Duquesne's office and the two men exchanged details on the German espionage network to which they belonged. Over the course of their next several contacts, Duquesne reported defense-related intelligence on the United States and information on ships bound for British ports, which Sebold was responsible for encoding and sending via clandestine radio to Germany.[14]

In May 1940 the FBI installed a shortwave radio station on Long Island and began transmitting contrived "secret" messages to Sebold's handlers in Germany and receiving from them Abwehr's instructions for the spy ring. During its 16 months of operation, the radio station sent more than 300 controlled messages to Germany and received about 200 in return.[15]

The members of the Duquesne Spy Ring numbered 33 in all, and Sebold had direct contact with many of them. Most of them were German natives who had become naturalized U.S. citizens, although a Russian and Frenchman of Germanic extraction were counted among them. From these agents Sebold received all manner of intelligence for submission to the Abwehr.[16]

The spy ring had been active for at least two years before Sebold's arrival. In the 1930s one of the agents, Herman Lang, had developed access to design specifications of the top secret Norden aerial bombsight. During a conversation with Sebold in 1940, Lang alluded that he had sent the Norden material to the Abwehr back in 1938.[17]

Perhaps the oddest member of the ring was Lilly Stein, a Viennese Jew who had escaped Austria in 1939 with the help of a U.S. diplomat.[18] Sebold met with Stein and received intelligence from her for transmission to Germany. She also allowed the Abwehr to use her residence as an accommodation address[19]—not unlike the ostensible arrangements at Grete Rotter's apartment in Vienna, where in 1944 Issakides was lured and ambushed by the Gestapo.

One may only speculate about Stein's justification for helping a country that was rounding up and trying to exterminate all of Europe's Jews. Her reasons were likely prosaic and banal, such as a need—or worse yet, merely a desire—for money. Egocentrism is one of the most common root-level motivations for betrayal.

Another oddity was the only member of the ring who had been born in the United States. Arkansas native Evelyn Lewis cohabitated with Duquesne and shared his strong anti–British sentiments. And if hating a key U.S. ally weren't enough, she was also anti–Semitic. (One may assume that Lilly Stein either never met Lewis or avoided chatting about religious issues with her.) Despite her ideological compatibility with the spy ring, Lewis apparently didn't steal any U.S. secrets for Germany, but she willfully aided and abetted Duquesne's espionage activities.[20]

Eventually the FBI had enough evidence to build a watertight case against all 33 members of the spy ring and arrested them in a coordinated sweep. Nineteen of the spies pleaded guilty but the remaining 14 were given a trial by jury in New York City beginning on 3 September 1941, about three months before Germany declared war on the United States. On 13 December 1941, the jury announced that they had found all 14 of the spies guilty. On 2 January 1942, the 33 members of the Duquesne Spy Ring received prison sentences totaling more than 300 years; individual sentences ranged from one year for Evelyn Lewis to 18 years each for Duquesne and Lang. No one was sentenced to death.[21]

In fewer than ten years after the war, two of the ring's top agents would be free men. Herman Lang was deported to Germany in September 1950,[22] and in 1954, because of his failing health, Duquesne was released from prison.[23] He died a couple of years later.

Some might argue that the Duquesne Spy Ring operated before the formal commencement of hostilities between Germany and the United States, and that its members therefore were not subject to harsh wartime punishments for espionage. On the other hand, the members of CASSIA were guilty of spying for a declared enemy of the Third Reich and had betrayed secrets that had—or might have had—a deleterious effect on Germany's national security.

These are valid contentions, at least up to a point, but do not take into account the announcement of verdicts for the Duquesne spies two days after Germany declared war and the passing of their sentences three weeks after that. The American public, which at that time had great contempt for Germany, would have certainly supported a decision by the sitting judge or an intervention by President Roosevelt to invoke very harsh punishments of the ring's members, to include death sentences for its leaders and most culpable subordinates.

Between these two examples, then, we have sufficient information to make a reasonable comparison between the wartime justice systems of the United States and the Third Reich. Most people—save for a few contrarians, perhaps—would probably conclude that the spies whom the FBI arrested were given a fairer trial than were the spies whom the Gestapo arrested. "Fair" is of course a loaded term: It is not an absolute, means different things to different people, and as such can prompt strong emotions. Although the word is admittedly definable only in terms of relative and transitory standards, it still has a common-sense applicability in this case. Perhaps the best test is to ask yourself, if you were accused—rightly or wrongly—of espionage, to which judicial system would you rather be subjected, that of the United States in the early 1940s or that of the Third Reich.

It is this work's contention that, if the members of CASSIA had been tried and sentenced by a judiciary similar to that of the wartime United States, you would now probably be reading a memoir by the likes of Maier or Messner, and the speculations, omissions, and other errors of this narrative would have never been.

23

The Survivors

Legradi remained in prison until the final week of the Soviet Red Army's taking of Vienna.[1] He was freed from the Liesl on 6 April 1945,[2] a day before the Soviets also decided to release a young American prisoner, Harald Frederiksen. Legradi was later reunited with Sokal, with whom, over the course of their wartime adventures, Legradi had fallen in love, and she with him. After the war, Legradi and Sokal were married.[3]

Of the CASSIA members whom the People's Tribunal sentenced to death, only Ritsch and von Pausinger would avoid execution. On 15 January 1945 the two men were transferred from Vienna to Berlin, where, drawing on von Pausinger's legal acumen, they filed several appeals for retrial and secured a stay of execution while the court conducted further inquiries into their cases. In the event that the court dismissed their mental-capacity pleas and found no other extenuating circumstances, the standing death sentences against Ritsch and von Pausinger would be enforced. However, on 27 April 1945, advancing Allied military units liberated Ritsch and von Pausinger from their cells in Berlin, and after Germany surrendered, both men were repatriated.[4]

During her incarceration, Issakides developed a stomach disorder, had great difficulty eating, and grew ever more gaunt. The Gestapo finally brought her to the offices of a "Dr. Franke" and, while he recognized her symptoms as indicating only dyspepsia, he diagnosed Issakides with a more serious condition, a duodenal ulcer, in a quiet effort to help her.[5] The doctor's ruse worked, for Issakides was sent to a prison hospital, not back to her cell[6]; the Gestapo had learned its lesson with Sokal, who had been checked in to a civilian hospital for treatment and had escaped.

Unknown to Issakides at the time, Kurt Grimm in Switzerland had been secretly communicating with powerful lawyers whom he had known in Vienna before the war, trying to find some way to get her released but failing, time and again.[7]

It has been suggested that Issakides's hospitalization, which apparently lasted until the Red Army's occupation of Vienna, may have saved her from eventual execution.[8] After her diagnosis, Issakides's court date was delayed for a month.[9] It is unclear if she would have ever faced the guillotine, gas chamber, or gallows, but her illness certainly saved her from further interrogations and the misery of sitting through a rigged trial.

After the war, U.S. Army Lieutenant Alfred C. Ulmer Jr., who had worked in OSS's Austria-Germany section in Bari, an Italian port city on the Adriatic Sea, found a still-thin but recuperating Issakides in Vienna. Once she had recovered her health, Issakides performed a piano concert in Vienna, and OSS sponsored an extravagant reception after the event. It was the last public performance that Issakides would ever give. Her health deteriorated and her anguish returned. Though her condition would later improve, Issakides never again returned to the concert hall.[10]

Despite her frailty, Issakides helped the OSS with its postwar investigation into CASSIA's catastrophic end and into the possible war crimes by those who oversaw the torture, show trial, and executions of the group's members. With Issakides's help, the OSS and U.S. military intelligence units identified two key at-large witnesses: Abwehr agent Grete Rotter (later Grete Felix[11]), in whose apartment the Gestapo had entrapped Issakides, and Gestapo-Vienna forensic assistant Egon Nohl,[12] who had firsthand knowledge of the Gestapo's activities and who, after the Soviet occupation of Vienna, had allegedly gone into hiding with Rotter.[13]

In early 1946 the Americans finally caught up with Rotter and Nohl in Vienna and placed them in the custody of the U.S. Detailed Interrogation Center. According to a cable from the Strategic Services Unit, OSS's first postwar successor, on 3 February 1946, when USDIC guards were transporting the couple from Vienna to the U.S. occupational zone (probably to SSU-Salzburg) for questioning, the Soviets seized the two prisoners at a checkpoint on the grounds that Rotter and Nohl "lack[ed] papers to transit [between] zone[s of occupation]." The SSU cable further lamented that Rotter and Nohl were "our only sources as to betrayal of Messner Group."[14] However, about a month later the United States regained access to Rotter and Nohl, and the resulting interrogations revealed the details of Rotter's role in Issakides's arrest.[15]

OSS officer Alfred Ulmer's searching did not stop with the musician. In the summer of 1945 he found the priest's mother, Katharina (née

Giugno). In her old age Mrs. Maier was living very simply but was still reluctant to accept any recompense from the United States.[16] Maier's father, who had been a railroad employee,[17] had died in 1939[18] and probably left Katharina a small pension, but with her son's death, she no longer received any additional assistance. Every month, from his salary of about 300 Reichmarks—worth U.S.$1,200 in 2016—Maier had sent his mother 50 Reichmarks (U.S.$200).[19]

At the time of Ulmer's visit, Mrs. Maier was living in "Moravia"—the part of Czechoslovakia that the Nazis had renamed the Protectorate of Bohemia and Moravia. Shortly after her husband's death, Katharina had left the family home in Grossweikersdorf, a town of fewer than 3,000 people in Lower Austria, about 30 miles (48 kilometers) northwest of Vienna, and had moved in with her daughter Elfriede, who would have been 35 years old when Ulmer showed up on her stoop.[20]

Only after many glowing remarks about the bravery and patriotism of Heinrich and after much coaxing and persuading was Ulmer able to convince Katharina to accept $2,500—about $33,000 in 2016 purchasing power—as a death benefit for the loss of her beloved son.[21] At the time Austria was suffering from great privation, and the value of U.S. dollars on the black market would have substantially exceeded the official exchange rate. (As an interesting aside, as an officer of the OSS's ultimate successor, the CIA, Ulmer would become the first chief of station in Austria.[22])

Back in middle November 1944, only two weeks after the People's Tribunal in Vienna had acquitted Fulterer, the Gestapo in Bregenz, Vorarlberg, rearrested him and for good measure arrested his wife, Trudi,[23] on unspecified charges. On 15 November 1944, the couple was then transferred to the Gestapo prison in Innsbruck, the capital of Tyrol, where they were questioned for three days.[24] Having failed again to establish Fulterer's complicity in resistance activities, the Gestapo released him and his wife, and they returned to Vorarlberg.

As noted previously in this story, many of the involved Viennese buildings and landmarks remain unchanged as of 2016, and one of them, perhaps the most notorious of the lot, did not stand to see the war's end. The old Hotel Métropole, which Gestapo-Vienna used as its headquarters, was destroyed during the Red Army's Vienna Offensive in April 1945.[25] Today, the building on this site—a residential structure called Leopold-Figl-Hof, which was constructed in the middle 1960s—has an inconspicuous mural, in relief, depicting the miseries that were once endured there; the mural bears the Roman numerals for 1938 on one end and for 1945 on the other.

Across the street from the previous site of the Métropole, on a corner shaded by a copse of trees, stands a simple monument, fashioned from blocks of granite from the Mauthausen quarry, which shelter the bronze statue of a prisoner. Etched into one of the stones is a dedication, in German:

> Here stood the Gestapo house.
> For the Austrians, it was hell.
> For many, it was the vestibule to death.
> Like the Thousand-Year Reich, it has sunk into ruins.
> But Austria has risen again,
> And with her our dead, the immortal victims.[26]

The Liesl prison building, vaguely reminiscent of a white-stone castle, was severely damaged during the war but was later fully restored. It is now used as a police detention center. As touched on earlier in this narrative, shortly after the First World War, the name of the street running along the length of the prison, Elisabeth-Promenade, was changed to Rossauer Lände, but the nickname Liesl—derived from Elisabeth—stuck.

The sites of both the old Gestapo headquarters and the Liesl now overlook popular biking and walking lanes that run along the Danube Canal. Every day thousands of people in vehicles and on foot pass these places with no awareness of the gruesome business that was once practiced there, of the multitudes of men and women—some still in their teens—who began the ends of their lives there.

Upon the Allied defeat of Hitler's vile Reich, CASSIA's battered survivors stood quietly victorious. Theirs was not a cause for wild celebration; too many of them were absent. The eulogy was triumphant, but it was still a eulogy: Though the trumpets had sounded, the dead remained dead.

24

The Actor and the Architect

As 1944 drew to a close, after CASSIA's show trial and death sentences, after Fritz Molden, back from the grave, materialized in Vienna as Wehrmacht Sergeant Hans Steinhauser, 20-year-old American student Harald Frederiksen searched for the remnants of CASSIA, armed only with a name—John Sekler. Frederiksen, whom OSS-Bern had assigned codename/number DIANA 1004, was now an official OSS sub-source.[1]

As noted previously, after their last meeting, Dulles had assigned Messner two codenames and a code number, to be alternated for security's sake. One of these was DIANA, which suggests that administratively OSS-Bern was linking Frederiksen to CASSIA.

But finding the survivors wasn't Frederiksen's only task: Molden had also asked him to facilitate contact between a Vienna-based Yugoslav resistance group and elements of the O5 umbrella organization, which included representatives of "FFOe."[2] (FFOe may be a reference to some prospective elements in Vienna of the Styrian partisan group *Österreichische Freiheitsfront*, the Austrian Freedom Front, or to a like-named cross-party resistance group, both of whose acronyms were rendered ÖFF or OeFF.[3])

Molden hadn't chosen Frederiksen randomly for this mission. He knew that in 1943 Frederiksen had met a fellow medical student named Dornik, whose ethnicity the Gestapo later described simply as "Croat." Presumably after confirming Frederiksen's claims of anti–Nazi resistance dating back to his time at grammar school, Dornik had revealed that he was a member of a secret Yugoslav loyalist group led by Dormile Petrin. That was the very group, Molden told Frederiksen, with which O5 endeavored to join forces.[4]

But before Frederiksen could make much progress on either of these assignments, the Gestapo arrested Dornik and under interrogation—and probably torture—he divulged that Frederiksen was a U.S. intelligence agent. So on 15 January 1945, the same day that Ritsch and von Pausinger were transferred to Berlin, Frederiksen was also picked up and aggressively questioned by one of *Kriminalrat* Sanitzer's subordinates, Wilhelm Weiss, at Gestapo-Vienna Headquarters.[5] (The infamous Sanitzer made his first appearance in this story in *The Executions* in reference to Messner's villa and OSS officer Jack Taylor.)

Frederiksen had assumed that Petrin, not Dornik, had fingered him, but a postwar statement by Weiss clearly points to Dornik's confession as having led the Gestapo to Frederiksen. And a line in Weiss's statement suggests that Sanitzer himself had been directly involved in Frederiksen's case.[6]

Either Frederiksen convinced his captors that he was just a student, or the Gestapo had insufficient evidence without his confession to proceed, or the Gestapo feared that, as a U.S. citizen, he might actually be an OSS officer, whose help might be needed as the Eastern and Western Allies converged on Austria from opposite directions.[7] While the Gestapo eased up on the interrogations and decided against a late-war show trial, it still wasn't ready to cut Frederiksen loose. Thus in the Liesl he remained until 7 April 1945, when the Soviets, Vienna's new overlords, released him.[8]

As described in the opening chapter, Frederiksen wasn't a free man for long. Once the Red Army took full control of Vienna, its security personnel remembered the young American whom the Gestapo had accused of being an OSS officer. Suspected of gathering intelligence on Soviet activities in Vienna, Frederiksen was once again detained and questioned first by a Major Sokolov, "the Soviet Political Commandant" for Vienna's 18th District, and a few weeks later by Soviet intelligence.[9]

Although Frederiksen was uncertain exactly who these latter interrogators were, they may have been officers of the People's Commissariat for State Security (NKGB), which in 1945 was responsible for Soviet intelligence and counterintelligence. In 1953/54, these functions were assumed by a new Soviet agency, the KGB.

As also noted previously, Frederiksen was later paroled and fled to the zone in Austria that was controlled by the Western Allies, where the OSS debriefed him.

So who was this mysterious John Sekler, the single link to the surviving members of CASSIA? Frederiksen's papers provide no clues, and Sekler is not mentioned in any of Molden's published accounts of the resistance. No Sekler—or any variant of that name—appears in Gestapo interrogation reports or in Sokal's postwar writings. Was Sekler an alias, an invention with no precedent? If it was, how was Frederiksen expected to find him?

Similarly the name is not found in the archives or databases of the *Dokumentationsarchiv des österreichischen Widerstandes* (DÖW)—the Documentation Centre of Austrian Resistance—or in any of the other published volumes on Austrian resistance activities during the Second World War. An exhaustive search—using terms that defined time-frame, anti–Nazi beliefs/activities, and name variants—yielded nothing, until....

A biographical blurb offered these intriguing details:

> Eduard Jakob SEKLER was born on September 6, 1880 in Brünn, Moravia [now Brno, Czech Republic], and died on November 15, 1976 in Vienna. He was an actor.
>
> After completing his education at the Elevenschule of the Deutsches Volkstheater in Vienna (1897–1899), Sekler performed for six years on Central European stages (Ljubljana, Budweis, Göttingen, Znojmo, St. Pölten, Mödling, Olomouc) and then in 1905 returned to Vienna. With interruptions (from 1938 to 1945, the Nazis barred him from acting), Sekler played at the Theater in der Josefstadt in Vienna until his death. He also worked as a director at the Volksoper and of Austrian silent films made during the 1920s, and in 1933 he co-founded and became the senior director of the Theater der Jugend.[10]

But there was no evidence that this Sekler had ever engaged in resistance activities, despite a Nazi ban that kept him from his vocation. Still, based on extensive research, Eduard Jakob Sekler appears to be the only Sekler still in Vienna in 1944 who had any bone to pick with the Nazis. For that possibility alone, he was worth a second look.

One investigative technique is to start at the end, which is often known and immutable, and to work backward, to look for discrepancies, possible points of commonality and intersection, and the like. Eduard Jakob Sekler's story ended at Sievering Cemetery in Vienna's 19th District.[11] He is interred with two other family members: Elisabeth, his wife, who died in 1974 at age 93, and Johann Seckler [sic], who died on 29 December 1919. Further examination revealed that the Seklers had a daughter, who died in childhood, and a son, Eduard Franz Sekler, who was born 30 September 1920 in Vienna.[12] Since Eduard Franz turned 18 in the year of the Anschluss, he too merited scrutiny.

In 1938 Eduard Franz Sekler finished his secondary education at Schottengymnasium, a highly respected preparatory high school in Vienna associated with Schottenstift, a Benedictine abbey founded in the 12th century. It was in this school where Sekler learned English from a priest named "Father Willibald."[13] After the war Sekler recalled that Willibald "spoke English perfectly," having "spent time in England," and that the priest "looked like a medieval monk with his short-cropped hair."[14] In addition to his English vocabulary, perhaps young Sekler's worldview was expanded by this well-traveled monk.

After high school, Sekler completed his compulsory military service as a radio operator and in 1941 began studying architecture at Vienna University of Technology.[15] In the final year of the war, he and his friend Sepp Stein, a fellow architecture student at the university, joined the O5 resistance group. Sekler and Stein wanted to do their part to preserve Vienna from destruction and to facilitate its declaration as an open city that could be peacefully handed over to the Allies. In a postwar interview, Sekler elaborated slightly on how he and Stein had helped the cause of resistance: "Our task was to get information and [to] pass it on to people who had their contacts."[16]

Sekler and Stein continued their secret work until the spring of 1945, when the resistance suffered a crippling compromise.[17] With the Soviet Red Army advancing on Vienna, Major Karl Biedermann (1890–1945), a senior member of a Wehrmacht resistance group led by Major Carl Szokoll (1915–2004), was preparing to play a key role in an important resistance operation, codename RADETZKY. The primary goal of RADETZKY was to smooth the way for the Red Army's occupation of Vienna, thereby sparing the city unnecessary damage and casualties.[18]

But before the operation could be executed it was betrayed by, according to Sekler, a "swine who survived [the war] and afterwards was an editor of an illustrated periodical."[19] This betrayal implicated Biedermann, who in early April was arrested, tried and found guilty by court martial, and sentenced to death. On 8 April 1945, Biedermann and two of his coconspirators, Captain Alfred Huth and Lieutenant Rudolf Raschke, were publicly hanged.[20] Their bodies—posted with signs that read "I made a pact with the Bolsheviks"—were left dangling to dissuade any further attempts at collaboration with the enemy. "After that," Sekler said, "Sepp Stein … and I didn't sleep at home anymore. We kept moving around because [the Nazis] were now arresting people in the street."[21]

Eduard Franz Sekler never made public the finer details of his resistance work, and except for his friend Sepp Stein, he never mentioned any other resistance members with whom he associated. (The author's inquires in June 2016 to Dr. Eduard Franz Sekler, who at the time was 95 years old, went unanswered.) Was he or his father, Eduard Jakob Sekler, whom the Nazis had barred from his profession, identifiable with John Sekler, the man who was supposed to help Frederiksen find the remnants of CASSIA? Did Sekler father or son take the *nom de guerre* "John," after the given name of a relative, Johann Seckler, then dead for some 25 years? (Such a small change in one's name is not unknown to espionage: It has been altered enough to provide a bit of deniability, but not enough to remain undetectable to fellow resistance members who might seek contact.) To complicate matters further, the name Johann Seckler in Vienna City burial records might well be the result of typographical error. According to Eduard Franz Sekler, he had an older sister who died before he was born.[22] Could Johann Seckler, who died nine months before Eduard Franz's birth, actually be Johanna Sekler?

If Eduard the son was John Sekler, then the mystery is mostly solved, save for a few details on the nature of his association with Fritz Molden and why he—as opposed to a more experienced resistance member with relevant access—was enlisted to investigate CASSIA. The same questions would apply to Eduard the father, but confirmation of his involvement with the resistance might prompt additional lines of inquiry. For example, if his dealings with the underground predated the formation of O5 and Molden's work with the OSS, did he have direct contact with any members of CASSIA? If so, did he gain such entrée through Curate Maier, whose circle of acquaintances was large and varied, or through fellow performer Barbara Issakides?

Short of a conclusive statement by Eduard Franz Sekler, now a nonagenarian, such questions—based as they are on speculation—may only be answered through the discovery of an obscure document in an over-stuffed archive, or of an unpublished memoir or forgotten letter in someone's dusty attic.

While CASSIA-related manuscripts and affidavits fail to mention any name that even approximates John Sekler, these materials did include the following people in a context that suggested their having sympathized with or provided assistance to members of CASSIA. Perhaps one of these people used the alias John Sekler. Or perhaps none of them did. Perhaps John Sekler immigrated to the United States after the war and became a prominent architectural historian and educator at Harvard University. (A biographic summary of Eduard Franz Sekler appears in a subsequent chapter titled *The Coda*.) Or perhaps John Sekler, once a respected actor in Vienna, now rests on a hill among vineyards and vacation cottages, having eluded researchers as he once eluded the Gestapo.

Members of the Legradi-Sokal Group

Habietinek, attorney (given name unknown)

Paulick, attorney (given name unknown)

Redlich, attorney (given name unknown)

Knoch, attorney (given name unknown)

Wozak, attorney (given name unknown)

Brixy, attorney (given name unknown)

Adolf Lindner, professor of pharmacology, University of Vienna (please also see "Linder/Lindner" in the following section)

Fritz Stiava, lawyer, who fled the Nazis first from the Sudetenland[23] and then from Prague but whose subsequent residency in Vienna the Legradi-Sokal group was able to legalize

Schneider, district judge, Tulln an der Donau, Lower Austria (given name unknown)

Tintara, judge (given name unknown)[24]

People Who Helped Sokal After Her Escape

Hilda Orlofska

Olga Novakowich

Leopoldine Grünsfeld

Annemarie Schlee

Frieda Förster

Fritz and Josefine Pospischil

Paula Schicht[25]

Other Resistance Members Connected to Sokal

Johann Jahoda

Josephine Meister

Dimiter Gagowsky, Bulgarian student

Pateff, Bulgarian student (given name unknown)

Ilarionow, Bulgarian student (given name unknown)

Robert Schützenhofer

Kronholz, judge (given name unknown)

Peinsipp, a Swiss-German military physician (given name unknown)

Lizzi Berner

Erwin Ratz

Hermine Wernhardt, described as "a Catholic physician" and as a resistance member

Viktor Stehr

Karl Schwind[26]

Names Revealed by Maier Under Interrogation

Ludwig Ennemoser: Maier described Ennemoser as an acquaintance from his church with whom he had never spoken about "political" issues.

Riccabona (given name unknown; associated with Caldonazzi; Maier claimed that Riccabona was not aware of CASSIA): Riccabona is possibly identifiable with Max Riccabona, born in Feldkirch, Vorarlberg, on 31 March 1915. Max Riccabona, a resistance member in Vienna, was arrested in May 1941 by the Gestapo, and was held in prisons in Vienna and Salzburg. On 16 January 1942 Max Riccabona was deported to Dachau concentration camp where he suffered great privation, abuse, and life-threatening disease until he was liberated by advancing U.S. troops on 29 April 1945.[27]

Herbert Adelsberger, an engineer (associated with Klepell; Maier claimed that Adelsberger was not aware of CASSIA)

Linder or Lindner (given name unknown; connected to Grimm): Grimm was in contact with prominent Austrian Social Democrat Anton Linder (1880–1958), who since 1934 had lived as a political refugee in Switzerland.[28] Another less likely possibility is Austrian-American OSS officer Ed Lindner.[29] Also, please note Professor Adolf Lindner in the preceding section.

Ferenc Keresztes-Fischer, Hungarian Interior Minister imprisoned in a concentration camp after the German occupation of Hungary in 1944 (mentioned by Messner to Maier as a person with whom CASSIA should attempt to establish contact)

Zeno von Libel or Libl, the print manager of the Viennese publisher Löcker Verlag (associated with Maier): Maier confessed that he had once mentioned Libel/Libl to Caldonazzi as a recruitment prospect but that he had never confided in Libel/Libl about CASSIA's plans and activities.[30]

Other Sympathizers

Heinrich Scheer
Hugo Zörnleib
Udo Lodgman-Auen, Semperit
Otto Löcker, Semperit
Franz Eidelpes, Semperit[31]
Clemens Holzmeister, a famous Austrian architect and stage

designer: Holzmeister lived in exile in Istanbul from the 1938 Anschluss until the 1950s. Before the war, Holzmeister and Rüdiger had become friends, and the Holzmeister and Rüdiger families remained close in Turkey during the war.[32] Holzmeister, who had connections to the communist resistance,[33] may have also served as one of Rüdiger's sub-sources and may be identifiable with DOGWOOD network agent OLEANDER.[34]

Geraldis, the wife of an Argentine consular official in Vienna (given name unknown; associated with Messner and possibly with Rüdiger): Mrs. Geraldis was allegedly involved in trying to facilitate—through the Argentinian legation in Switzerland—the provision of a U.S. radio transmitter to CASSIA.[35] Please see Appendix I for further details on CASSIA's ostensible plans to acquire a U.S. radio transmitter.

Gina Böhm,[36] manager of Semperit's office in Budapest[37]

Vilma[38] Heindl, Semperit (Vienna)[39]

Part Four: The Benediction of Tragedy

25

Operational Analysis—CASSIA

CASSIA was once called "a group of brave but naive resisters."[1] Brave, by all means and very, but the evidence does not support the charge of their having been naïve.

At first, the members of CASSIA were inexperienced at the tricky game of espionage, as are most new spies, with the notable exception of intelligence professionals who betray their employer and work clandestinely for another country (e.g., Dulles's agent Hans Bernd Gisevius, an Abwehr officer). Still, CASSIA's founders, relying only on their instincts, did almost everything correctly, save for their neglect of a few quality-control issues concerning intelligence collection.

By the time that Maier and Messner began to build CASSIA, the Gestapo had established in Vienna a vast network of informers and *V-Mann* agents, and had infiltrated and destroyed most Austrian resistance groups. Perhaps the most notorious case involved Otto Hartmann. In 1940 Hartmann, a smalltime actor and well-paid Gestapo *V-Mann*, facilitated the arrest of about 200 resistance members, of whom a dozen were executed, helping to ensure that any larger Austrian resistance was stillborn.[2]

Such was the atmosphere in Vienna, where neighbor suspected neighbor, where a careless word could easily find its way to the Gestapo's ears, where private pursuits could be misconstrued as subversive activities. Everyone was filled with doubt and paranoia. This was hardly the safest time for men and women to embark on a secret venture to undermine the state, but it was, as the priest had stressed to the merchant, the *right* time to act.

As noted previously in this work, a good case officer acts accordingly as an agent's employer, financial advisor, psychiatrist, friend, marital counselor, and religious guide. The qualities that make a good agent handler also make a good agent recruiter, which is exactly what Curate Maier was.

Unlike DOGWOOD principal agent Schwarz, who introduced a number of foxes into the henhouse, the record suggests that all of Maier's recruits were genuine and remained so *To the Bitter End*—as Gisevius would title his memoir of the war.

The layman may well ask, how did Maier, a young priest from a neighborhood church, accomplish this astounding feat? While we will never know exactly how Maier plied his hidden trade, for he took those secrets to the grave, successful recruiters of intelligence agents share proficiency in a uniform set of skills.

Effective recruiting begins and ends with effective persuading, and tight operational security begins and ends with the recruiter's ability to assess accurately the psychology of the prospective agent, such as his or her trustworthiness, motivations, and resiliency. If the recruiter works for or is otherwise supported by an intelligence or security service, this agency can fortify the assessment process.

Often, intelligence recruiters first take a broad view of an agent candidate: Does she or he have current or prospective access to information of interest; is he or she truthful and reliable; is she or he properly motivated; and is he or she fundamentally suitable for this work? The first two questions are self-explanatory, but the second and third merit a much closer look and further elaboration.

Motivations are a knotty subject, and only a skillful operator can accurately appraise what drives another human. For example, revenge might be an appropriate motivation if an agent candidate is cool-headed, logical, and patient. But a recruiter should know that vengefulness expressed with rage (even if that rage is at the moment quietly simmering), irrationality, haste, and anxiety cannot be controlled and is dangerous.

In Maier's case, if an agent prospect had been disadvantaged or otherwise injured by the Nazis, but if that person also longed to exact revenge without regard for the risks and consequences, he or she was incompatible with intelligence work. If, on the other hand, someone was opposed to the Nazis and willing to work tirelessly *and* discreetly toward their defeat, that candidate was properly motivated for the delicate tasks that Maier had in mind.

Suitability, in intelligence jargon, refers to the prospect's overall psychological disposition. An agent candidate may have excellent access to state secrets and may possess solid motivations in perfect measure, but may be unable to cope with the stresses and strains of living a so-called double life. Or the prospect may reveal that she or he simply must confide everything in his or her best friend, who just happens to be a notorious gossip or who, in turn but unknown to the agent candidate, also shares everything with a third confidant, who is a Gestapo informer. The list of suitability disqualifications is long and sometimes sordid, but these examples convey an idea of their general nature.

What of these skills of persuasion[3] that Maier obviously possessed in abundance? First and foremost, some distinctions are in order. Many people, even in the intelligence business, confuse the terms persuasion and manipulation. Both have a place in the trade, but they are not interchangeable. Maier, a highly principled man, likely did not swim in the murky, disorienting waters of manipulation, which—in the business of intelligence operations—is an effort to achieve a desired result through the provision of inaccurate information.[4]

An intelligence officer may feel compelled to manipulate an agent or a prospect at some point, perhaps to nudge the person into full compliance or to offer a boost of encouragement, but recruiters and handlers must use manipulation with the utmost care. A crusty intelligence officer once warned, "You can never remember the number of a bus you never took." The finer details of lies—particularly lies based on lies—are easily forgotten and even more easily misremembered. Hard-won trust will evaporate when one is caught in even a small lie. Usually, manipulation is used to achieve a short-term gain, when no other reasonable options are available and when questions of perishability are secondary at best.

Persuasion, though, is a different animal altogether. It is based firmly on trust and its results will endure. It is a virtual certainty that Maier was a master at the art of persuasion. He likely honed his skills from the pulpit when he tried to convince a jaded and weary congregation that one must always love his or her nasty neighbor, that humility may not get you any profit but it still trumps pride, and that there is great honor in poverty and suffering. One must remember that many of Maier's flock had lost loved ones in the First World War or had seen their loved ones return from combat forever disfigured (internally and externally), that all of them felt diminished and embarrassed by the aftereffects of the Treaty of Versailles, and that the Great Depression had made the hollow ache of hunger an everyday reality. Such misery, despite Maier's contentions, did not seem so noble.

And as Maier built his congregation, so too he built CASSIA. No one books passage on a stormy cruise unless they trust the captain. That applies equally to the voyage to salvation and to the voyage to victory in war. Both are fraught with certain danger and hardship. If trust doesn't exist, the ship never leaves the dock.

Lessons on persuasion can—and do—fill many volumes of textbooks and many hours of lectures, but a few points on this elusive art, relative to how Maier probably operated, are warranted. As mentioned above, trust comes first. It does not come easily, for it must be built, bit by bit and over time, and it always remains susceptible to erosion, but it must exist before any other elements of persuasion are exercised. Trust is born from honesty and consistency, and with trust comes comfort and openness. Maier was an expert at building trust in his relationships. Everyone in CASSIA trusted him, from the merchant in the beginning to the soldiers near the end.

Good persuaders are always good listeners. Maier was a trained and practiced counselor and confessor. He understood that people will eventually tell you what they want and need, if only you create an environment of honesty and confidentiality, and seek to hear what they mean (which is sometimes different from what people say). Maier knew that if he dominated conversations with parishioners and prospects, laboring to convince them of something, he would fail to hear the fact, idea, or answer that they were explicitly or implicitly offering up to him.

On one last point, Maier was, to many people, an authority figure. Many people turned to him for guidance on the most important issues and decisions of their lives, and confessed to him their deepest secrets. Maier probably used his standing in the community—with nuance, of course, to avoid coming off as arrogant—to good effect. His confident words of wisdom were likely sought out and respected.

Thus Maier was able, right under the ubiquitous eyes of the Gestapo, to form a secret group dedicated to subverting the Nazi cause and to bringing an early end to the war. The members of this group were not only recruited clandestinely; in Vienna, ground zero for Gestapo activities in Austria, they also communicated and operated secretly. The group's internal correspondence was never intercepted, and its meetings were never discovered. The group twice sent envoys abroad to establish contact with the Allies, and developed a secret platform in Istanbul to facilitate the exfiltration of intelligence from the Reich. At no point were CASSIA's clandestine activities detected through any inherent operational deficiency in the group's tradecraft.

At this point, one might well ask how a parish priest was able to succeed where an intelligence agency and its worldly principal agent failed. In the case of OSS, the reason is centered on its officers' inexperience. But perhaps the organizational culture of OSS—more specifically, in modern military parlance, the OSS chief's "command climate"—also deserves some blame.

The OSS chief, "Wild Bill" Donovan, rewarded creativity and audacity, but at times he also encouraged the furthest reaches of these qualities by seriously considering even the absurd and the foolhardy.[5] "Woe to the officer who turned down a project because, on its face, it seemed ridiculous or at least unusual," OSS Colonel David K.E. Bruce once said.[6] (Bruce was OSS chief of European operations and a great admirer of Donovan.) Such feedback often ignited bouts of bravado in Donovan's subordinates. In some cases, such boldness and bluster likely masked great deficiencies.

That kind of atmosphere may well have discouraged officers' expressions of doubt; they may have feared being labeled timid. MacFarland and Coleman may have realized that they were trapped on a runaway train but couldn't summon the fortitude to admit that they had no idea how to repair their situation and to ask for help. In some cases, exercising moral courage in a bureaucracy can be more difficult than being valorous on a battlefield.

Of course OSS-Istanbul alone wasn't stocked with operational greenhorns. Virtually none of that agency's officers had experience with the abstruse art of agent recruiting. It was, after all, very ticklish work. Its concepts were vague and variable, and as such were troublesome to teach. Mastery came, if it ever did, only after hundreds of hours of practice on the street, which was more than enough time for a new officer to generate a few disasters before everyone concluded that he or she had no aptitude for the trade.

Since the Second World War, many field-operations trainees have wearied of their instructors' stock response to the most vexing scenarios—"It depends." But no matter how often those words are repeated, they are never hackneyed, for their significance cannot be diminished through use. And "It depends" is more than an accurate answer to many of complicated questions; its utterance also serves as a litmus test for those who might try their hand at this curious profession. Intelligence fieldwork is the wrong job for those who derive comfort from the predictable and the unambiguous.

The steps of the idealized recruiting process may be tallied and worded in many different ways, but they usually break down along the following lines: spotting prospects, carefully and incrementally developing relationships with them, assessing them at every step, scrutinizing their backgrounds and their potential for duplicity, ascertaining if they have access to desired intelligence and the disposition to leverage that access to service collection requirements, and prudently moving them into an optimal position for formal recruitment and then "pitching" them—jargon for hiring them as agents.

And now, after enduring that litany, one might still venture to ask what exactly "pitching" means. In its essence it is a quid pro quo: You give me secrets and in return I will give you something that you value. Agents are often suborned—in other words, they are given money to spy—and less frequently they are convinced to cooperate based solely on "ideological" grounds, which suggest an agent's political or philosophical beliefs but in practice may include highly personal reasons. In a case built on an agent's ideology, the something-of-value-in-return might be an emotional or intellectual reward.

In the example of CASSIA, Maier was far more experienced at recruiting than were any of the involved OSS officers, to include Dulles. During the war the OSS officers of this story spent the lion's share of their time fielding offers—talking to multitudes of volunteers and to people whom other U.S. and foreign agencies had referred. This was time-consuming and arduous work, certainly. It involved confirming or refuting the volunteers' claimed access and initial offerings of intelligence. And if the intelligence seemed to be genuine, OSS officers then had to determine its potential worth to the Allied war effort.

These tasks, while difficult and exacting, drew on different skills from those used in recruiting. Volunteers were usually eager and decided, but recruitment prospects were sometimes edgy and reluctant—due to doubts or fears—to betray the things and people to whom they had pledged fealty, even if that pledge had been perfunctory. In sum, the temperament and circumstances of a typical recruitment target were frequently antithetical to those of the standard volunteer, and thus demanded from the operations officer discrete approaches and expertise.

During the Second World War, the commission—or sometimes even only the suspicion—of espionage carried the threat of summary execution. In many cases death came after harsh interrogation and torture, and in some cases death was welcome. Prospective spies knew well about all of these staggering risks. Convincing someone to do the "right" thing—especially in wartime when right is not always easily distinguishable from wrong—can be a monumental task. In some cases it is impossible, even if the involved operations officer is highly competent and experienced.

Maier's successes in recruiting, then, were not a foregone conclusion. Many highly trained, talented, and much-practiced operations officers have devoted copious amounts of time, energy, and reflection to developing relationships with prized "targets"—as jargon has labeled them—only to have these prospects reject even the most basic terms of a secret pact. We will likely never know Maier's success rate at recruiting, for his tentative probes and abandoned forays were never recorded, but one could sensibly offer that he was quite accomplished at this esoteric business.

As for the sophisticated and seasoned Schwarz, a few lines from the U.S. War Department's postwar analysis of OSS operations offer clues why he was duped, time and again: "'Dogwood' had such extraordinary self-assurance that he apparently thought that he need only take a double-agent into his confidence in order to gain his support." The analysis added, "[Schwarz's] self-confident garrulity, unchecked by the mission chief [MacFarland], was responsible [for allowing penetration of DOGWOOD by German double agents]."[7]

In short, Schwarz's ego got in the way of his ability to recruit effectively. And even if Schwarz had recruited loyal sub-sources, he lacked the necessary discretion for doing secret work: He was excessively talkative, a flaw that OSS-Istanbul failed to rectify.[8] A handling officer with even a modicum of skill would have seen from the start that Schwarz was fundamentally unsuitable for any kind of role in intelligence operations. It is no wonder that German double agents flocked to his door.

But Maier knew how to operate clandestinely *and* suffered from no such damning pridefulness; he had no undue confidence in his intellect or powers of oratory that might have warped his perspective. And so he embodied another immutable requirement for this arcane task: A good recruiter is keenly self-aware, in that he or she knows well what strengths and weaknesses he or she has, and proceeds accordingly.

26

Operational Analysis—OSS

In the end, CASSIA was not betrayed from within, but from without, through the efforts of the earnest but bumbling intelligence officers who were charged with protecting it.

As one author described these officers' dodgy record, "Seventeen foreign intelligence services competed in Istanbul, of which the most resolutely inept appears to have been the American."[1] Even as early as the spring of 1944, some OSS officers would have agreed with this damning statement.

One such critic was James G. O'Conor, who replaced MacFarland and served as interim chief of OSS-Istanbul from 1 April to 30 May 1944. A week before he left Istanbul, referencing MacFarland, O'Conor wrote to Whitney H. Shepardson (1890–1966), the head of Secret Intelligence at OSS Headquarters, "I wonder why a person of such casual bearing should have [had] such an important assignment." In this same note O'Conor described OSS-Istanbul's operations as being "of junior status, bordering on mediocre" and the office's star agent, Schwarz, as being "a political and not an intelligence agent."[2] In terms of context, O'Conor drafted these opinions long before the postmortem on DOGWOOD produced even its most preliminary results.

After the war, an OSS officer, never assigned to Turkey and commenting on the agency in general, provided some clues for the failures in Istanbul: "We were all amateurs. It was a boy scout affair, you have to understand. Nowadays, in the intelligence business, you go through years of training.[3] [OSS chief William Donovan] recruited a bunch of cowboys and amateurs like myself, who had to improvise and learn as we went along."[4]

OSS-Istanbul's grand errors shook the ground beneath not only the OSS; its mistakes threatened to derail productive relations with the United States' most important intelligence partner, the British. According to the

U.S. War Department's postwar analysis of OSS operations, "Various British intelligence officers had privately voiced criticisms of the insecurity of OSS/Istanbul during the CEREUS operation. In May 1944 [about the time that O'Conor replaced MacFarland], a meeting of representatives from all British agencies had decided to minimize relations with the [OSS] mission [in Istanbul], pending some improvement in security in both business and personal activities."[5]

As that final line implies, the British were aware of more security problems at OSS-Istanbul than only those concerning the DOGWOOD network. A postwar analysis of MacFarland's operations concluded, "A ... notable penetration of OSS was effected by one Mrs. Hildegarde Reilly, reputed to have been the most successful female agent working in Istanbul during 1944 and 1945. Mrs. Reilly came in contact with an OSS officer, and, although she was known to be a double-agent, the mission chief [MacFarland] approved the association, hoping that some information on German activity could thus be acquired. The project backfired inasmuch as Mrs. Reilly is known to have reported to the Germans on OSS personnel and activities. Other similar penetrations were accomplished by various female spies in the city."[6]

That concluding sentence was ominous, and rightly so. As it turned out, German-born Reilly, who had acquired her surname through marriage to an Englishman, was far from being alone in her seamy work. Just as she plied her trade in an Istanbul bar where Western expatriates—to include OSS-Istanbul officers—went to blow off steam after long days in the office, so too did other female German agents.[7]

In one case, the Turkish authorities charged a Hungarian hostess with working as a German agent and deported her, and the OSS later determined that she had engaged in trysts with various Americans in Istanbul. So successful were these honey-trap operations that at one point the Abwehr actually financed a bar, using it both as a meeting place for German agents and as a targeting venue, where naïve men from Allied countries could be softened up and picked clean of their secrets.[8]

It appears that MacFarland did not issue—or at least did not rigorously enforce—an edict against mixing incompatible covers. His officers operated under a wide assortment of guises: "By mid–1944, the mission consisted of 43 members under State Department, FEA [Foreign Economic Administration—a wartime agency tasked with centralizing and coordinating all US foreign economic operations], Military Attache, business, press and other covers."[9] In the fishbowl of wartime Istanbul, officers who were ostensibly businessmen fraternized openly with officers who worked in the consulate.

This unchecked and unmonitored socializing did not stop with the U.S. expatriate community. Some OSS-Istanbul officers also associated freely with—and in some cases philandered with—British subjects, Turks, natives from a hodgepodge of other countries, and some people whose national origins were at best unclear. While interacting with a large and diverse number of people is an operation officer's job, so too is exercising professional discrimination, circumspection, and intentionality in his or her dealings with those contacts.

The bottom line is that MacFarland and his officers ran too fast and loose in Istanbul. While at the time MacFarland may have thought that the bar-crawling and love affairs were all in good fun or were chances to exhibit some vocational cleverness against the enemy, in the end these poorly considered actions only added to the whopping sum of OSS-Istanbul's counterintelligence errors.

But OSS-Istanbul's misadventures even went beyond DOGWOOD's double agents and its officers' readily succumbing to the wiles of Abwehr's Mata Haris. In the latter part of the war OSS learned that "two chauffeurs, one assigned to the mission chief's [MacFarland's] car, were in Russian service" and that "the X-2 [OSS counterintelligence] chauffeur reported regularly to the Turkish police on X-2 activities."[10]

From the start OSS-Istanbul had been outmatched by German intelligence (and to a lesser degree by the Russian and Turkish services), and at least one of its officers suspected as much: "[Abwehr operatives] ... have as many aliases as a rainbow has colors.... The city is riddled with their agents; one's movements are frequently watched and occasionally followed." So wrote OSS-Istanbul officer Cedric Seager, whose family had lived in Istanbul since the middle 1800s.[11] Because of his ease with Turkish language and ways, Seager was charged with handling OSS's official liaison with the *Milli Emniyet Hizmeti*,[12] Turkey's intelligence agency from 1926 to 1965. From these dealings he had gained unique insights on the scope of German espionage in Istanbul and was greatly unsettled by what he had learned.

OSS-Istanbul was not an unruly outlier. Other OSS offices and units also made mistakes, some of them as calamitous as those committed in Turkey, but the agency had its share of successes as well. Several of Dulles's operations in Bern were very effective, as was some OSS work with resistance groups in Europe—notably with those in France and Norway—usually done in concert with the British. OSS's unit in Japanese-occupied Burma,

Detachment 101, excelled at a broad range of activities: gathering intelligence, serving as scouts for larger units, conducting sabotage and ambushes against Japanese regular forces, and rescuing downed Allied pilots. In fact, for its many and commendable accomplishments, Det-101 received a Presidential Distinguished Unit Citation after the war.[13] These triumphs, though, do not efface other tragedies.

As this study and others have demonstrated, OSS-Istanbul's blunders are easily counted and dissected. After digesting many pages of such criticism, one could rightfully ask how MacFarland and his men might have done better. As it turns out, the answer, though comprised of a few component elements, is straightforward, accessible, and cost-effective.

OSS's first and most serious error was to fold CASSIA into the metastasizing DOGWOOD network. Trained, proven, and well-covered OSS officers should have directly—and exclusively—handled CASSIA. Coleman's cover job with *The Saturday Evening Post*, if it had been properly maintained (i.e., not cross-contaminated with other officers' incompatible covers), would have been perfect for this assignment. The case involved no compelling security or handling reasons for using a principal agent.

Schwarz's German language skills comprised an insufficient justification to insert him into a sensitive case where his middleman services were not truly needed. Like his colleagues in Istanbul, Dulles was not proficient in German, but to ensure that his operations ran securely and productively, he scoured the U.S. expatriate community in Switzerland and found suitable bilingual prospects.[14] Then he checked them out thoroughly, received approval from OSS headquarters, and hired them onto his staff. Certainly Switzerland had a greater number of U.S. citizens who could speak German than did Turkey, but for such an important operation, either MacFarland or the OSS beyond Istanbul could have found the right officer for this critical job. Further, Rüdiger and Issakides were fluent in English, and Messner, a well-educated international businessman, almost certainly had ample proficiency in the language.

Likewise, any other proposed reasons for using Schwarz, for example as an OSS proxy for meeting directly with Messner, needlessly complicated the operation and in so doing introduced additional risk. In Switzerland through Grimm, and in Istanbul through Rüdiger, OSS already had the means to convey instructions to Messner for a meeting with the designated OSS handling officer, Archibald Coleman, in a safe house or hotel room, acquired under an innocuous pretext. On his way to meet with Messner (or any other agent), Coleman would have needed to take a long circuitous—but not alerting—route through Istanbul to confirm that no one was following him, and he would have needed to instruct Messner and Rüdiger on the basic principles and practice of such techniques. These few precautions alone—directly handling agents, employing basic surveillance-detection methods, and meeting in appropriate locations—would likely have kept the members of CASSIA out of prison and alive until the end of the war.

Perhaps the most succinct statement of what went wrong with DOGWOOD was included in the U.S. War Department's postwar analysis of OSS operations: "The careless handling of agents eventually resulted in the arrest of many of the OSS/Istanbul contacts in Europe." CASSIA was singled out as one of these casualties. And on this point the War Department elaborated, "A further weakness in the intelligence resulted from the centralizing of operations through 'Dogwood.' Since the latter [Schwarz] was not a member of the OSS office, he could not have available the facilities and data necessary for [agent] briefing and training. CEREUS members and contacts [i.e., Coleman's sources and sub-sources in DOGWOOD] received therefore none [i.e., no such support and training], and their intelligence reports showed the lack. Had they been operated directly by OSS instead of through a doubtful sub-agent, many would have been released after X-2 vetting, and others might have been developed into excellent sources." Interestingly, a footnote to this passage elaborated that "this affair provided one of the main reasons for the OSS directive of 19 June 1944, requiring that all agents hired in the field be vetted against X-2 files."[15]

But Coleman demonstrated that he *could* establish and maintain secure contact with an agent of the DOGWOOD network. In September 1943, Coleman first met CASSIA's man in Istanbul, Rüdiger, in a closed-down summer resort on the Sea of Marmara,[16] courtesy of one of Rüdiger's biggest fans, DOGWOOD agent PERIWINKLE—Josef Lehrner, the Austrian who worked for Philips & Co. in Istanbul.[17] One could argue that such a location, while likely free from prying eyes and ears, reeked of Hollywood cliché and may well have worked against Coleman's earnest efforts at discretion, in that two foreigners lounging around a villa in an otherwise vacant resort might draw some attention. But still, these arrangements suggest that Coleman was at least thinking about operational security, was doing his best, such as it was, to keep the meeting secret, and as a result was getting a firsthand look at a DOGWOOD sub-source.

Although Coleman's appraisals of Schwarz and the greater DOGWOOD network proved to be sorely lacking, his comments about Rüdiger are nevertheless of interest, since they add another perspective about

CASSIA's mysterious front man in Istanbul. In his post-meeting report, Coleman wrote that Rüdiger "looks and dresses like an Englishman" and described him as "smart and honest" and "responsible." Coleman also mentioned Rüdiger's good sense of humor, and added that women found Rüdiger attractive.[18]

Coleman lauded Rüdiger as an accomplished business executive and noted that he had prominent family connections in Austria—a reference, no doubt, to Rüdiger's father-in-law, former Chancellor Otto Ender. Before the war, Ender had moved in the country's most exclusive circles, and through these contacts Rüdiger had probably gained entrée to people who had not only influence and but also access to intelligence.

After Coleman's seaside conversation with agent STOCK, despite having shown that OSS officers could securely meet and debrief penetrations of the Reich in Turkey, he largely surrendered responsibilities for handling the network's sources to Schwarz. Although OSS records suggest that Coleman met with Rüdiger four more times before late December 1943, when Coleman was temporarily removed from duty because of illness, he often allowed Schwarz to dictate how the CASSIA operation was run and how its intelligence was handled. Worse yet, during Coleman's absence, MacFarland took over the DOGWOOD case but exercised even less control over Schwarz than Coleman had.[19]

For the sake of argument, if regular direct contact was unfeasible for some cogent reason and if the only remaining course of action was to use DOGWOOD, Coleman would have needed to play the game at a much higher level than he ever did. When one considers his lack of training and relevant experience, that level of performance was well beyond his grasp. That he was so far out of his depth explains why Coleman made such rookie mistakes: He ceded too much control and responsibility to Schwarz, and otherwise failed to manage the operation in a prudent way.

Schwarz's role was not confined to managing DOGWOOD's cover mechanism and to recruiting and handling the network's multifarious collection of agents. Coleman also allowed Schwarz to gather all of the network's intelligence without oversight, and to write and process all of the reports, most of which Coleman never even read.[20] Even when things began to go sideways, Coleman neglected to identify the problems quickly, when the operation was still salvageable, and to take decisive action toward the lasting correction of these deficiencies.

Coleman and his boss, MacFarland, clearly considered Schwarz to be—once again in intelligence jargon—a "vetted" contact, an agent whose background OSS had once checked and pronounced worthy. But "running counterintelligence checks," suggesting a single procedure frozen in time, was—and always is—insufficient. Counterintelligence is adeptly practiced as a pervasive and enduring awareness. A good officer is always sensitive to changes in an agent's counterintelligence profile and demeanor, as well as to changes in the overall counterintelligence environment—which in Coleman's case meant Istanbul, but also extended into the Reich where CASSIA operated. A good officer not only remains vigilant to such changes, but also assiduously records every salient incident, appraisal, observation, and comment. And such an officer regularly takes a step back and scrutinizes these data in their aggregate, to determine if any unsettling patterns are beginning to emerge. Watchful is the diligent officer's watchword.

A focused counterintelligence unit, such as OSS's X-2, can support these activities—by, for example, searching for correlations in archival holdings and in other sources' reports, and occasionally offering a fresh and objective opinion—but counterintelligence officers are not ultimately responsible for the health of an operation. That responsibility lies with the handling officer, the only person with his or her eyes on the agent or agents, the only person walking the streets of some foreign city, taking calculated risks and guiding other people safely through such risks. For CASSIA, that person was Coleman and more often than not he was asleep at the wheel.

During CASSIA's life and after its demise, some OSS-Istanbul and X-2 officers grumbled that DOGWOOD worked against their efforts to monitor the network. Indeed, he did so by withholding details on his sub-sources, which thwarted efforts to run traces that could inform assessments. In the postwar years OSS's official history elaborated, "Despite the presence of an X-2 representative [in Istanbul] from October 1943, the mission chief [MacFarland] supported 'Dogwood' in his refusal to allow X-2 vetting of CEREUS recruits [sic; while this reference suggests that Coleman recruited all of the network's sub-sources, it actually means that those sources were attributed to him as DOGWOOD's handler]."[21]

But such complaints border on the absurd. A paid agent is employed by the handling agency (and *only* that agency) and must be responsive to it. If the agent works at cross-purposes to his employer, he or she is first warned, is then reprimanded, is subsequently punished, and, if he or she still refuses to comply, is fired—"terminated" in the vernacular. And that agent is terminated promptly *even if the handling agency risks losing important intelligence*, for if the warning signs are ignored and an agent "goes bad," not only is the current flow of information staunched, but also a dark shadow of doubt is cast on all previously collected intelligence. Neither Coleman nor MacFarland grasped that corruption of a part can lead to decay of the whole, and that sometimes the only cure is amputation.

Perhaps even more egregious in the case of Laufer the Mole, X-2 *had* derogatory information on him but was unable to retrieve it, or possibly had lost it. One could justifiably charge that, when it came to providing support to the CASSIA case, OSS-Istanbul, OSS-Cairo (whose chief, Lada-Mocarski, served as MacFarland's direct supervisor and had signed OSS's Memorandum of Agreement with CASSIA), elements of OSS-London, and OSS Headquarters were doing little else than tripping over one another, bumping into walls, and falling on their faces. For these offices, it was not so much an operation as it was slapstick. OSS Headquarters was particularly culpable. It should have *quickly* noticed the problems, launched an exhaustive investigation, demanded explanations from OSS-Istanbul, dispatched capable officers to make firsthand observations, and then ordered MacFarland to get his house in order or replaced him.

Despite their shoddy performance, these OSS offices were not always silent on the matter. There were a few voices of dissent about DOGWOOD, decrying Archibald Coleman's handling skills, and charging that his operation had grown too large, that he had lost control of it, and that he had likely allowed German double agents to penetrate it. But almost all of these criticisms came after the worst damage was done and failed to provide any hard evidence of DOGWOOD's infiltration by enemy agents.[22]

At one point, even Coleman proved capable of providing an accurate—if not fully substantiated—counterintelligence assessment. On multiple occasions he advised Schwarz not to use Laufer for DOGWOOD-related operations. But Schwarz simply brushed off Coleman's guidance, arguing how valuable Laufer was to the network.[23]

It is astounding—unfathomable, actually—that a handling officer would have so little control over a principal agent that his or her directives would be easily ignored, discounted, or reversed. A professional officer *issues* such instructions to and *levies* requirements on an agent. Such orders are often given tactfully and thoughtfully, but they are still orders and as such are beyond debate. And while in certain circumstances an officer might offer advice to an agent on a suitable adjunct topic, he or she never merely suggests anything that approximates *operational* guidance. The professional intelligence officer is fully responsible for and thus fully in charge of an operation, and does not erode his or her authority or an agent's confidence in him or her by *proposing* how the operation should best be run. (The preceding italicized words, which some readers may find excessive, not only provide emphases on how operations should be run but also represent the author's stupefaction and dismay at how DOGWOOD was chronically mismanaged.)

Regarding such directives, one notable exception—in terms of its proofs and the force of its delivery—was a message, sent in early January 1944, from OSS chief Donovan himself to MacFarland. The British had collected irrefutable evidence from a trusted counterintelligence source that at least one DOGWOOD agent was working for the Germans: Hatz, codename JASMINE. The British first brought the report to MacFarland, who dismissed it, explaining that Hatz only dealt with the Germans to enhance his cover. Befuddled by MacFarland's response, the British sent the report directly to Donovan, who was outraged and immediately cabled MacFarland, explaining that Hatz was a confirmed double agent and ordering MacFarland to terminate him, post haste. But MacFarland ignored the evidence and the instruction, and instead argued fatuously on Hatz's behalf. It would take two more blistering messages from Donovan before MacFarland finally began taking steps to distance OSS from Hatz, but by that time the Germans already had what they needed to take down CASSIA.[24] While Donovan's message arrived in Istanbul a couple of weeks before Caldonazzi's arrest, even if it had prompted MacFarland to take immediate and decisive action, it came much too late to thwart the Gestapo's planned actions against most of CASSIA's members.

Donovan's case was even stronger than he apparently realized. From his own office in Bern, he had corroboration that the British warning was valid. OSS-Bern chief Dulles had collected from one of his best agents, Berlin-based German Foreign Ministry penetration Fritz Kolbe, the names of several German double agents who were on OSS's books, to include a Hungarian lieutenant colonel named Otto Hatz.[25] If Donovan had put two and two together and had grasped the full gravity of the situation, he may well have not suffered any such telegraph-message volleying on the subject with MacFarland.

Other than Donovan's charges, which fingered Hatz but lacked any critical deduction—based, for example, on Hatz's intimate links to other agents—that DOGWOOD was likely riddled with enemy spies, all other OSS suspicions were founded on a fallacy: Inaccuracies in reporting, which were caused not by nefarious intent but by inexperience and a lack of training. In short, some OSS officers were looking at the wrong problems and were misinterpreting their causes, but still reaching the correct conclusion.

As snitch Romen's accusations against Messner and Rüdiger demonstrated, even a blind chicken can occasionally find a kernel of corn.

Regardless of the internal debate, of who in OSS said what and when, the fact remains that no decisive action was taken on DOGWOOD until—at least for CASSIA—it was far too late.

In the immediate aftermath of the CASSIA disaster, OSS groped for answers to what had gone wrong. MacFarland's first successor, O'Conor, was quick to offer his opinion: "[S]ome people in [DOGWOOD's] Hungarian chain might have been instrumental in 'Cassia's' arrest." To explain how such a thing could have happened, O'Conor pointed to a lack of compartmentalization, charging that Schwarz had exposed CASSIA to another part of DOGWOOD and that "the Hungarian chain ... should have been maintained distinctly separate" from the Austrians.[26]

Unfortunately, although O'Conor's first toss at the DOGWOOD dartboard was respectable, the passage of time did not improve his accuracy. On 24 August 1944 in *Report on My Istanbul Mission*, O'Conor erroneously deduced, "Cassia's material came to us through Stock [Rüdiger], who was the manager of Cassia's Istanbul branch. But Stock's office associate and close friend was one Herock [Fred Herok[27]], a bad and dangerous Gestapo agent. Cassia was arrested in Budapest.... This might very well have been caused by Herock."[28] But according to research by an accomplished Austrian historian, "American classified research after the war showed, however, that in summer 1944 the German security services doubted Fred Herok's loyalty to the Reich, brought him back to Vienna with a number of other suspects, and made charges [probably of treason] against him. Only when the Soviet Red Army occupied Vienna was he freed from prison."[29] O'Conor's assertion that "Gestapo agent" Herok was to blame for CASSIA's demise still finds its way into research on OSS operations,[30] but it is highly improbable that the Gestapo would have had any cause to arrest and imprison its supposed star agent—the man who, as alleged by O'Conor, had brought down the OSS's largest spy ring in Austria. But O'Conor's instincts were not completely off base: CASSIA was betrayed, in part, by a Semperit insider—Sigismund Romen in the company's Vienna headquarters, not Fred Herok in its Istanbul sales office.

Meanwhile, as the rest of OSS-Istanbul was coming to terms with the scope of its intelligence failure, ever-credulous Coleman, refusing to believe that he had been duped, submitted his position for the record: "The arrest of 'Cassia' was not related to 'Jasmine's' [Hatz's] group in any way whatsoever."[31] For Coleman, any other conclusion was unacceptable; to admit that Hatz was a traitor was to admit his own role in a debacle that delivered a dozen CASSIA members into the hands of the Gestapo. In its official postwar report on OSS, however, the U.S. War Department found credence in O'Conor's views and, in so doing, summarily discounted Coleman's assertion: "Due to insufficient OSS security, the Hungarian agents gained knowledge of other Istanbul contacts, and caused the subsequent collapse of CEREUS [Coleman's] operations."[32]

Another important fact merits mention. DOGWOOD was set up and operated for money. OSS provided the startup capital, operating costs, and salaries, and DOGWOOD produced intelligence. Schwarz ran DOGWOOD like a dynamic business because OSS allowed him to do so and because he was a businessman. Commerce was what he knew. Companies are designed to grow and to generate more profit, and this is precisely how Schwarz designed DOGWOOD to work. But as one intelligence adage counsels, "Big is bad," which means, among other things (e.g., the proverb "too many cooks spoil the broth" is also implied), largeness and loudness and obviousness are anathemas to clandestine operations.

Despite Schwarz's great efforts—one can accuse him of many things but not of being lazy—and despite similar attempts in the decades since the Second World War, the running of intelligence operations does not meld well with, and in some cases is incompatible with, standard corporate practices. For CASSIA, however, one exception merits highlighting: Unlike anyone else associated with group—possibly aside from Legradi, whose role in the group seems to have been fairly limited—Messner performed well as both a businessman and an agent. But his was a rare combination of skills. In different circumstances, he may have also excelled at service as a principal agent or, given the chance, even as a case officer or field supervisor of intelligence operations.

Many have tried, and as many have failed, to introduce business jargon, which is often even more vapid than government lexicon, into the intelligence trade, usually in some misguided attempt "to improve efficiencies." But even that lofty goal—which apparently means "to make more efficient"—is too ambiguous to be useful, and thus fits awkwardly if at all into the world of espionage, which is often naturally indistinct and thus begs for infusions of clarity. As a devised example of this discordancy, there is no commercial profit in spending one million dollars to get a blurry photograph of a high-school laboratory centrifuge, but depending on the circumstances, particularly on where and how that centrifuge is being used, there may very well be a compelling intelligence justification—"operational profit," perhaps—for that cost. For the right photograph at the right time, an intelligence agency might even consider one million dollars to be a bargain.

On one last point, different offices and organizations among and within the Western Allies tried to impugn CASSIA's fidelity to the Allies. Those entities—in the OSS and, to a lesser degree, in the USAAF—were mostly looking in the wrong places and misinterpreting what they saw, but were also failing to notice and take action on the real problems of the DOGWOOD network. Meanwhile Schwarz continued to run his money-making enterprise, with no thoughtful parental control, until he had run it off the rails and into a deep ravine.

Amidst all of the carping about CASSIA, one even-keeled professional offered the most accurate wartime appraisal of the group, based not on adroit counterintelligence analysis or on scrutiny of aerial photographs, but solely on his honed assessment skills. In a secret cable dated 14 March 1944, Allen Dulles wrote, "[Messner] impressed us [OSS-Bern] very favorably. We are convinced that he is worthy of all our support and we will make arrangements to give him some modest financial assistance from here if he requests it."[33] Then, in an 8 May 1944 secret cable, unaware that CASSIA was already doomed, Dulles added, "[Messner's] honesty, I feel, cannot be doubted. He gives a very fine personal impression. It is not probable that he would operate in behalf of [Germany] for money, in view of his standing in the community. The possibility that he may be a Nazi by ideology or temperament is one which I discount."[34]

27

The Coda

As maintained in the preface, some tragic stories never really end. This sad tale may live on through its compelling examples of courage and its enduring lessons, but all of its characters—with the possible exception of John Sekler—have died. Some passed violently, as described in *The Executions*, others strangely, and still others peacefully. The following passages provide a few more facts on the men and women of this story—additional biographic details, insights on what a few of the survivors did after the war, and how some of them died and where they are buried.

In the 1940s, Harald Sattler Frederiksen looked like an average young man: He was slender, had wavy dark hair and an innocent face, and wore round wire-rimmed spectacles that suggested—stereotypically but, in his case, correctly—an interest in scholarly pursuits. But nothing about him was ordinary.

Frederiksen was born on 2 May 1924 in Cristóbal, U.S. Panama Canal Zone, to Frederik Peter Frederiksen (1874–1965), a naturalized U.S. citizen born in Vejle, Denmark, and Anna Catharine "Annie" Frederiksen (née Sattler) (1897–1987), a naturalized U.S. citizen born in Vienna, Austria. Frederiksen had one sister, Gunhild (1930–2010), who later took the married surname Glass. Frederik worked as an engineer on the Canal from 1905 to 1936, and then retired on a U.S. Civil Service pension.[1]

In 1936 the Frederiksen family embarked on a tour of Europe "for recreational and educational reasons," at one point stopping to visit Annie's relatives in Vienna. In Austria Frederik fell seriously ill, and the family's scheduled return to the United States was delayed. While he was recovering, Hitler annexed Austria. The family remained unmolested in Vienna until the United States entered the war in 1941, when the Reich placed the Frederiksens under a type of arrest that restricted their movements to the city.[2]

In 1942 the Reich arranged for Frederik's repatriation, having worked out some sort of prisoner exchange with the United States, and promised to send the rest of the family on the next available transportation. Probably due to his fragile health, Frederik departed alone at the first opportunity, while the rest of the family remained in Vienna, waiting for the Third Reich to issue Catharine an exit permit. She was essentially stateless: married to a U.S. passport holder but unable to apply for U.S. citizenship, since uninterrupted residence in the United States—not in a U.S. territory like the Panama Canal Zone—was a requirement of the naturalization process. Just before the family's scheduled departure, the Third Reich cancelled their repatriation, and Harald, his mother, and his sister were trapped in Austria for the remainder of the war.[3]

In Vienna, Harald completed grammar school—where he met Fritz Molden—and preparatory high school. As noted earlier in this narrative, in 1942 he was admitted to the medical school of the University of Vienna, and two years later he was expelled for having obstructed a recruiting lecture designed to entice foreign students to join the SS. Some of Frederiksen's professors, however, took great risks to continue to provide him informal instruction. After the war, the University of Vienna awarded him full credit for both his official and off-the-books wartime studies.[4]

In September 1945, after his OSS debriefing in Salzburg and subsequent stopovers at OSS offices in Paris and London, Frederiksen traveled to New York and was reunited with his father. Six months later Frederiksen returned to Vienna and resumed his studies.[5]

On 4 May 1946, Frederiksen began to work again for U.S. intelligence—specifically for the 430th CIC Detachment in Vienna—and in 1947 attended the European Theater Intelligence School in Oberammergau, a town of some 5,000 residents in Bavaria, Germany. For his intelligence work, Frederiksen was awarded two commendations, both classified secret. In 1948 he completed his medical degree but remained in Vienna for an additional year of postgraduate work.[6]

In 1949 Frederiksen returned to the United States and worked for 11 months at the Staten Island Public Health Service Hospital—formerly known as the U.S. Marine Hospital Service and currently called the Bayley Seton Hospital. Then, in the summer and fall of 1950, he spent three months in the surgery wards of the U.S. Marine Hospital in Cleveland (closed in 1953).[7]

In October 1950, Frederiksen headed the U.S. Public Health Service unit at the U.S. consulate in Liverpool, United Kingdom. He also attended public health courses the University of Liverpool and, at the end of 1951, passed the Certified in Public Health (CPH) examination. But Frederiksen, still in his late 20s, didn't spend all of his time in Britain working and studying. He also met an Irish nurse, Kate, who would become his wife.[8]

In December 1951, Frederiksen and his bride moved to the United States and he began working for the Communicable Disease Center in Atlanta, Georgia, which would evolve into today's Centers for Disease Control and Prevention. Throughout the 1950s and 1960s Harald and Kate traveled the world. After a life filled with intrigue and adventure and untold dangers, Harald and Kate settled down in northwest Washington, D.C., and later purchased a second home in rural Virginia near the town of Leesburg.[9]

On 9 August 1970, while pruning trees and bushes in the backyard of his country home, 46-year-old Frederiksen disturbed a hive of wild bees. In a matter of moments, he suffered an acute allergic reaction to the bee stings and died.[10] Such was the astonishing end of Harald Frederiksen, who had defied the Nazis and the Soviets, only to be killed by insects.

The Danish side of Frederiksen's family was devastated by the news of his untimely and unusual death. Years later, one of Frederiksen's Danish cousins remembered him as having been extremely intelligent and incisive, but also as having been shy, gentle, and polite. Frederiksen had been the first in the family to obtain a university degree, and his Danish relatives had always admired his many academic and professional accomplishments.[11]

Frederiksen was buried in the Gettysburg National Military Park in Pennsylvania (Annex, Site Number V-22). Almost 19 years later, on 6 April 1999, Frederiksen's wife Kate passed away. She was buried by his side.

Three of Fritz Molden's family members were also involved in resistance activities during the war: His father, Ernst, the deputy editor-in-chief of Viennese newspaper *Neue Freie Presse*, which because of its Jewish management the Nazis closed down in 1938; his mother, Paula Preradović, an author and poet who wrote the lyrics to the Austrian national anthem; and his older brother, Otto.[12]

After the war, as mentioned earlier, Molden married Dulles's daughter Joan, but the couple later divorced. At the time of his death Molden was wedded to his fourth wife, an Austrian author whose works appear under the name Hanna Molden. Molden had five children, to include two sons of some repute in Austria: Ernst, a musician and novelist, and Berthold, a professor of history at the University of Vienna.[13]

Molden was born on 8 April 1924 in Vienna and died on 11 January 2014 in Schwaz, a town of about 13,000 people in the Austrian Tyrol. He is buried in a Grave of Honor in Vienna's Central Cemetery (Group 32C, Number 42) with his father, mother, and brother.

Allen Welsh Dulles (7 April 1893–29 January 1969) became the fifth Director of Central Intelligence in 1953, an office that he held until 1961. He headed the CIA for longer than any other director to date.

After the war, unidentified friends of Curate Heinrich Maier (born 16 February 1908), Dr. Josef Wyhnal (born 22 February 1903), and Hermann Klepell (born 19 June 1918) found the three men's remains in a common grave at the Central Cemetery, in Vienna's southern outskirts, and reburied them in Neustift am Wald Cemetery in the 18th District. The Neustift graveyard, a 30-minute walk from Gersthof Parish Church, runs along the crest of a pine-covered hill that overlooks the vineyards and villas of the 19th District.

The City of Vienna later designated the burial plots of Maier, Wyhnal, and Klepell as Graves of Honor (Group E, Row 1, Numbers 13, 14, and 15, respectively). Maier's uncle Oskar (1894–circa 1972), whom Maier credited—under the duress of a Gestapo interrogation—with introducing him to Theodor Legradi, is buried with Maier.

In 1949, probably at the urging of the Catholic Archdiocese of Vienna,

The graves of Klepell (left), Wyhnal (center), and Maier (right) in Neustift am Wald Cemetery, Vienna (taken by the author, 2016).

a residential street near the cemetery was named Dr.-Heinrich-Maier-Strasse. In 1995 a plaque explaining Maier's resistance work was added at the street's intersection with Khevenhüllerstrasse.

Also in the 1990s, Maier's grandnephew, Gerald Spitzner, composed a beautiful musical tribute titled *Heinrich Maier Oratorium* and premiered it in 1995, "the year of tolerance," at the Vienna Regional Court, where 50 years earlier Maier had been guillotined.[14]

As of 2016, Maier's Gersthof Parish Church at Bischof-Faber-Platz 7 appeared much as it had during the war. In the church a plaque bears Maier's particulars and the inscription "Beheaded for Christ and Austria"; a large headless sculpture, symbolizing his sacrifice, stands in a side aisle against a wall; and in the courtyard a tree was planted and in front of it another commemorative plaque announces, "This gingko was [planted on the occasion of] the Austrian Millennium on 15 May 1996 as a memorial life-tree for resistance fighter Curate DDr. Heinrich Maier." (The Austrian Millennium was the country's 1,000th anniversary celebration in 1996 of the name "Austria."[15])

Because Franz Josef Messner (born 8 December 1896) was gassed and cremated at Mauthausen in April 1945, his widow, Franziska "Franka" Messner, was required to petition the Vienna Regional Court to declare her husband "legally dead." The court issued a death certificate for Messner in late 1946.

On 23 May 1946, more than a year after her husband's murder, Franka Messner, with support from Semperit (whose offices at the time were listed as Helferstorferstrasse 9/16 in Vienna's 1st District), printed a memorial to Messner, detailing his ultimate sacrifice for Austria's freedom and voicing Franka Messner's hope that his memory would be bound to better days in Austria's future. The notice announced a requiem for Messner on 7 June 1946 at nine o'clock in the morning in the church of the Benedictine abbey of Schottenstift[16] (from whose high school, as noted earlier, Eduard Franz Sekler graduated in 1938). The 17th century church was the perfect choice for such a solemn occasion: its respectful baroque architecture, its ornate ceiling with beautiful ecclesiastical paintings, its majestic altar, its location on a prominent corner of the abbey, its key part of an institution known for contemplative silence.

The author of this work was unable to find a single memorial to Messner in Vienna—nothing at his villa at Hasenauerstrasse 61, nothing at Semperit (although he is mentioned in some of the company's literature), no streets named in his honor, no memorial grave. If one exists, it is exceptionally well hidden. Even loathsome Otto Hartmann (1904–1994), the actor and Gestapo *V-Mann* who betrayed about 200 resistance members, was pardoned in 1957 and was allowed to live a full life, dying peacefully at the ripe old age of 90. Even he was given a decent burial in his family grave in Vienna's Hernals Cemetery (Group 40A, Number 61) and his name etched on the plot's granite headstone.

Since the war, Messner's villa has had a facelift or two but gazes still over the beauty and serenity of Türkenschanzpark. Its peaceful setting belies the pitched battles of conscience that Messner fought within its walls and the rough trade that the Gestapo later practiced there.

Though now under private ownership, the villa would be a perfect place for a museum of the Austrian resistance, if good men and women of influence and means would only open their minds and loosen their purse strings to that end. Further, if it would not hurt such a cause, the U.S. government should offer funding and archival and artifact donations to realize the establishment of a museum. Such gestures would help to repay the great debt that the United States still owes—and will always owe—to CASSIA.

As former OSS officer George Howe so eloquently put it, as he did many things in his espionage novel of the Second World War, *Call It Treason*, "A man is alive as long as he is remembered, and killed only by forgetfulness."[17] The memory of Messner deserves to be kept alive.

As for Messner's wife Franka, according to DÖW's digitized files of the *KZ-Verband*, an Austrian project in the immediate postwar years to create a roll of victims of Nazi persecution, she never registered as a widow of a resistance member. Franka Messner was not alone in her neglect to stake such a claim. Many survivors of resistance members, whose wartime work was necessarily furtive, had little—if any—understanding of their deceased relatives' contributions. Other family members comprehended those activities but were cowed by strong sentiments in Austria that branded former resistance members as collaborators, spies, and traitors.[18]

Franka, who was born on 21 January 1889, died on 26 November 1983 in Altenmarkt an der Triesting, a quaint village of about 2,000 residents an hour's drive southwest of Vienna. She never changed her married name.[19]

Helene Sokal was born on 26 March 1903[20] in Znojmo (Znaim in German), a town in the Czech Republic near the Austrian border.[21] Theodor Legradi, with whom she founded a communist resistance cell and later shared her life, was born on 1 April 1880.[22]

Sokal's father, Rudolf Mirna (born 1863), was a teacher, and her mother, Franziska (née Urschler in 1855) was a women's rights advocate and school director. Sokal had one sibling, a brother, who was much older than she. After Sokal's birth, the family moved to Vienna. In 1926 Sokal received a doctorate in political science, and in 1936 a law degree.[23]

As noted previously, in 1945 Sokal married Legradi, 23 years her senior; thereafter she was often called Helene Sokal-Legradi or Helene Legradi. She had two sons and one daughter.[24]

In 1999, German investigative journalists discovered that Sokal had been a clandestine source of East German intelligence for several years during the 1980s, when she was in the last of her three decades as the director of the Austrian East-West Trade Bureau. The recruiting agency, the East German Ministry for State Security, widely known as the Stasi (a contraction derived from *Staatssicherheit*—State Security), codenamed Sokal PRINCESS. The sources for this revelation were, according to the investigative report, a former Stasi officer and "recently discovered [Stasi] magnetic [data or voice] tapes."[25]

According to the investigative report, from "her palatial office in [Vienna's] Prinz-Eugen-Strasse 4,"[26] Sokal had direct access to "the boardrooms of the Austrian economy" and thus to the economic security intelligence in which such high officials routinely traded. In Vienna, Sokal was handled by case officers from the Stasi's foreign intelligence division, known as the Main Directorate for Reconnaissance, headed by the notorious spymaster Markus Wolf (1923–2006). According to the investigative report, "Wolf's scouts [had] targeted [Sokal] … because … she unswervingly glorified the Soviet system, Mao's China, and North Korea."[27]

But she was apparently motivated by more than political idealism. A former East German courier revealed that the Stasi often delivered an envelope to Vienna containing "converted 10,000 Deutsche Marks [about U.S.$5,500] for [its] PRINCESS."[28] It seems that Sokal, codenamed with a monarchist title, was both a strident communist and an enterprising capitalist.

Sokal died in Vienna on 28 January 1990, about two months after the December 1989 de-facto collapse of communist East Germany. Shortly before Sokal's death, pro-democracy protestors seized control of Stasi Headquarters and its vast collection of files on internal informants and foreign agents. If Sokal had lived beyond the opening of these damning files, she may well have experienced a few espionage-related difficulties with the Austrian authorities.[29]

According to the announcement of Sokal's death, her remains were cremated at the Vienna-Simmering Crematorium on 6 February 1990, in a ceremony organized by one of her sons, Johannes Sokal, and his wife, Eidvile, and Sokal's grandchildren, Maria-Theresia Sokal, Richard Sokal, and Edith Holzer.[30] Her ashes were then interred at Vienna's Inzersdorf Cemetery (Group D, Number 194).

Karl Seitz, whom Sokal credited with introducing her and Legradi to Heinrich Maier, was the mayor of Vienna from 1923 to 1934. In 1944, due to his contact with one of the suspected plotters of the 20 July 1944 assassination attempt against Hitler, Seitz was deported to Ravensbrück concentration camp in northern Germany.[31] He survived the war and was repatriated. In the last years of his life he remained dedicated to the Social Democratic cause and involved in Austrian national politics.[32]

Seitz, who was born in Vienna on 4 September 1869, died on 3 February 1950 and was laid to rest in a Grave of Honor in Vienna's Central Cemetery (Group 24, Row 5, Number 2).

After the war, Barbara Issakides married Dr. Karl Fellinger (1904–2000), a prominent Viennese physician. (In 1940, Dr. Fellinger was drafted into the Wehrmacht and served as a military doctor near the front in Russia and Poland. He returned to Austria in late 1944.[33]) Issakides went back to school and from the University of Vienna received a Juris Doctor degree, although it appears that she never devoted herself to a career in the law.

An Austrian historian provided a glimpse of Issakides—relative to her role in the intelligence trade—in the immediate postwar years:

> In OSS files, Barbara Issakides's name was associated with a few sour notes, which provide a good example of the significant difficulty that comes with the handling of intelligence sources. In April 1946 British counter-espionage gave its American counterpart in Salzburg, [SSU] X-2, the following information: "…a Greek [sic] woman called Madame Issakides, a pianist by profession, is believed by the Swiss police to be a Soviet agent"; furthermore, Issakides had a brother who, since September 1941, had owned a company in Istanbul "which [according to the British] might have been used as a post box for the German Intelligence Service." [During the war] the British Ministry of Economic warfare blacklisted this company, which was owned by [Issakides's younger brother] Aristides Issakides.[34] In November 1945, the Americans had removed the company's name from the blacklist, ensuring that Barbara Issakides's wartime contributions to the Allied cause were not in any way diminished.[35]

Although her wartime experiences had doused Issakides's interest in performing, and in fact she actively shunned the limelight, her husband sought exposure in Austria and on the world stage. Beginning in 1946, Dr. Fellinger held sundry prominent positions, primarily at Vienna's Medical University Hospital and at the University of Vienna, and became president of Rudolfinerhaus, an exclusive private hospital in Vienna's 19th District.[36]

Among his famous patients were Saudi Arabian King Abd-al-Aziz ibn Saud, Persian Shah Mohammad Reza Pahlavi, Afghan King Zahir Shah, Moroccan King Hassan II, Pakistani President Zia-ul-Haq, and the patriarch of Constantinople (Istanbul), Opel Athenagoras I. Dr. Fellinger had become acquainted with many of these luminaries and strongmen while serving as a visiting professor in Cairo during the early 1950s.[37]

Also, for two years in the late 1970s, Dr. Fellinger designed and hosted a television series for the Austrian Broadcasting Corporation (ORF) called *Der gläserne Mensch* ("The Transparent Man"). In each episode Dr. Fellinger imparted medical knowledge "in an exciting way" to the general public.[38]

In 1975, after receiving a request for an interview from former DÖW Director Herbert Steiner, Issakides sent her regrets, explaining that she couldn't bring herself to discuss those wartime events: "I was suffering from shock and could only get back on my feet by forgetting and repressing again."[39]

Despite her reluctance, in the fall of 1977 American author Joseph E. Persico (1930–2014) persuaded Issakides to sit for an interview in Vienna. She did not, however, immediately consent to that meeting. At first, Issakides told him in a letter dated 3 September 1977, "[N]ow, more than 30 years after that dark period, I really wish to forget these days and have tried all the time, to cut out these years from my memory," and "I have been imprisoned by the Gestapo for nearly one year under constant threat of death (many of my very best friends were actually executed) and every attempt to recall the detail of these times would mean a real stress and even shock to me." Persico was persistent, though, and finally convinced her that the story needed to be told—not only for her sake but also for the memory of her fallen friends. In a letter after the interview, Issakides told Persico how much she and her husband had enjoyed speaking with him; the interview was, apparently, much less traumatic than Issakides had anticipated.[40]

In 2002, two years after her husband's death, Issakides instigated the founding of a nonprofit association in his name to promote cancer research. Its offices are located in Rudolfinerhaus.[41]

As of the late 1970s, Issakides and her husband lived in an exclusive neighborhood in Vienna's 18th District, at Starkfriedgasse 27, across the street from the Cottage Tennisclub Pötzleinsdorf.[42] From the right spot on the properties that run along the south side of Starkfriedgasse, one may see the spire of Maier's Gersthof Parish Church, an easy 20-minute downhill stroll from the Fellinger residence. Issakides must have been reminded from time to time, as she gazed down at her old neighborhood, of the life-altering events of those wartime years.

Issakides, who was born on 31 May 1914 in Vienna, died on 29 August 2011 and is buried in her husband's Vienna Grave of Honor at Döbling Cemetery (Group 24, Row 2, Number 1). The gravestone, which details some of her husband's accomplishments, records Issakides's fascinating life simply as "Dr. Barbara Fellinger 1914–2011."

The Issakides family plot, in which Barbara's grandparents, parents, and sister-in-law are buried, lies on a gentle slope in Neustift am Wald Cemetery. After the war, when Issakides visited the plot to leave flowers, she would have passed by the graves of Maier, Wyhnal, and Klepell.

As of 2016, Issakides's wartime home at Scheibenbergstrasse 61, though a bit worn and chipped, appeared much as it had more than 70 years before.

After Germany's surrender, Kurt Grimm returned to Vienna and his job as advisor to Josef Joham, who—as described previously—had been one of Grimm's wartime intelligence sub-sources and who despite postwar upheaval in Austria was still a senior executive at Austrian bank Creditanstalt-Bankverein. Upon Joham's death in 1959, Grimm became Creditanstalt's director.

For this lofty position, Grimm maintained an office in the bank's headquarters at Schottengasse 6 in Vienna's 1st District. As of 2016, after mergers and buyouts, UniCredit Bank Austria AG held most of the old Creditanstalt shares and occupied this same building, the address of which is now designated Schottengasse 6–8.

As an interesting aside, across the street from Schottengasse 6–8 is the former palatial residence of Baron Ignace von Ephrussi (1829–1899), the founder of a European banking dynasty that had rivaled that of the Austrian Rothschilds, the prewar owners of Creditanstalt. In 1938, because of the Ephrussi family's Ashkenazi Jewish heritage, the Nazis seized of all its properties.[43]

Grimm, who was born in Vienna on 5 May 1903, died on 20 September 1984 and is buried in Döbling Cemetery (Group 15, Row 7, Number 1), not far from the grave of Barbara Issakides (Fellinger), whom he met in Zurich to launch the ill-fated venture of CASSIA.

Shortly after the end of the war, British authorities arrested banker-extraordinaire Josef Joham in his native Carinthia (Kärnten in German), Austria's southernmost state known for its ideal location in the Eastern Alps, which stretch from Switzerland to Slovenia, for its splendid alpine lakes, and for its medieval castles. There was apparently an outstanding warrant for Joham, alleging that through his position at Creditanstalt he had been involved in abetting war crimes in Yugoslavia.[44]

The United States quickly intervened in the case, explaining that Joham had been a U.S. intelligence agent during the war whose reporting had assisted Allied bombing raids against key targets in the Reich. Without further ado, the British released Joham from custody, and the charges of war crimes against him were never investigated.[45] After this brief but probably unnerving interlude, Joham again landed on his feet, just has he had when the Nazis appropriated the Rothschild family bank, and he resumed control of Creditanstalt-Bankverein, first on 28 June 1945 as its "public administrator" and then on 26 February 1948 again as its director.[46]

A few years later, in the early 1950s, Joham was at the center of a scandal that involved maladministration of Marshall Plan funds, which at the time totaled some U.S.$900 million (worth about $8 billion in 2016).[47] Although Joham was the subject of an extensive Austrian Parliamentary inquiry into the affair, he was allowed to remain the director of Creditanstalt until his death.

During his postwar tenure at Creditanstalt, Joham approved a number of loans to Semperit, which with additional Marshall Plan funds was rebuilding its factories and warehouses. By August 1945, through their dogged efforts to collect war reparations, Moscow's apparatchiks in Austria had shipped much of the company's machinery and materials to the Soviet Union.[48]

Joham, who was born on 21 February 1889 and died on 7 April 1959, was laid to rest in Neustift am Wald Cemetery (Group A, Row 19, Number 3), not far from the graves of Maier, Wyhnal, and Klepell.

The Amelungia Catholic Student Fraternity and others have done much to preserve the memory of Walter Caldonazzi (born 4 June 1916). The fraternity sponsored the writing of an article (in German) of Caldonazzi's background and resistance activities; Amelungia conducted some of its research for this piece in the archives at DÖW. Also, memorials to Caldonazzi have been established in Vienna and in the Austrian Tyrol.

In 1947, Amelungia arranged to have Caldonazzi's remains exhumed from a common grave in Vienna's Central Cemetery and reburied at Breitenfurt Monastery, not far from the city's westernmost limits. In 1975, his remains were again transferred, this time to the family grave of his sister, Herta, in Eastern Cemetery (Pradl), Innsbruck.[49]

After the war, after having been temporarily resettled in Cairo, Gustav Rüdiger returned to his wife and son in Turkey. He was shocked and greatly saddened by news of his friend Messner's death.[50]

DÖW archives contain a letter—dated 1 August 1945, on Semperit letterhead and signed by five Semperit officials (to include resistance member Vilma Heindl)—attesting to Rüdiger's ownership of an apartment at Doblhoffgasse 9/6 in Vienna's 1st District, a property that the Nazis may have seized after the CASSIA arrests.[51] At the time, Rüdiger had no plans to occupy the property, but one of his sisters, Hilde Gabriel, and her family needed a place to stay; their apartment in Vienna's 9th District had been damaged during the war.[52]

In late October 1946, while still living in Turkey, the Rüdigers welcomed a second son into the world: Gustav Thiemo Carolus, called simply Thiemo, who like his brother Thomas arrived two months early.[53]

In late August 1947, Rüdiger and his family left Turkey and joined Otto and Maria Ender, his parents-in-law, at their home in Bregenz, Vorarlberg. In June 1948, the Rüdigers moved permanently to Vienna and took up residence in Gustav's old apartment at Doblhoffgasse 9/6.[54]

In June 1948 Rüdiger began working for *Phoenix Krawatten* ("Phoenix Neckties"), a store in Vienna's 1st District owned by Austrian men's clothing company *Theodor Friedmann's Nachfolger*. The director of *Theodor Friedmann's* was Karl Westermayer, the husband of Rüdiger's sister Hermine. Upon the death of Westermayer later that year, Rüdiger took over management of the company and worked there as a senior executive until February 1975.[55]

Gustav Rüdiger, who was born in Vienna on 23 May 1894, died on 16 March 1975, about one year after his having suffered from a stroke and only one month after his last day at *Theodor Friedmann's*.[56] Four days later he was interred in the Westermayer-Rüdiger family grave in Vienna's Central Cemetery (Group 42G, Number 24). The headstone bears the name Gustav Rüdiger but no dates of birth or death. Buried in this same grave are his wife, Margaretha "Gretl" (27 October 1912–11 January 1989[57]), his sister Hermine (1889–1975), and his brother-in-law, Karl Westermayer (1876–1948).

The Rüdigers' first son, Thomas, became an attorney and practiced law for many years in Vienna's upscale 1st District, a short stroll from his father's postwar office at *Phoenix Krawatten* and also from Saint Stephen's Cathedral, where his parents had married in 1941. His generosity is evidenced by this narrative's revelations about his father. Thomas Rüdiger is now retired and lives with his wife in Vienna.

OSS formally terminated DOGWOOD—Alfred Schwarz and his network—on 31 July 1944.[58]

After decades of silence, in 1987 Schwarz granted his first interview about his wartime activities to author Barry Rubin (1950–2014). Rubin met Schwarz, who was then 83 years old, in the former OSS principal agent's home near Lucerne, Switzerland. Rubin found him to be welcoming and eloquent. Rubin learned that Schwarz, who had lost his whole family to the Holocaust, had stayed on in Istanbul for many years after the war before becoming a banker in Switzerland and Austria. As for his recollections of CASSIA, Schwarz's skirting the truth or selective memory or both is described in this study's afterword.[59]

Lanning MacFarland was born on 15 January 1898 in Chicago, Illinois, into a life of economic comfort. His father was the owner of Law Bulletin Publishing Company, which produced (and still produces) a newspaper called *Chicago Daily Law Bulletin*—claimed to be "the oldest daily courts newspaper" in the United States—and a monthly legal magazine called *Chicago Lawyer*.[60]

After his service in the First World War and postwar time in the Balkans, described earlier in this work, MacFarland took a degree from Harvard University and in 1921 joined Chicago-based commercial bank Northern Trust Company. He remained at Northern Trust until his service in the Second World War. In 1945 he left the OSS with the rank of lieutenant colonel.[61]

After the war, MacFarland returned to his job at Northern Trust and worked there until 1953, when he became chairman of the family company, Law Bulletin Publishing. Over the next 18 years, he held other titles, sat on a few boards, and served as a trustee for several organizations—educational, charitable, healthcare-related, and interest-specific (i.e., clubs).[62]

MacFarland did not limit himself to success in the fields of banking and publishing: In June 1947, when he was still at Northern Trust, MacFarland, along with veterinarian D.M. Warren and medical doctor Horace H. Koessler, founded Intermountain Lumber Company, based in Missoula, Montana, which in its prime was one of the state's largest lumber companies. At the time of his death he was still listed as vice president and director of Intermountain, and as director of Bear Brand Hosiery Company of Chicago.[63]

The now-defunct Bear Brand was formed in 1922 from a reorganization of the Paramount Knitting Company, which had its factory in Kankakee, Illinois, some 30 miles—about 96 kilometers—south of Chicago. Bear Brand, which was quite successful when silk stockings were all the rage, produced parachutes during the Second World War. It appears to have gone out of business in the late 1970s.

In the postwar years, MacFarland developed a keen interest in Greece. He devoted considerable time and energy to informally advising the Greek government on their business and banking laws and practices.[64]

MacFarland, a resident of Wilmette, a northern suburb of Chicago, died on 12 October 1971 and was cremated at Oak Woods Cemetery on Chicago's South Side. He left behind a wife, Virginia, three sons, and a daughter.[65]

Archibald Coleman was born on 21 February 1900 in St. Paul, Minnesota. After studying at the University of Minnesota, Coleman entered the U.S. Military Academy at West Point, New York, but remained there for only two years. He then returned to Minnesota and took a degree in English literature.[66]

After graduating, Coleman ventured to hot southern climes, first managing a banana plantation for the United Fruit Company in Guatemala and then working for a subsidiary of Standard Oil in Mexico. After a few years in the private sector, Coleman decided to try the public. His business experience in Latin America and his fluency in Spanish landed him a job as the U.S. Trade Commissioner in Mexico.[67] Coleman committed five years to government service, and then struck out on his own, running a company involved in the oil business.[68]

In 1940, as America's inevitable entry into the war approached, Coleman returned to the United States and signed on again with the government. At some point, probably in the late summer or fall of 1941, he met with some intelligence functionaries, presumably from then-Colonel Donovan's office of the Coordinator of Intelligence, which in middle 1942 would be renamed the OSS.[69] How he had secured this appointment was suggested by research of OSS files at the U.S. National Archives: "Coleman [was] an old friend of William Donovan."[70] Coleman signed on with this nascent group and later embarked on his aborted assignments to Mexico and Spain.[71]

Upon returning to the United States, Coleman was assigned to a new OSS training facility nicknamed "The Farm." Established in spring 1942 and officially designated RTU-11, The Farm was located on a large country estate near Clinton, Maryland, some 20 miles (approximately 32 kilometers) south of Washington DC. After serving for a few months as a "chief instructor," Coleman became The Farm's director.[72] In other words, in a portent of more OSS ineptitude to come, a man with little relevant experience and sketchy performance in the field was put in charge of training operatives who were destined for some of the war's riskiest missions. (Another possibility is that Coleman failed as a tradecraft instructor and was moved to a face-saving senior administrative position, and that his friendship with Donovan won him the subsequent assignment to Istanbul.)

After almost a year at The Farm, Coleman packed his bags, the blind having apparently led the blind for long enough, and was dispatched to Istanbul on his third and final OSS assignment. In a photograph taken shortly before he arrived in Turkey, Coleman was bald with a neatly trimmed mustache (which he sported from his university days until old age), oval face, and prominent nose and ears.[73]

In an interview several years after the war, describing his service in Istanbul, Coleman claimed to have "recruited and supervised 75 espionage agents."[74] For casual readers the number was very impressive; for those familiar with DOGWOOD and practiced in the intelligence profession, it was preposterous. And Coleman carefully neglected to say anything about the good agents whose lives were lost due, in part, to his vocational deficiencies.

At some point after the war, Coleman settled in Virginia Beach, Virginia, and became "a successful businessman." In the middle 1960s he also appeared regularly on the local Public Broadcasting Service channel, teaching an economics course.[75]

Coleman died on 4 October 1980. He is buried with his wife at Eastern Shore Chapel Cemetery in Virginia Beach.[76]

In a turn of cosmic justice, the Snitch did not live to see the execution of his main nemesis, Messner. Sigismund Romen was killed during an Allied air raid on 7 February 1945,[77] in what may have been the single most effective use of an aerial bomb during the Second World War.

Police sergeant Andreas Hofer was born in Innsbruck on 24 August 1915.[78] After he was shot near Stein an der Donau, Hofer's remains were likely buried with the other executed prisoners in an unmarked mass grave.

As noted earlier in this narrative, Wilhelm Ritsch, born on 15 February 1915,[79] was one of two condemned CASSIA members, along with Clemens von Pausinger, to survive the war.

On 28 June 1948, a sensational mass-murder trial began at the Vienna Regional Court, "Dr. Clemens Pausinger" presiding. How his fortunes had changed in three years, from being a condemned man to being a judge in the very court where his friends had been murdered.

The trial concerned events of late March 1945 along the Hungarian-Styrian border near Rechnitz, a town of about 3,000 residents some 80 miles—130 kilometers—due south of Vienna in Burgenland.[80] That picturesque landscape, with its rolling hills and vast vineyards, was the scene of great suffering for more than 1,000 Hungarian Jewish forced laborers.

Accounts of what happened on the night of 24/25 March vary, but it seems that a few local personages, including some Nazis, gathered for a party hosted by Countess Margareta "Margit" von Batthyány (1911–1989) at her residence, Castle Rechnitz. Things got out of hand, which things tended to do when Nazis partied, and a few firearms were produced. The armed gang—led by *SS-Sturmscharführer* (Sergeant Major) and Rechnitz area Gestapo representative Franz Podezin—marched out, found the hapless Jewish laborers, and set about beating them. Podezin and his pals then decided to murder some of the defenseless folk, and once the gunfire stopped between 175 and 200 of the laborers were dead. After the war, a few witnesses stepped forward and an investigation was launched.[81]

Brought to stand trial before Judge von Pausinger were "the main culprits"—46-year-old Stephan Beiglböck, 46-year-old Kaufmann Ludwig, 51-year-old Josef Muralter, 29-year-old Hildegard Stadler, and 29-year-old Hermann Schwarz.[82] A few other Rechnitz notables—to include Countess Margit herself—were also strongly suspected of having played a role in the slaughter, but at that time courageous witnesses were few and far between.

As for *SS-Sturmscharführer* Podezin, he was no longer around and thus was not named as a defendant in this trial. According to German historian and journalist Stefan Klemp, who also implicated local Nazi Party member Eduard Nicka in the massacre, Podezin survived the war and later relocated to the northern German city of Kiel.[83]

On 25 July 1948, 28 days after the trial began, which were 26 more days than he had gotten in 1944 from the People's Tribunal, Judge von Pausinger announced the verdict and sentencing.[84] It was not a satisfying end, but considering that one witness was shot to death and another seems to have disappeared, it was probably the best that von Pausinger could do.

Of the first four defendants, only Ludwig Groll was found guilty of "remote complicity in the crime of murder," and was sentenced to eight years in prison. Stephan Beiglböck, Hilde Stadler, and Johann Muralter were acquitted of the crime of murder for "lack of conclusive evidence of guilt," but Muralter was found guilty of "high treason" and sentenced to five years in prison. Beiglböck and Stadler were immediately set free, but the court advised, "the suspicion of their involvement in the murders is not completely exhausted" by the judicial process. The case of the fifth defendant, Schwarz, was apparently excluded from these proceedings when his attorney unexpectedly withdrew a few days after the trial began.[85]

In a 2010 German magazine article, Sacha Batthyany, the great-nephew of Count Margit, wrote that, in addition to these criminal sentences, "On July 15, 1948 … Eduard Nicka [was also sentenced] to three years. Podezin and [Batthyany estate administrator Hans-Joachim] Oldenburg, the two alleged main perpetrators, [were still] on the run."[86]

The Nazis and their sympathizers in the dock must have grasped the great irony: The former Gestapo prisoner, convicted of treason against the Reich and sentenced to death, was sitting in judgment over them. Now it was he who held their fates in his hands.

Von Pausinger, who was born on 5 July 1908, died on 18 July 1989. He is buried in Vienna's Hietzing Cemetery (Group 55, Number 147), adjacent to the grounds of Schönbrunn Palace, the Habsburg Dynasty's summer residence.

As a post script to the first trial of the perpetrators of the Rechnitz Massacre, in the early 1960s a new investigation led straight to *SS-Sturmscharführer* Podezin's stoop in Kiel, but several curious delays in arresting him gave Podezin time to flee Germany. He finally landed in Johannesburg, South Africa, where he found work with Hytec, which calls itself the region's "largest supplier of hydraulic components and systems." Podezin later retired to the small Eastern Cape coastal town of Alexandra, where he reportedly died in the middle 1990s, having never answered for his horrid crimes.[87]

In 1956 in Lustenau, a town in Dornbirn District (where alleged CASSIA conspirator Karl Fulterer was born), Austrian state of Vorarlberg, a "Dr. Karl Fulterer" founded a company called "Fulterer Drawer Slide Systems," which manufactures metal runners for drawers, such as those in desks and other pieces of furniture. In 1988 Manfred and Heinz Fulterer—probably founder Karl's sons—assumed management of the company. As of 2016, the Fulterer company, still headquartered in Lustenau, maintained offices in the United States (High Point, North Carolina) and in Switzerland (St. Margrethen).[88]

While this Karl Fulterer is likely identifiable with the acquitted Fulterer of the CASSIA show trial, the author's inquiries to the company about its founder went unanswered.

By the end of May 1944, OSS declared DOGWOOD fully compromised and ceased all contact with František Laufer. As Germany's defenses crumbled, Laufer was spotted—probably in or near Prague—in the company of the retreating Wehrmacht.[89]

One might imagine that an exceptional survivor like Laufer would have ended up in a community of German exiles in South America. But his great reserves of luck finally ran out. Shortly after the war, Czech resistance fighters tracked down Laufer and executed him and all of his aliases.[90]

But is that really how the mole met his end? Another reference suggests that at the end of the war Laufer ended up in Prague's central jail, where his recruiter, Abwehr Captain Klausnitzer, shot him "because he knew too much," or that Laufer may have survived the war and been recruited by the SSU in Vienna. (By this time, apparently the last quarter of 1945, SSU had replaced the OSS.) According to this version, the SSU ran Laufer as an agent in its anti–Soviet operations.[91] The first possibility has the ring of the fanciful about it, and the second reeks of the conspiratorial, but still, where Laufer was concerned, anything was possible.

During the summer after the war, Lieutenant Jack Taylor, USNR, tried to remain in the OSS, which was already beginning to restructure to meet the emerging threats of the Cold War. However, because he spoke no foreign languages, and perhaps also because of his uneven—though courageous—performance on several intelligence missions, Taylor was discharged in October 1945. He returned to the dental practice that he had built before the war in Santa Monica, California. Taylor later received the Navy Cross, the U.S. Navy Department's second highest decoration for valor after the Medal of Honor.[92]

About a year after mustering out, Taylor was recalled to active duty, was promoted to lieutenant commander, and was dispatched to Europe to testify in the war-crimes trials against his former captors at Mauthausen concentration camp. His eyewitness testimony provided some of the most damning evidence against the defendants, and played a crucial role in the court's reaching several guilty verdicts—very possibly including that against *SS-Oberscharführer* Niedermayer, the Mauthausen guard who had led Messner to the gas chamber. Taylor was once again discharged from the Navy and resumed the practice of dentistry.[93]

Accounts of Taylor's health indicate that he suffered from chronic anxiety and restiveness—common symptoms of post-traumatic stress syndrome.[94] Few in the immediate postwar world, and virtually none today, can imagine what Taylor had endured and what haunted him still: the inestimable tension of missions behind enemy lines; the great privation of Nazi captivity; the constant threat of death from starvation or illness or execution; the daily horrors of a forced labor camp that was quickly transforming into a death camp; the vicious physical and psychological torture.

Taylor once revealed that he grasped just how close he had come to perishing at Mauthausen: "After the Americans had liberated us, I discovered that I should have been executed on 28 April 1945, along with 27 other prisoners from Block 13. A friendly Czech, Mylos [Milos Stransky], who worked in the political department had, unknown to me, removed my paper and destroyed it so that I was not included with the 27."[95] It is a testament to this man's astounding resiliency and depth of character that he was able to function so well—as a son, husband, father, and breadwinner—in the years after the war.

Taylor's quiet anguish never dampened his passion for the sea and seamanship, which years before had brought him to the U.S. Navy and then to OSS's Maritime Unit. After the war, he founded a "marine specialties" company, but it seems that he was unsuccessful at business. He later focused on his dental practice and family.[96]

Taylor, who was born on 9 October 1908 in Kansas, died in an automobile accident on 10 May 1959 in Imperial County, California, not far from his residence. He was survived by his parents, John and Theodosia (née Lofinck); a sister; his wife; and a daughter. Taylor is buried in Resurrection Cemetery in Montebello, California.

On 3 May 1945, two days before a reconnaissance unit from the U.S. 11th Armored Division entered Mauthausen, Messner's murderer, *SS-Standartenführer* Franz Ziereis (born 13 August 1905 in Munich), slipped away with his wife—who had once sought macabre amusement at the gas-chamber peephole—and went into hiding in the mountains of Upper Austria. On 23 May, a U.S. Army unit found and detained Ziereis, but he later attempted to escape and was shot. American soldiers brought him to a field hospital that the U.S. Army had set up at the Gusen I sub-camp, located about 3.75 miles—some six kilometers—west of the main Mauthausen camp.[97]

The next day, on 24 May 1945, Ziereis died from his wounds. His place of death, Gusen I, had held prisoners, all malnourished and many ill, who had been forced to toil at the nearby granite quarry, where they had hauled large blocks of stone on their backs up the 186 "Death Steps" cut into the side of the quarry, many of them collapsing from exhaustion and crushing other prisoners as they toppled back into the pit.[98]

At a U.S. Military Court trial in Dachau that began in March 1946, *SS-Oberscharführer* Josef Niedermayer (born 11 April 1920), who assisted Ziereis in the execution of Messner, was found guilty of "Violation of the

Laws and Usages of War," specifically for "acting in pursuance to a common design to subject ... persons ... to killings, beatings, tortures, starvation, abuses, and indignities ... at or in the vicinity of the Mauthausen Concentration Camp."[99] Niedermayer, whom testifying former prisoners—certainly to include Lieutenant Commander Jack Taylor—had frequently singled out for his acts of "excessive cruelty,"[100] was sentenced to death and hanged in the spring of 1947.[101]

Eduard Franz Sekler, the son of actor Eduard Jakob (1880–1976) and Elisabeth (1881–1974) Sekler, finished his architectural studies at Vienna University of Technology in 1945. In the late 1940s he began graduate studies at the Warburg Institute, University of London, from which he earned a doctorate in art history.[102]

In the early 1950s, Sekler traveled to the United States as a Fulbright fellow and by the middle of the decade was a visiting professor at Harvard University. In 1960 he became a full professor of architecture in Harvard's Graduate School of Design, and embarked on a career that would win him renown as an architectural historian and an educator.[103]

During a visit to Nepal in the early 1960s, Sekler developed an enduring interest in the preservation of the traditional architecture of Kathmandu Valley. To codify his work in Nepal, in 1990 Sekler founded the Kathmandu Valley Preservation Trust, for which as of 2016 he was still serving as an honorary board member. He retired from Harvard in 2004.[104]

As of 2016, Sekler was living in Massachusetts with his wife, Patricia Sekler (née Mary Patricia Olivia May in Cumberland, Maryland, in 1932). Patricia Sekler, who is a painter, photographer, and art historian, received a doctorate in fine arts from Harvard in 1973.[105]

Sepp Stein, Sekler's classmate and fellow resistance member, continued his architectural studies after the war, receiving his doctorate in 1954 from the Vienna University of Technology. During his long career, Stein designed important buildings in Vienna and abroad. Stein, who was born on 4 September 1920, died on 31 May 2008 in Vienna.[106]

Afterword

Some readers may think this work's criticisms of OSS-Istanbul are unduly harsh. I would only offer that, when intelligence officers make mistakes that lead to the deaths of six loyal agents, strong criticism is not only warranted; it is also obligatory.

OSS too recognized the gravity of the overall DOGWOOD failure, of which CASSIA was a significant part. The agency reassigned MacFarland[1] to recover downed aviators in Yugoslavia; Coleman was recalled to the United States where he later resigned from the OSS; and OSS terminated its contract with Schwarz.[2] But these were minor setbacks; all of them went on to live regular lives. "To live" is the key verb.

Both MacFarland and Coleman, who had thrived professionally before the war, went on to be even more successful after the war. (Their triumphs in business and tragedies in intelligence operations may lend further support to the contention that the two trades—commerce and espionage—are usually incompatible.) On at least one occasion, Coleman went so far as to brag about his supposed prowess in espionage, and MacFarland's 1971 obituary lauds his time in the OSS, noting that in 1946 he received the Legion of Merit, the sixth highest U.S. military award, for his wartime service in "intelligence operations."[3]

Considering such revisionism, one may well wonder if any of the three were penitent about their fatal lapses with the DOGWOOD network. Principal agent Schwarz seems not to have been: During an interview in 1987, he claimed to have met Laufer only a few times and to have stopped handling DOGWOOD some eight or nine months before its disastrous end in 1944.[4] He was wrong on both counts, either through prevarication or convenient memory loss. The interviewer reached the same conclusion: "Schwarz had either rewritten or successfully blotted out large portions of his past."[5]

Perhaps, over the years, the two OSS officers experienced occasional pangs of a guilty conscience, or maybe they suffered greatly, replaying time and again for the rest of their lives the sins of omission and commission that sent good men to the guillotine, gas chamber, and firing squad. Or maybe they felt nothing at all. One cannot see what is in another's heart.

But even with so much damning evidence against these men, it was difficult for me to enumerate their shortcomings, particularly those of the two OSS officers. After all, MacFarland and Coleman answered the call and served bravely—if not very effectively—during the Second World War. In finding fault with them, I had the luxury of drawing on my much-tested professional experience and on decades of hindsight; I had access to details not only on what they were doing but also on what the enemy was doing. But my discomfiture does not excuse my responsibility, so my appraisal still stands: These three men—MacFarland, Coleman, and Schwarz—were inept at the conduct of field intelligence operations.

There is another, personal reason that the story of CASSIA spoke to me. Three of my uncles and one of my aunts served honorably in the war, three of them in the Pacific Theater and one in the European. The latter fought across the Continent and into Austria. A reconnaissance element from this uncle's division was the first Allied force to reach the gates of Mauthausen, some 12 days after Messner's execution, and to discover its unimaginable horrors. Thereafter, the leaders of that unit, the 11th Armored Division, made sure that all of its men visited Mauthausen, to see firsthand what evil they had been fighting.[6]

I have also served in times of war. I know that, in exigent circumstances, decent well-meaning men and women sometimes fail to measure up and sometimes make critical mistakes. I think, then, that it is best to assess events and people as they were and are, not as we might wish them to have been or to be. Such wishing leads to errors in memory, and such errors threaten to condemn us to repeating old mistakes. Accountability is more than word; it is a virtue possessed by and practiced by those who do not shrink from their blunders and from any resulting censure.

So how might CASSIA's lessons of yesterday be applied today? Even a good operation might go bad, no matter how beautifully it is designed, but poorly planned and executed intelligence operations *will* go bad, sooner or later, and sometimes the results will be lethal.

Working from the example of CASSIA's death toll, the reader may want to review instances since the Second World War in which at least six intelligence officers or agents have been killed due to bad decisions and other errors of judgment. Such events likely provide opportunities to learn from avoidable tragedies in the field of intelligence operations.

> *It is those who are*
> *morally right but never achieve*
> *success who appeal to me....*
> —Stefan Zweig[7]

Appendix I
Gestapo-Vienna Final Report on the Interrogations of Heinrich Maier

On 22 June 1944, Gestapo-Vienna officer K.S. Kaiser[1] filed his final report on the interrogations of Maier, which he had supervised for the previous three months. Affixed to the report was a summary, detailing what Kaiser thought that he had successfully extracted from Maier about CASSIA.[2] The People's Tribunal was now responsible for sorting through the evidence as it built the Reich's case against the traitors.

Kaiser, who signed all of Maier's interrogation reports, remains a mystery. If he stayed in Austria and survived the Vienna Offensive of April 1945, the Red Army probably did not deal kindly with him and his Gestapo colleagues.[3] Kaiser may well have ended up at one of the Soviets' special "denazification" camps, where his prospects for survival would have been at best uncertain.

The following is the translated text of Kaiser's summary:

> In reference to: Dr. Maier, Heinrich, curate, born in Gross-Weikersdorf on 16.2.1908, DRA., rk.,[4] single, Vienna, 18th District, Bischof-Faber-Platz, Number 7, resident.
>
> Dr. Henrich Maier was born in Gross-Weikersdorf as the son of Heinrich Maier, who worked in the private sector, and Katharina, maiden name Giugno. He attended elementary school and high school in Leoben.[5] After graduating, he enrolled in the Department of Theology at the University of Vienna. In 1930, he acquired a doctorate of theology, and in 1939, he was awarded a doctorate of philosophy.[6]
>
> In 1932, Dr. Maier was ordained and assigned as curate to Schwarzach am Steinfeld.[7] Later, he worked as priest in Reichenau an der Rax[8] and in Mödling.[9] In September of 1935, he came to Vienna [and began working at] Gersthof [Parish Church], where he was, until his arrest on 28.3.1944, active as a curate. From the time of his arrival in Vienna [1935] until 1938, he taught religion at many different Viennese high schools.
>
> In terms of politics, Dr. Maier's position since his youth favored a clerical legitimism. He was a member of the Ostmärkischen Sturmscharen, the Österreichischen Jungvolk,

and the Vaterländischen Front.[10] In the two first mentioned associations he was active as a chaplain.

In 1942, Dr. Maier again turned toward politics and made contact with likeminded comrades. His main goal was to unite many oppositionist political groups, except the communists, under the concept of fighting for an independent Austria, or put another way, [Maier's primary objective was] to build cohesion among the different, existing [oppositionist] groups. It was clear to him that the establishment of a new independent Austria, based on democratic values, could only be possible by combining—with the help of enemy military force—the defeat of Germany and the creation of a new order in Europe.

Dr. Maier explained this idea to lawyer Dr. Helene Sokal,
maiden name Mirna,
born on 26.5.1903 in Znaim, DRA., evangelic, divorced,
Vienna, 10th District, Sickingengasse, 20, residence,

And to the director of Wander Gesellschaft GmbH, Dr. Theodor Legradi,
born on 1.4.1880 in Vienna, DRA.,
21st District, Smolagasse, 1, residence,

And confirmed their agreement [with him] in the matter.

In the summer of 1942, Dr. Maier entrusted Mrs. Sokal to give, on the occasion of her business trip to Switzerland, an oral message to Jesuit Dr. Otto Karrer, so that he could pass along the message to the English Commission in Bern. The message was as follows:

"Mutual suffering has brought the Austrian nation to the point of overcoming its ideological differences. The parties, on both the left and the right, now find themselves on a common platform. They all support an independent and democratic Austria. We are ready, after the war, to take our place in the newly ordered European family of nations and wait for your call as soon as the time is right."

[It was Maier's intention that] this message, which expresses clearly the political objectives of its originator and his followers, would also be publicized by Austria just after the end of the war.

Furthermore, in order to sustain this contact [with the Allies], in September of 1943 Dr. Maier sent through Dr. Otto Karrer a new message to the aforementioned enemy organizations in Switzerland. This text had the following content:

"We still live and await the right moment that the call for assistance will come to us."

Dr. Theodor Legradi was the person in charge of mediating this message, because during that time he had business dealings in Switzerland.

In the summer of 1943, Dr. Maier met District Police Sergeant Andreas Hofer,
born on 24.8.1915 in Innsbruck, DRA.,
Vienna, 19th District, Philippovichgasse, 1/I/II/10, residence

And Engineer-Diplomate Walter Caldonazzi,
born on 4.6.1916 in Malles, South Tyrol, DRA.,
Vienna, 18th District, Cottagegasse, 94, residence,

They [Hofer and Caldonazzi] assembled a group with legitimist tendencies. Through Hofer and Caldonazzi, Dr. Maier subsequently met an individual with a medical background, Josef Wyhnal,

born on 22.2.03 in Vienna, DRA.,
Vienna, 1st District, Wildpretmarkt, 1/8, residence,

And Corporal Hermann Klepell,
born on 19.6.18 in Vienna, DRA.,
Vienna, 18th District, Ferrogasse, 16/11, residence,

Finally, Dr. Maier was introduced to Senior Lance Corporal[11] Dr. Wilhelm Ritsch,
born on 15.2.15 in Brez, South Tyrol, DRA.,
Vienna, 7th District, Sigmundsgasse, 16/II/15, residence

During conversations with the aforementioned people, Dr. Maier explained that different oppositionist political movements have now merged into a resistance organization. A central committee, composed of representatives from each of these movements, directs this organization. They have at their disposal [existing] contact with the Anglo-Americans and have already informed [these Allied powers] about the fusion of Austrian [resistance] elements.

In the beginning of 1943, Dr. Maier met through his friend, pianist Dr. Barbara Issakides,
born on 31.5.1914 in Vienna, DRA.,
Vienna, 18th district, Scheibenberggasse, 61, residence,

the General director of Semperit-Werke A.G. Dr. Franz Messner,
born on 8.12.1896 in Brixlegg, Tyrol, bras. St. A.,[12]
Vienna, 18th District, Hasenauerstrasse, 61, residence

Maier found in Dr. Messner a comrade. He shared with Messner all of his political endeavors and asked Messner, because of his many business trips abroad, to acquire information about the locations and activities of emigrated former Austrian politicians.

On the occasion of Dr. Messner's [planned] business trip to Switzerland in December of 1943, Dr. Maier asked him to meet a Jewish lawyer living in Zurich:
Dr. Hollitscher
Dr. Maier told Messner to ask [Hollitscher] how he sees the current political situation [with regard to the war and its likely outcome]. Further, he should inform Dr. Hollitscher about the conceptual establishment of a resistance movement. Dr. Messner agreed to fulfill this requirement. After Messner's return from Switzerland, he explained to Dr. Maier that Dr. Hollitscher expressed fascination at the idea of an Austrian separatist movement and explained that he and his people would support the installation and operation of a radio transmitter in Ostmark. [Hollitscher] had, at his disposal, such a transmitter, an American Army transmitter, but noted that Dr. Maier and his people would need to be responsible for smuggling this transmitter—which supposedly is in Vaduz[13]—into Ostmark. Furthermore, Dr. Messner reported to Dr. Maier that Dr. Hollitscher publishes in Switzerland a newspaper with Austrian legitimist leanings and that Hollitscher intended to smuggle copies of it into Austria. Also, [Messner said that] former Austrian minister and professor at the Jewish University Dr. Dobretsberger was part of [Hollitscher's activities]. Finally, [Messner reported] that in England there was an [Austrian] Emigrants' Committee, of which a certain Schneider, a certain Nova, and a Dr. Herz are members—they are part of the Christian Socialists, or rather, [they have] Socialist and Democratic tendencies.

> Dr. Maier discussed with Hofer and Caldonazzi the possibility of smuggling the aforementioned transmitter, and also held counsel [on the matter] with Hermann Klepell and Dr. Ritsch. The plan was not successful because, according to Dr. Ritsch, the Swiss-German borders maintained excessively heavy surveillance.
>
> In September of 1943, Dr. Maier and Dr. Ritsch decided to reveal [to the Allies] the most important industrial areas in Ostmark. On the one hand, [this revelation] was supposed to be the resistance movement's contribution to helping the Allied forces to win [the war]. On the other hand, [such information would also] prevent the destruction by enemy air raids of industries and non-militarized cities until a [postwar] peacekeeping force could assume control over the territory.
>
> (Translated by Nicole Dieterich and Fernando Silveira Ruiz Diaz, and edited by the author.)

Kaiser's summary reveals that, despite his having grilled Maier for months, he still had an incomplete picture of CASSIA. He grasped the basic conspiracy against the Third Reich, but lacked awareness or had a skewed understanding of some of the case's specifics. Maier's subterfuge was to blame for these missing or ill-fitting pieces of the puzzle.

It is likely that other CASSIA members—notably Messner, Issakides, and Caldonazzi—were similarly resisting. It was a dangerous game, since none of them knew what the others were saying, and as a result they certainly contradicted one another on occasion and then paid for such transgressions, painfully. It appears, however, that their admissions about the group's core activities were sufficiently consistent to have given the Gestapo a degree of false corroboration.

How exactly did Maier and his cohorts, working from such great disadvantage, mislead the Gestapo? As described in previous chapters, Maier and other CASSIA members convincingly fabricated revelations from whole cloth, omitted key pieces of information, and altered genuine details to misdirect their interrogators. Often, it seems, the primary goal of these efforts was to conceal or reduce the culpability of other members of the group, their family members, and the group's sympathizers.

These clever prevarications, exclusions, and modifications did nothing, of course, to divert the Gestapo from its mission to deliver the traitors to the courtroom, where the People's Tribunal waited with its predetermined verdicts. But it is very likely, as also suggested previously, that such acts of resistance saved Issakides from execution, muddied the cases against Ritsch and von Pausinger, and may have played a role in Fulterer's acquittal.

As an example of his distorted understanding of CASSIA, Kaiser concluded that Maier's group sought to unite representatives from the full spectrum of Austrian ideologies, "except for the communists," into a single resistance movement. This statement reveals that the Gestapo had failed to define the political proclivities of Sokal and Legradi, and to identify any of the several leftist sub-sources whom they had integrated into CASSIA.

Austrian communists were very persistent—if not always successful—in their actions against the Nazis, and as such were a priority target of the Gestapo. If Kaiser had confirmed a communist presence in CASSIA, the Gestapo would have probably concluded that the group represented a more extensive and pervasive threat—one likely supported at least in part by the Soviets—and may well have launched an exhaustive search for additional coconspirators. And had Sokal and Legradi been labeled communists, they would have certainly been subjected to much greater misery at the Métropole: The Gestapo was known to exercise particularly vicious interrogations of its communist captives.

Kaiser also recorded that Issakides introduced her friend Maier to Messner in early 1943. In reality, Maier and Messner had become acquainted some six years earlier and had worked for many months to build a resistance organization. Further, it was Maier who introduced CASSIA cofounder Messner to his friend Issakides when the priest was looking for a new courier to deliver a second message to the Allies.

These details may seem minor or even inconsequential, but they are evidence of Maier's attempts to confuse the Gestapo about CASSIA's origins and longevity, and about the roles of certain members. According to what Maier "confessed" to Kaiser, the group had begun to coalesce a scant year before Caldonazzi's arrest and thus had been fully operational for a fairly short time.

By compressing CASSIA's functional lifespan, Maier was implying that the group hadn't had the chance to engage in a greater breadth and depth of subversive activities. In fact, even in those interrogations when Kaiser confronted Maier with other members' admissions (e.g., the drafting of a site map of an armaments factory), Maier would explain that, while he had conceptually discussed such activities, the group hadn't had the time or opportunity to follow through on any of these plans.

Also, the report's errant focus on Swiss-based Austrian attorney Hollitscher and on an aborted plan to smuggle a radio transmitter from Liechtenstein into Austria attests further to Maier's efforts at misdirection. In these instances he strove to draw his questioners' attention with intriguing but unverifiable claims and with adroitly delivered partial truths. (In particular Maier's references to Hollitscher's Jewish faith probably played to the Gestapo's anti–Semetic proclivities.) In short, Maier baited his interrogators with insignificant or amended information to distract them from learning other, more damning details, to include, for example, Messner's and Issakides's repeated visits to Switzerland for meetings with Grimm (and later with Dulles).

Had Maier been unable to deflect repeatedly his interrogators' lines of questioning, to keep them occupied with spurious subjects, Kaiser would have resorted more frequently to his selection of intensive techniques, to include torture. And if Maier had been subjected constantly to such methods, he would have eventually divulged other sensitive information—such as the group's provision of intelligence on the V-weapons facility at Peenemünde, large-scale death camps, and Germany's use of slave labor in military industries—and the fact that some of CASSIA's tactical intelligence had informed U.S. and British planning for air raids. Not only would such confessions had warned the Germans what parts of their war machine were at the greatest risk from aerial bombardment, but they would have also implicated any number of sub-sources who had been involved in the front-line collections of that intelligence.

Curiously absent from the summary is mention of Messner's contact with American "General Mac Farlane" in Istanbul—a name that Maier confessed in an earlier interrogation session, almost certainly under great duress. Perhaps Kaiser dismissed this information, as he did other revelations that he deemed suspect, considering it to be a fanciful attempt by Maier to mislead the Gestapo. That Maier did, in fact, provide a phonetic version of MacFarland's name is interesting, in that he seems to have gone to some lengths to avoid mentioning Dulles. Perhaps Maier understood, as Messner had also deduced, that OSS-Istanbul was fully to blame for the disastrous end of CASSIA and thus had no reservations about exposing that part of the group's activities.

In the trial of CASSIA's members, the People's Tribunal introduced much more evidence than what appears in Kaiser's summary. The prosecution drew on the full scope of admissions from the group, on reports from snitches like Romen and double agents like Laufer, and on the results of traditional police work. As described previously in detail, these sources provided insights, for example, on the group's fraternization with and attempts to assist prisoners of war, preparation of maps of war industries, distribution of anti–Nazi and antiwar propaganda, and medical interventions to excuse conscientious objectors from combat. The People's Tribunal allowed any information that would further "justify" its settled decision to murder the defendants.

Appendix II
Contact Between CASSIA and the British in Istanbul in 1943

In his seminal work (in German) on SOE operations in Austria, *Subversion deutscher Herrschaft*, University of Vienna history professor Dr. Peter Pirker devoted a section to the contact in 1943 between Istanbul-based SOE officer G.E.R. (George Eric Rowe) Gedye (1890–1979) and agent STAR—Gustav Rüdiger, the Semperit representative in Istanbul. In his correspondence to SOE Headquarters, Gedye—who before and after the war was a journalist and book author of some renown—wrote that he first met Rüdiger through another British agent, Schwarz, codename LEONARD, who was running an agent network of Bulgarians, Romanians, and Greeks. At this introductory meeting, Rüdiger told Gedye that he represented a group of Austrians who were engaged in resistance work against the Nazis.[1]

Gedye later wrote that, in May 1943, Rüdiger also established contact—again through Schwarz—with the new OSS office in Istanbul. Then, in August 1943, after Rüdiger returned from a visit to Austria, he informed Gedye that 14 prominent Social Democrats and Christian Socialists had organized an "Action Committee" to conduct resistance activities in Austria. The Committee's long-term goal was to prepare for a free and independent Austria after the country had been liberated from Nazi Germany.

At some point between May and August, Gedye tasked his two principal Austrian charges in Istanbul, exiled Social Democrats Karl Hans Sailer (1900–1957) and Stefan Wirlandner (1905–1981), to look into Rüdiger and Messner and their claims. Pirker noted that Wirlandner had worked for Semperit in 1939, implying that he could readily develop a pretext for contact with Rüdiger and Messner. But despite their best efforts Sailer and Wirlandner were unable to come up with any conclusive findings.

After his meeting with Rüdiger in August, Gedye sent a cable to SOE Headquarters in which he conveyed his doubts about STAR's claims: "Firstly, I have never been convinced that the 'members' of this Committee know the use STAR is making of their names, and secondly, I suspect that the Social Democrats are being used without their knowledge as cover for STAR's director [Messner] and dividend-loving friends.... I have told STAR that we want more 'Action' and less 'Committee'; LEONARD [Schwarz] has thereupon persuaded him [Rüdiger] to sell his proposition to the more amenable GROSVENORS [Americans]."[2] In late August 1943, Gedye advised London that Rüdiger had stopped meeting with the British and was cooperating solely with OSS-Istanbul.

In other correspondence to SOE Headquarters, further justifying the hardline stance that he had taken with Rüdiger, Gedye disparaged the conditions that Rüdiger had placed on his cooperation with Britain: "It was obvious from the first that his [Rüdiger's] main object was to reinsure himself. He had a grossly exaggerated idea of his importance to the British, and put too high a price on his co-operation. Not the least of this was that the British Government should guarantee not to bomb the Semperit Rubber Factory, of which he was a manager."[3]

Gedye's criticisms didn't stop with Rüdiger; he also lambasted the way that Schwarz was handling his network, and suspected that it was vulnerable to German infiltration. While Gedye's comments about Rüdiger and Messner ranged from duly cautious to unfairly censorious, his views on DOGWOOD highlighted the very flaw that would destroy the network and that would leave the members of CASSIA to their fates.

Appendix III
Background on the Austrian Committee of Liberation and Memorandum of Agreement Between CASSIA and OSS

Austrian historian and intelligence expert Dr. Siegfried Beer provided additional details on Rüdiger's pitch to the OSS in the fall of 1943, which culminated in the 1944 agreement between OSS and CASSIA: "[Rüdiger] had managed to convince his immediate interlocutor, Schwarz, that a united and representative independence movement existed in Austria. [Messner] … had been able to create, starting from a core group known as the Freedom Committee of Fourteen, an organization whose anti–Nazi members represented virtually the whole spectrum of Austrian politics."[1] In this regurgitation of his earlier proposal to the British, Rüdiger—apparently at Messner's behest—was seeking to expand CASSIA's work beyond its core mission of collecting intelligence, writing and distributing propaganda, excusing conscientious objectors from frontline service, and assisting foreign prisoners of war in Austria. Rüdiger was imploring the OSS to believe that the group also included a robust political component.

Beer explained that, after Rüdiger made his pitch, Schwarz and MacFarland christened the group the "Austrian Committee of Liberation"—a loose translation of the German name that Rüdiger had used, *österreichischen Freiheitskomitee.* In its subsequent correspondence, OSS often called the group ARCEL,[2] which was an expedient codename derived from the vocalization of the acronym ACL, but OSS also continued to use the codename CASSIA, usually when referring to the group's existing intelligence-collection activities in Austria.

Drawing from OSS-Istanbul report number 373, dated 16 February

1944, Beer noted that—according to Rüdiger—ACL was comprised of four cells, each representing an Austrian political bloc: Center Party (30 percent of ACL), Social Democratic Party (10 percent of ACL), Revolutionary Socialists (35 percent of ACL), and Communist Party (25 percent of ACL)—and each with a chief and a spokesman.[3] In this same report, OSS-Istanbul described the interactions between the cells as follows:

> Each group is represented by a committee of 5 members, headed by a Chief who is not a member. For reasons of security, the Committees maintain no direct communication, and their members do not know of each other's functions in the organization. The Chiefs also are unknown to each other. The necessary intercommunication between the Committees is ensured through 'Spokesmen' who act as liaison officers and couriers between the Committees, but are not members. They are known only to their Chiefs and to each other. The chiefs are interconnected through the Head [Messner], who also knows the names of the Committee members and is in direct contact with some of them. The Committees are the central exponents in charge of subordinate units like factory cells, terrorist and sabotage organs, peasant groups, etc., according to the character and degree of organization of the Party concerned. These subordinate units are kept separate from each other in the same way as the top organs.[4]

In summary, the ACL proposal claimed that a large, well-organized independence movement existed in Austria, that it represented virtually all Austrian political interests, that influential people were among its members, and that, for reasons of security, it adhered to strict rules of compartmentalization. The origins of these assertions were, at least in part, the great diversity of CASSIA's members and sympathizers, and the clandestine tradecraft that the core members of CASSIA practiced.

It is important to point out that Rüdiger first tabled the ACL concept *before* the October/November 1943 Moscow Declaration, which stated—among many other things—that, in the Allies' eyes, the Anschluss was null and void, and that in time the Allies would see to the re-establishment of a free and independent Austria. On this point, for resistance-inclined Austrians, the Declaration included a very important caveat: "Austria is reminded, however that she has a responsibility, which she cannot evade, for participation in the war on the side of Hitlerite Germany, and that in the final settlement account will inevitably be taken of her own contribution to her liberation."[5]

After MacFarland submitted a summary of Rüdiger's proposal, a few months passed before OSS chief Donovan responded. On 23 January 1944, unknowingly echoing what SOE officer Gedye had told SOE Headquarters in August 1943, Donovan wrote, "Our organization's work does not call for speech but for action.... Position of our Government was made clear in the Moscow Agreement. Be firm but just in stating our position and such words as negotiations and protocol should be avoided."[6]

In the final analysis, the defects of the ACL proposal, the suspicions about the true intentions of Rüdiger and Messner, and the possible embellishment of ACL's membership are inconsequential. The only relevant fact about CASSIA is that it performed well as an OSS clandestine intelligence source inside Austria. And Beer spelled out the only salient—and sorrowful—fact about OSS's part in the operation: "The primary reasons behind the rapid and tragic end of ARCEL/CASSIA were that OSS failed to compartmentalize sufficiently information and allowed its agent network to be severely penetrated by a host of enemy double agents."[7] For an intelligence agency, there can be no greater condemnation.

But before the tragic end of CASSIA were heady days of international intrigue—great derring-do, secret codes, and furtive meetings. The involved men and women were no simpleminded adventure-seekers; while their motivations were many and personal, they were all dedicated to subverting the German war machine, ousting its corrupt overlords, and rehabilitating Austria. The strategy, tempered by political expediency and bureaucratic caution, to reach these goals was preserved in the agreement that Messner and OSS-Cairo chief Lada-Mocarski signed in early 1944.

The document's bland prose—a style familiar to those with time in government—tends to downplay the gravity of its sundry points, which obligated CASSIA to conduct all manner of perilous work behind the lines while OSS agreed to provide some radio sets, codebooks, and money.[8] And though the memorandum mentions that CASSIA must prepare "landing places ... for Allied parachutists" and "Documents such as Identity Papers, ration cards etc." for such infiltrated personnel, OSS's responsibility on this subject is more loosely worded: "in due course [OSS] will despatch representatives to Austria to work with ARCEL."

Further, OSS decisively quashed the political ambitions of the ACL proposal: "It is understood and agreed that [OSS] has no authority or the desire to make any commitment on political matters" and "It is clearly recognized by both parties that this memorandum agreement is limited in scope to the development of collaboration between the two groups and under no circumstances is to be interpreted as a political instrument; and that there are no implied agreements." These lines must have disappointed Messner, but as an experienced businessman he was familiar with not getting everything that he wanted, so he decided to take what he could get from OSS.

This imbalance of obligations reveals a standard practice of intelligence services, which endeavor to protect themselves from the inherent dangers of their associations, which in terms of reliability and risk run the gamut. It is a form of organizational compartmentalizing, the building of a firewall between the extreme heat of the engine and the sensitivity of its controls. Accepting such an arrangement is typically the price of admission for playing the game of espionage.

Memorandum of Agreement reached by CASSIA, representing ARCEL, and JUNIPER [Lada-Mocarski], representing OASIS [OSS], at their meeting on February 3, 1944, 4 February 1944

1. PURPOSE

On the basis outlined in subsequent paragraphs ARCEL and OASIS agree to collaborate in bringing about the defeat of Nazi Germany and the liberation of Austria. In this undertaking OASIS is acting under the proper authority to conduct subversive activities in enemy countries, using resistance groups only on the basis of their willingness to cooperate, without any regard to ideological differences or political programs.

ARCEL is a committee representing responsible groups of Free Austrians engaged in underground warfare against Germany.

In reaching this agreement ARCEL has pledged itself to supply OASIS currently with military, economic, and political intelligence, and to create and organize subversive groups in preparation for action at a time to be agreed upon in the future.

2. PROVISION FOR LIAISON

For the purposes of carrying out this agreement ARCEL will send representatives to Istanbul as early as possible, and in due course OASIS will dispatch representatives to Austria to work with ARCEL. Communications will be maintained by radio, telegraph, and overland couriers.

3. INTELLIGENCE REQUIREMENTS

Without in any way seeking to limit the scope of intelligence desired, the following subjects were particularly discussed:

A. Military Intelligence
   1. Current Order of Battle intelligence
   2. Present German garrisons in Austrian territory, by division and regiment, including officer personnel, if possible.
   3. Prompt notification of withdrawals, transfers, reinforcements, etc.

B. Passage of troops and material through Austria to other fronts.

C. Military Depots
   1. Arms and ammunition stores.
   2. Liquid fuel supplies.
   3. Airdromes, including units occupying same, and A/A defenses.
   4. Positions of A/A defenses and searchlights on all defense areas.
   5. Detailed information regarding all fortified positions existing or being constructed.
   6. Regular supply of meteorological information.

D. Intelligence on German war industries
   1. Raw materials, their production refining, and transshipment.
   2. Liquid fuels, including refineries, production statistics etc.
   3. Armament plants manufacturing airplanes, tanks, locomotives, arms (both large and small) etc.
   4. Production of U-boats, U-boat parts, machine tools, secret weapons, and all other items of war importance.
E. Prompt notification of transfer of war plants to or from Austria.
F. Detailed information of destruction caused by air raids.
G. Political intelligence
   1. Current information on political developments within Austria and Germany.
   2. Information on strikes, axis sabotage, riots etc.
   3. Current information regarding the labor supply, including percentage of foreign workers, prisoners of war etc.
   4. Current information regarding the morale of the population in Austria and Germany and occupied countries.

4. ARCEL undertakes to organize active subversive warfare against the enemy on the following lines:

A. Patriotic groups will be organized for military action at a time to be agreed upon as suitable for the successful use of such groups.
B. Sabotage groups will be organized for the execution of sabotage against German industrial and war economy in accordance with directions to be given by OASIS in the course of future developments. This planning shall include preparation for the interruption of the Austrian communication system including railroads, highways, canals, telephone and telegraph trunk communications etc.
C. Secret depots of arms and ammunitions shall be created for use by ARCEL at the proper time.
D. Groups will be organized to assist the Allied effort in the distribution of material dropped by airplanes, and landing places shall be prepared for Allied parachutists.
E. Documents such as Identity Papers, ration cards etc., shall be made available.

Under the terms of this agreement adequate channels of communication shall be set up between ARCEL and OASIS, presumably through radio stations to be supplied by OASIS together with ciphers, broadcasting instructions etc. Mutually agreed upon codes will be used in the transmission of messages by commercial telegraph. ARCEL undertakes by this agreement to develop a Courier service to Istanbul or other possible points, to insure a regular flow of the substantial volume of required intelligence. OASIS undertakes as well, to broadcast instructions to ARCEL over Allied stations in Algiers, London, or Bari.

5. It is understood and agreed that OASIS has no authority or the desire to make any commitment on political matters. It will maintain records of the intelligence supplied by ARCEL and evidence of cooperation on subversive activities which will be made available to the American Joint Chiefs of Staff.

6. OASIS will agree to supply necessary financial assistance in amounts to be agreed upon from time to time by the representatives of ARCEL and OASIS.

7. It is clearly recognized by both parties that this memorandum agreement is limited in scope to the development of collaboration between the two groups and under no

circumstances is to be interpreted as a political instrument; and that there are no implied agreements.

8. It was agreed that in due course the nature of this agreement will be fully disclosed to the proper authorities of Great Britain and the USSR, so that as the plans contemplated by this agreement proceed, it will become a cooperative affair.[9]

(Beer retrieved the preceding document from the U.S. National Archives, Record Group 226, Entry 190, NARA Microfilm Publication 1642, Roll 83.)

The ACL proposal may have been the first effort to convince the Allies that a substantial anti–Nazi political movement existed in Austria, but it would not be the last. Less than year later Fritz Molden would venture to persuade OSS-Bern chief Allen Dulles that an umbrella resistance organization, O5, was in place and viable, and that O5 and its political counterpart, the Provisional Austrian National Committee (*provisorische oesterreichische Nationalkomitee*, POEN), were ready to work with the Allies in displacing the Nazis and setting up an interim political and administrative system. Because Molden and many of his prominent associates survived the war, their story is fairly well known—at least in Austria—while the sad tale of CASSIA and its ambitious offshoot, the Austrian Committee of Liberation, is all but forgotten.

Chapter Notes

Epigraph

1. Epictetus, *The Golden Sayings of Epictetus*, trans. Hastings Crossley (New York: P.F. Collier & Son, 1909), p. 56, item CXXVI.

Preface

1. Blaise Pascal, *Pascal's Pensées*, trans. W.F. Trotter (New York: E.P. Dutton & Co., 1958), p. 47, item 159.

Introduction

1. George Washington, letter to his friend John Armstrong who had served as a senior officer in the Revolutionary War and as a delegate to the Continental Congress, 26 March 1781; the text of this letter is available through the U.S. Library of Congress website at memory.loc.gov/cgi-bin/query/r?ammem/mgw:@field(DOCID+@lit(gw210400)).

Chapter 1

1. Harald Sattler Frederiksen, "Harald S. Frederiksen Papers," collection identifier GTM. GAMMS450, *Georgetown University Library Special Collections Research Center* (donated by Harry P. Travis, 2002), Box 1, Folders 3, 8.
2. Frederiksen, "Papers," Box 1, Folders 3, 8.
3. Frederiksen, "Papers," Box 1, Folders 3, 8.
4. Frederiksen, "Papers," Box 1, Folders 3, 8.
5. Frederiksen, "Papers," Box 1, Folders 3, 8.
6. Frederiksen, "Papers," Box 1, Folders 3, 8; Fritz Molden, *Fires in the Night*, trans. Harry Zohn (Boulder: Westview Press, 1989), p. 61.
7. Fritz Molden, *Exploding Star: A Young Austrian Against Hitler*, trans. Peter and Betty Ross (New York: William Morrow & Company, 1979), p. 159.
8. Molden, *Star*, pp. 177–178.
9. Molden, *Star*, pp. 179–180.
10. Molden, *Star*, pp. 179–180.
11. Wolfgang Neugebauer, *The Austrian Resistance: 1938–1945*, trans. John Nicholson and Eric Canepa (Vienna: Edition Steinbauer, 2014), p. 217.
12. Molden, *Fires*, pp. 82–83; Neal H. Petersen, ed., *From Hitler's Doorstep: The Wartime Intelligence Reports of Allen Dulles, 1942–1945* (University Park: Pennsylvania State University Press, 1996), pp. 434–436; Neugebauer, *Resistance*, pp. 217–218.
13. Molden, *Fires*, pp. 60–61; Frederiksen, "Papers," Box 1, Folder 8.
14. Helga Thoma, *Mahner-Helfer-Patrioten: Porträts aus dem österreichischen Widerstand* (Klosterneuberg: Edition VA bENE, 2004), p. 141; Joseph E. Persico, *Piercing the Reich: The Penetration of Nazi Germany by American Secret Agents During World War II* (New York: Barnes & Noble Books, 1997), p. 56; Siegfried Beer, "'ARCEL/CASSIA/REDBIRD': Die Widerstandsgruppe Maier-Messner und der amerikanische Kriegsgeheimdienst OSS in Bern, Istanbul und Algier 1943/44," in *Jahrbuch 1993* (Vienna: Dokumentationsarchiv des österreichischen Widerstandes [DÖW], 1993), p. 77.
15. Frederiksen, "Papers," Box 1, Folder 8; Molden, *Fires*, pp. 60–61.
16. Frederiksen, "Papers," Box 1, Folder 8.
17. Molden, *Star*, pp. 92–96.
18. Molden, *Star*, pp. 92–96.
19. Molden, *Star*, pp. 101–102, 106–107.
20. Molden, *Star*, pp. 109–159; Central Intelligence Agency, Center for the Study of Intelligence, "Office of Strategic Services (OSS)

Oral History Project Transcripts: Fritz P. Molden," interviewed by Siegfried Beer on 5 November 1996 (College Park, Maryland: U.S. National Archives), p. 21.

21. Frederiksen, "Papers," Box 1, Folder 8.

Chapter 2

1. A 1944 court document (*Volksgerichtshof-Urteil*, p. 3) asserted that Maier began working at the church in 1938, but this date is at variance with Maier's statements and with Gestapo investigative findings, which record 1935 as the year that Maier was transferred to Gersthof parish.

2. Geheime Staatspolizeileitstelle Wien (Gestapo), hereinafter "Interrogations," a 29-page sheaf of interrogation reports and related documents on Heinrich Maier, prepared by Gestapo-Vienna officer K.S. Kaiser, dated 28 March 1944, 29 March 1944, 5 April 1944, 7 April 1944, 25 April 1944, 27 April 1944, 5 June 1944, 10 June 1944, and 22 June 1944 (Vienna: DÖW archives); retrieved circa 2010 by Austrian author Hans Schafranek from Bundesarchiv Berlin, Aussenstelle Dahlwitz-Hoppegarten; Persico, *Piercing the Reich*, p. 56.

3. Thoma, *Mahner-Helfer-Patrioten*, p. 142.

4. Gestapo, "Interrogations"; Thoma, *Mahner-Helfer-Patrioten*, p. 144.

5. According to the University of Vienna records, Maier was required to sit for a series of oral examinations: on 6 July 1939 in moral and pastoral theology, on 25 June 1941 in Biblical studies, and on 16 July 1942 in dogmatic theology. Then, on 25 July 1942, he received his Doctorate of Catholic Theology. Maier had received his first doctorate—in scholastic philosophy, as noted previously—on 16 July 1930 from the Pontifical Gregorian University in Rome, where one of his fellow students had been Cardinal Franz König (1905–2004), who in 1956 became the Archbishop of Vienna. (Source: Katharina Kniefacz and Herbert Posch, "Heinrich Maier," in *Gedenkbuch für die Opfer des Nationalsozialismus an der Universität Wien 1938*, accessed on 10 October 2016, gedenkbuch.univie.ac.at/.)

6. Thoma, *Mahner-Helfer-Patrioten*, p. 146–147.

7. Beer, "ARCEL/CASSIA/REDBIRD," p. 77.

8. Beer, "ARCEL/CASSIA/REDBIRD," p. 77.

9. After the war Hurdes helped to found the center-right *Österreichische Volkspartei* (ÖVP), the Austrian People's Party, and also served a stint as the Austrian Minister of Education.

10. Beer, "ARCEL/CASSIA/REDBIRD," p. 77; Peter Broucek, *Militärischer Widerstand: Studien zur österreichischen Staatsgesinnung und NS-Abwehr* (Vienna: Böhlau Verlag, 2008), pp. 378–379, 408–409.

11. Volker Sartorti, *Biographie Dr. Franz Josef Messner* (Elmshorn, Germany: Eigendruck, 2003), p. 5.

12. These details, which were drawn from a Gestapo interrogation report, may be inaccurate: Maier may have misled his questioners about how and exactly when he met Messner—for example, to protect the person or device responsible for their introduction. However, a 1944 court document (*Volksgerichtshof-Urteil*, p. 6) suggested that "Messner called himself a Buddhist," so at least part of Maier's account appears to be genuine.

13. Gestapo, "Interrogations."

14. Persico, *Piercing the Reich*, p. 56.

15. Beer, "ARCEL/CASSIA/REDBIRD," p. 77.

16. G.C. Paikert, *The Danube Swabians: German Populations in Hungary, Rumania and Yugoslavia, and Hitler's Impact on Their Patterns* (New York: Springer Publishing, 1967), p. 114; Charles Ingrao and Franz A.J. Szabo, eds., *The Germans and The East* (West Lafayette, Indiana: Purdue University Press, 2007), p. 359.

17. Szabolcs Szita, *Trading in Lives?: Operations of the Jewish Relief and Rescue Committee in Budapest 1944–1945*, trans. Sean Lambert (New York: Central European University Press, 2005), p. 43.

18. Kermit Roosevelt et al., eds., *War Report of the OSS, Volume 2: The Overseas Targets* (Washington DC: U.S. Government Printing Office, 1949; New York: Walker and Company, 1976), p. 270.

Chapter 3

1. Sokal's surname appears in some documents as Sokal-Mirna, or incorrectly as Sokal-Myrna. Sokal's maiden name was Mirna, but after her divorce, she chose to retain Sokal, the surname of her former husband, also an attorney, probably because she was already known professionally by that name. Sokal's ex-husband, who was Jewish, fled Austria shortly after the Anschluss.

2. Helene Sokal-Legradi, "Widerstandstätigkeit der Gruppen Legradi-Sokal in Verbindung mit der Gruppe Dr. Heinrich Maier," unpublished manuscript dated circa

1963 (Vienna: DÖW archives, catalogue entry DOeW01553), p. 1.

3. Gestapo, "Interrogations."

4. Neugebauer, *Resistance*, p. 169.

5. Sokal, "Widerstandstätigkeit," p. 1.

6. Sokal, "Widerstandstätigkeit," pp. 4–5.

7. Beer, "ARCEL/CASSIA/REDBIRD," p. 77.

8. According to DÖW researcher Manfred Mugrauer, "Helene Sokal had belonged to the Communist Party since 1936 and subsequently had worked with Communist functionary Theodor Pawlin," which explains how Theodor's wife, Eva, became associated first with the Legradi-Sokal Group and later with CASSIA. (Source: Manfred Mugrauer, "Eine 'Bande von Gaunern, Schwindlern und naiven Leuten': Die Widerstandsbewegung O5 und die Kommunistische Partei Österreichs," in *Jahrbuch 2016* [Vienna: DÖW, 2016], p. 121.)

9. Dokumentationsarchiv des österreichischen Widerstandes (DÖW) searchable online data holdings, accessed extensively from 15 October 2015 to 15 September 2016, doew.at; referenced data were retrieved through the site's search tool, whose results often provided no specific web-page address; Theodor Pawlin, who was born on 22 June 1906, was buried in a shaft grave with fellow resistance member Johann Heinrich (1913–1943) in Vienna's Central Cemetery, in a section—Group 40—later dedicated to victims of the Nazis. On his headstone Theodor's surname is spelled Pavlin.

10. A 1944 court document (*Volksgerichtshof-Urteil*, p. 3) noted that Legradi "studied philosophy, chemistry, and physics and received [his] doctorate in 1922."

11. Sokal, "Widerstandstätigkeit," pp. 1–2.

12. *Urteil des Volksgerichtshof, 5. Senat* (Vienna: DÖW archives, 28 October 1944), p. 3; a scanned copy of this document, labeled *Volksgerichtshof-Urteil*, is also available at doew.at.

13. Gestapo, "Interrogations."

14. Sokal, "Widerstandstätigkeit," pp. 2–3.

15. Gestapo, "Interrogations."

16. Gestapo, "Interrogations."

17. Sokal, "Widerstandstätigkeit," p. 2.

18. Roosevelt, *War Report*, p. 277.

19. Sokal, "Widerstandstätigkeit," p. 3; Beer, "ARCEL/CASSIA/REDBIRD," p. 78.

20. Sokal, "Widerstandstätigkeit," p. 3.

21. Beer, "ARCEL/CASSIA/REDBIRD," p. 96.

22. S. Payne Best, *The Venlo Incident: A True Story of Double-Dealing, Captivity, and a Murderous Nazi Plot* (New York: Skyhorse Publishing, 2010).

23. Lucas Delattre, *A Spy at the Heart of the Third Reich: The Extraordinary Story of Fritz Kolbe, America's Most Important Spy in World War II*, trans. George A. Holoch, Jr. (New York: Grove Press, 2005), pp. 92–98.

24. Delattre, *A Spy at the Heart of the Third Reich*, pp. 83, 92–98; Petersen, *Hitler's Doorstep*, p. 12; Hans Bernd Gisevius, *To the Bitter End*, trans. Richard and Clara Winston (Boston: The Riverside Press, 1947), pp. 350–351.

25. Petersen, *Hitler's Doorstep*, p. 286.

26. Roosevelt, *War Report*, p. 274.

Chapter 4

1. Gestapo, "Interrogations."

2. Ilse Korotin, ed., *biographiA: Lexicon österreichischer Frauen, Band 02, I-O* (Vienna: Böhlau Verlag, 2016), pp. 1437–1438.

3. Thoma, *Mahner-Helfer-Patrioten*, p. 148; Beer, "ARCEL/CASSIA/REDBIRD," p. 78.

4. As of 2016, the Issakides family business still operated from this location.

5. Persico, *Piercing the Reich*, p. 55.

6. Persico, *Piercing the Reich*, p. 56.

7. Hans Jakob Stehle, "Die Spione aus dem Pfarrhaus," *Die Zeit*, Number 02/1996, 5 January 1996, accessed 28 October 2015, zeit.de/1996/02/Die_Spione_aus_dem_Pfarrhaus.

8. In the final year of the war, the Gestapo formulated a different hypothesis, possibly to strengthen its spotty case against her: Issakides had separately developed friendships with Maier and Messner, and in early 1943 she had introduced the two men (Source: Appendix I).

9. Persico, *Piercing the Reich*, p. 56; Gestapo, "Interrogations."

10. Persico, *Piercing the Reich*, p. 56.

11. Persico, *Piercing the Reich*, p. 56; Richard Breitman, "Other Responses to the Holocaust," in *US Intelligence and the Nazis*, ed. Richard Breitman et al. (Washington DC: National Archives Trust Fund, 2004), p. 51; Roosevelt, *War Report*, p. 270.

12. Neugebauer, *Resistance*, p. 168.

13. Persico, *Piercing the Reich*, p. 56; Beer, "ARCEL/CASSIA/REDBIRD," p. 78.

14. Persico, *Piercing the Reich*, pp. 54–56.

15. Persico, *Piercing the Reich*, p. 56.

16. Molden, *Fires*, pp. 78–79.

17. Persico, *Piercing the Reich*, pp. 54–55.

18. CIA, "Oral History Project: Molden," p. 66; Molden, *Fires*, pp. 71, 78–79.

19. Roosevelt, *War Report*, p. 277.

20. Beer, "ARCEL/CASSIA/REDBIRD," p. 77.

21. Thoma, *Mahner-Helfer-Patrioten*, p. 152; In his article *ARCEL/CASSIA/REDBIRD* (p. 78), Austrian scholar Siegfried Beer, draw-

ing on archived OSS documents, pieced together a slightly different sequence of events: Issakides and Grimm first met in November 1942 (through an undefined mechanism, perhaps as a result of Grimm's reputation) and Grimm was struck by her anti-Nazi views; Joham later verified (presumably through his resistance-minded contacts in Vienna) that Issakides was genuinely opposed to the Nazis and vouched for her to Grimm; and on Issakides's next visit to Switzerland in March 1943, she and Grimm met again and apparently engaged in a more substantial discussion. This article (p. 77) also records that Joham was counted among those of Messner's existing acquaintances who served as his own sub-sources of intelligence.

22. Sartorti, *Biographie-Messner*, p. 3.

23. Gerald D. Feldman, *Austrian Banks in the Period of National Socialism* (Cambridge: Cambridge University Press, 2015), p. 391.

24. Sartorti, *Biographie-Messner*, p. 3.

25. Feldman, *Austrian Banks*, p. 359.

26. Feldman, *Austrian Banks*, p. 28.

27. Some of Joham's later reports to OSS—passed through Grimm and Messner—are attributed to codename MANA, which may have been derived from the Pacific Islands concept of a personal spiritual force or supernatural power. Another possible origin of codename MANA may be the antiquated spelling of manna, the sustenance that God gave the Israelites during their desert wanderings. (Source: Siegfried Beer, *ARCEL/CASSIA/REDBIRD*, p. 98.)

28. Petersen, *Hitler's Doorstep*, p. 230; Renate Graber, "Ein übertypischer Österreicher," *Der Standard*, 30 November 2006, accessed on 6 October 2016, derstandard.at/2678171/Ein-uebertypischer-Oesterreicher.

29. Yale Law School, ed., "The Moscow Conference; October 1943," in *The Avalon Project: Documents in Law, History and Diplomacy*, Lillian Goldman Law Library, accessed on 27 October 2016, avalon.law.yale.edu/wwii/moscow.asp.

30. Oliver Rathkolb, *The Paradoxical Republic: Austria 1945–2005*, trans. Otmar Binder (New York/Oxford: Berghahn Books, 2014), p. 244.

Chapter 5

1. Persico, *Piercing the Reich*, pp. 56–57.

2. U.S. Allied Commission for Austria (USACA), Industry Report 22: "Semperit Gummiwerke A.G.," November 1947, two-page attachment on Semperit's foreign subsidiaries as of 1943; a scanned copy of this document is available at fold3.com.

3. From the German term *Land* or *Bundesland*, which is usually translated as "state" or "province."

4. *Volksgerichtshof-Urteil*, p. 5; Sartorti, *Biographie-Messner*, p. 2.

5. *Volksgerichtshof-Urteil*, p. 5; Sartorti, *Biographie-Messner*, p. 2.

6. *Volksgerichtshof-Urteil*, p. 5; Sartorti, *Biographie-Messner*, p. 2.

7. Franz Meßner, "Die Grundlagen des Kaffeebaues im brasilianischen Bundesstaat Sao Paulo, eine wirtschaftsgeographische Studie" (PhD diss., University of Vienna, 1934), Universität Wien Philosophischer Rigorosenakt 12155, in *VERZEICHNIS: über die seit dem Jahre 1872 philosophischen Facultät der Universität in Wien eingereichten und approbierten DISSERTATIONEN, Band I.* (Nendeln, Liechtenstein: Kraus Reprint, 1972), p. 236.

8. PH RA 12155 Messner, Franz Josef, 1934.04.24–1934.05.04, Archivinformationssystem, Archiv der Universität Wien, accessed on 27 September 2016.

9. Sartorti, *Biographie-Messner*, p. 3; Anna Lasinger-Guserl, Semperit Group, e-mail message to author, 25 October 2016.

10. *Volksgerichtshof-Urteil*, p. 5; In 1937 Messner would have received his salary in Austrian Schillings. After the Anschluss, his annual income was likely converted from around 150,000 Austrian Schillings to 100,000 Reichmarks, which in 1938 would have been worth more than U.S. $40,000—about $650,000 in 2016 purchasing power, as noted in the narrative. Some experts on the history of inflation and on the current values of past (and in some cases defunct) currencies might quibble about these figures, but nonetheless they give the reader a general idea of the relative value of Messner's salary. (Source: Harold Marcuse, "Historical Dollar-to-Marks Currency Conversion Page," 19 August 2005 [updated 9 February 2013], accessed on 4 November 2016, history.ucsb.edu/faculty/marcuse/projects/currency.htm.)

11. Roosevelt, *War Report*, p. 270.

12. Sartorti, *Biographie-Messner*, p. 4.

13. Hans Schafranek and Andrea Hurton, "Im Netz der Verräter," *Der Standard*, 5/6 June 2010, accessed 28 October 2015, derstandard.at/1271378203933/Im-Netz-der-Verraeter; *Volksgerichtshof-Urteil*, p. 5.

14. Carlos Dreyer is probably identifiable with Carl Ernst Dreyer (born in Germany to Johann Ludwig and Marie Elise Dreyer), a businessman in Manaós/Manaus who also served as the city's German consul. Carl

Dreyer's wife was named Rosa, and the couple had a son named Walter Johann Dreyer (1916–1998), who became a lawyer in Brazil. Carl Dreyer died in Rio de Janeiro, Brazil, in the 1960s. (Source: Genealogia Pernambucana, "Carl Ernst Dreyer," accessed 24 December 2016, araujo.eti.br/familia.asp?numPessoa=44232.)

15. Sartorti, *Biographie-Messner*, p. 3.

16. Cesar Campiani Maximiano and Ricardo Bonalume Neto, *Brazilian Expeditionary Force in World War II* (Oxford: Osprey Publishing, 2011), p. 5.

17. U.S. Coast Guard records indicate that, as of early June 1940, the *Conte Grande* was in Santos, Brazil (a major seaport in São Paulo state), and at that time she was engaged in a South American cruise. It is possible that earlier in 1940 the *Conte Grande* attempted an Atlantic crossing (a service for which she was originally designed), that the French intercepted her and detained some of her Axis passengers, and that after her impoundment in Casablanca she was sent back to Brazil. These same records also provided the following historical statement on the *Conte Grande*: "The *Monticello* (AP-61) was built as *Conte Grande* by Stabilimento Tecnico, Triestine, Trieste, Italy as an Italian-flagged passenger ship capable of carrying 7,798 persons. She was launched on 28 June 1927 and entered service with Lloyd Sabaudo of Genoa at Cantieri San Marco for service on the North Atlantic tourist and passenger trade. In 1933 she transferred to the South American tourist trade. Early in June, 1940 the *Conte Grande* was in Santos, Brazil, on one of her regular South American cruises. Here her officers held her awaiting developments after Mussolini's attack on France on 10 June 1940. On 27 February 1942 she was transferred to Brazilian registry and a Brazilian crew replaced the Italian crew who were interned. She was purchased on 16 April 1942 by the United States. She was commissioned the same day at Sao Paulo in Brazil under the command of CAPT Morton L. Deyo, USN." The ship was then refitted and saw extensive wartime service as a U.S. troop transport, and at war's end helped to repatriate Italian POWs who had been held in the United States. After the war, *Monticello/Conte Grande* was mustered out: "She decommissioned at Norfolk on 22 March 1946 and returned to the War Shipping Administration for disposal on 27 May 1946. She was returned to the Italian government in June, 1947." (Source: U.S. Coast Guard, "USS *Monticello*, AP-61," accessed on 24 December 2016, uscg.mil/history/webcutters/AP61_Monticello.pdf.)

18. Sartorti, *Biographie-Messner*, p. 3; *Volksgerichtshof-Urteil*, p. 5.

19. Barry Rubin, *Istanbul Intrigues: Espionage, Sabotage, and Diplomatic Treachery in the Spy Capital of WWII* (New York: Pharos Books, 1992), p. 178.

20. Sartorti, *Biographie-Messner*, p. 3.

21. Sartorti, *Biographie-Messner*, pp. 2, 3, 8.

22. Sartorti, *Biographie-Messner*, p. 3.

23. Sartorti, *Biographie-Messner*, p. 5; Schafranek and Hurton, "Netz."

24. Sartorti, *Biographie-Messner*, p. 2.

25. *Volksgerichtshof-Urteil*, p. 19.

26. Stehle, "Pfarrhaus."

27. Stehle, "Pfarrhaus."

28. Persico, *Piercing the Reich*, pp. 56–57.

29. Persico, *Piercing the Reich*, p. 57.

30. Michael J. Neufeld, *The Rocket and the Reich: Peenemunde and the Coming of the Ballistic Missile Era* (Washington DC: Smithsonian Books, 2013), p. 285–286.

31. Persico, *Piercing the Reich*, p. 57.

32. Stehle, "Pfarrhaus."

33. Feldman, *Austrian Banks*, p. 309.

34. The name *buna* is derived from a contraction of butadiene, an industrial chemical used in synthetic rubber production, and natrium (sodium). *Buna*, a polymerization of butadiene and styrene, was developed in 1929 by German chemical conglomerate IG Farben.

35. Stehle, "Pfarrhaus."

36. Rubin, *Istanbul Intrigues*, p. 179.

37. Stehle, "Pfarrhaus"; Persico, *Piercing the Reich*, p. 57; Rubin, *Istanbul Intrigues*, p. 170.

Chapter 6

1. Beer, "ARCEL/CASSIA/REDBIRD," p. 80.

2. Persico, *Piercing the Reich*, pp. 56–57; Molden, *Fires*, p. 61; Thoma, *Mahner-Helfer-Patrioten*, p. 152.

3. Petersen, *Hitler's Doorstep*, pp. 37–38.

4. Roosevelt, *War Report*, p. 280.

5. Roosevelt, *War Report*, pp. 280–281.

6. Roosevelt, *War Report*, p. 277.

7. Petersen, *Hitler's Doorstep*, p. 75.

8. Roosevelt, *War Report*, p. 270.

9. Petersen, *Hitler's Doorstep*, p. 6; Persico, *Piercing the Reich*, p. 57.

10. Joseph E. Persico, "Papers of Joseph E. Persico," collection identifier APAP-030, *M.E. Grenander Department of Special Collections and Archives*, State University of New York at Albany, Box 27, Folder 61 (Peenemunde).

11. Delattre, *A Spy at the Heart of the Third Reich*, p. 231.

Chapter 7

1. Roman Posch, "Walter Caldonazzi," Katholische Österreichische Hochschulverbindung (KÖHV) Amelungia, accessed on 20 December 2015, amelungia.org/site/pages/view/12; Karl Glaubauf, "Forstwirt Widerstamdskämpfer Walter Caldonazzi," accessed on 15 January 2016, austria-forum.org/af/Wissenssammlungen/Biographien/Caldonazzi,_Walter.
2. Posch, "Caldonazzi"; Schafranek and Hurton, "Netz."
3. Encyclopædia Britannica, ed., "Engelbert Dollfuss: Chancellor of Austria," accessed on 11 October 2016, britannica.com/biography/Engelbert-Dollfuss.
4. Posch, "Caldonazzi."
5. Mals is located near today's Italian borders with Austria and Switzerland. According to the 2011 census, almost 97% of the population of Mals speak German, while only 3% speak Italian. (Source: *Astat info*, No. 38, 06/2012.)
6. Glaubauf, "Forstwirt-Caldonazzi."
7. *Auszugsweise Abschrift aus dem Urteil des Volksgerichtshofes Berlin, 5. Senat, Geschäftszahlen* (Vienna: DÖW archives, 28 October 1944).
8. Rolf Steininger, *South Tyrol: A Minority Conflict of the Twentieth Century* (Piscataway, New Jersey: Transaction Publishers, 2003), pp. 8–10, 49–55; Molden, *Fires*, p. 101; CIA, "Oral History Project: Molden," p. 11.
9. The school's name in German is *Universität für Bodenkultur*, which translates literally as University *for* Agriculture.
10. Posch, "Caldonazzi."
11. Gerhard Jagschitz, "Kaplan DDr. Heinrich Maier," in *Hundert (100) Jahre Nibelungia: Festschrift zum hundertsten Stiftungsfest der Katholisch-Österreichischen Studentenverbindung Nibelungia zu Wien im ÖCV* (Vienna: ÖCV, 2008), pp. 25–30.
12. Posch, "Caldonazzi."
13. *Volksgerichtshof-Urteil*, p. 4.
14. Posch, "Caldonazzi"; Glaubauf, "Forstwirt-Caldonazzi"; According to a 1944 Nazi court document (*Volksgerichtshof-Urteil*, p. 4), Caldonazzi worked for an association of forestry firms in Vienna.
15. Gestapo, "Interrogations."
16. Thoma, *Mahner-Helfer-Patrioten*, pp. 148–149.
17. Gestapo, "Interrogations."
18. Thoma, *Mahner-Helfer-Patrioten*, p. 149.
19. Glaubauf, "Forstwirt-Caldonazzi."
20. Posch, "Caldonazzi."
21. Caleb Hornbostel, *Construction Materials: Types, Uses and Applications* (New York: John Wiley & Sons, 1991), pp. 146–148.
22. Posch, "Caldonazzi."
23. Rubin, *Istanbul Intrigues*, pp. 178–179.

Chapter 8

1. Richard Breitman, "Other Responses to the Holocaust," p. 51.
2. As of 2016, Rüdiger's two sons didn't know why their father chose the nickname Gustav. "Gustav Rüdiger" appears consistently in British wartime documents and in the 1941 edition of Lehmann's, the standard Vienna city directory of that time. However, Rüdiger often signed legal instruments as Josef Rüdiger, and his letterhead sometimes bore the initials G.J., to signify Gustav Josef. "G.J. Rüdiger" was also inscribed on a number of his luggage labels. In some studies, whose research was based on archived OSS materials, Third Reich court documents, and Semperit records, Rüdiger's surname is recorded as Ridiger or Riediger, and his given names appear variously as Josef, Franz Josef, and Hans. Due to these variations, and to the fact that the Rüdiger family also used the alternative spelling Ridiger, in early 1952 Gustav Rüdiger petitioned Saint Stephen's Cathedral—pursuant to a legal decision by the Vienna Regional Government—to standardize the spelling of his surname on his marriage certificate to Rüdiger. Saint Stephen's granted Rüdiger's request in April 1952. (Sources: The author's conversation with Thomas Rüdiger on 29 November 2016 in Vienna, and a copy of a revised marriage certificate—dated 7 April 1952—that Thomas Rüdiger gave the author at this same meeting.)
3. Thomas Rüdiger, e-mail message to author, 6 November 2016.
4. Thomas Rüdiger, e-mail message to author, 6 November 2016; USACA, "Semperit Gummiwerke A.G."
5. A 1944 German court document (*Volksgerichtshof-Urteil*, p. 11.2) asserted that in January 1941 Messner traveled to Istanbul under a business pretext, enlisted Rüdiger's help in contacting the "enemy," and shortly thereafter Rüdiger forged a relationship with the "Americans." (This document spelled Rüdiger as "Ridiger," despite the fact that its sources—Gestapo interrogation reports—referred to him only as Rüdiger.) While Messner may have recruited Rüdiger into CASSIA around this time (i.e., early 1941), Rüdiger's first contact with any of the Allies would occur about two years later.

6. Thomas Rüdiger, e-mail message to author, 6 November 2016.

7. Thomas Rüdiger, e-mail message to author, 4 January 2017.

8. Thomas Rüdiger, e-mail message to author, 6 November 2016.

9. Vorarlberg Chronik, ed., "Dr. Otto Ender 1875–1960," accessed 21 October 2016, apps.vol.at/tools/chronik/viewpage.aspx?viewtype=artikel&id=94&left=artikel.

10. Encyclopædia Britannica, ed., "Otto Ender: Chancellor of Austria," *Encyclopædia Britannica*, accessed on 16 September 2016, britannica.com/biography/Otto-Ender.

11. Encyclopædia Britannica, "Otto Ender."

12. Thomas Rüdiger, e-mail message to author, 6 November 2016.

13. Rubin, *Istanbul Intrigues*, p. 165.

Chapter 9

1. Richard Breitman, "Other Responses to the Holocaust," p. 49; Rubin, *Istanbul Intrigues*, p. 166; Tuvia Friling, "Istanbul 1942–1945: The Kollek-Avriel and Berman-Ofner Networks," in *Secret Intelligence and the Holocaust*, ed. David Bankier (New York: Enigma Books, 2006), p. 123.

2. Friling, "Istanbul-Networks," p. 123.

3. Richard Breitman, "Other Responses to the Holocaust," p. 49.

4. Chicago Pneumatic, "History: decades of innovation," accessed on 27 September 2016, cp.com/usen/whoweare/history/.

5. Rubin, *Istanbul Intrigues*, p. 167; Breitman, "Other Responses to the Holocaust," pp. 49–50.

6. Peter Pirker, *Subversion deutscher Herrschaft: Der britische Kriegsgeheimdienst SOE und Österreich* (University of Vienna Press, 2012), p. 254.

7. Shlomo Aronson, "OSS X-2 and Rescue Efforts During the Holocaust," in *Secret Intelligence and the Holocaust*, ed. David Bankier (New York: Enigma Books, 2006), pp. 71–72.

8. Friling, "Istanbul-Networks," p. 123.

9. Roosevelt, *War Report*, p. 269.

10. Rubin, *Istanbul Intrigues*, p. 167.

11. Rubin, *Istanbul Intrigues*, pp. 135–136; "Lanning MacFarland Dies at 73," *Chicago Tribune*, Wednesday edition, 13 October 1971, Section 2A, p. 6.

12. Roosevelt, *War Report*, p. 269.

13. Rubin, *Istanbul Intrigues*, pp. 163, 166; Persico, *Piercing the Reich*, pp. 57–58; Aronson, "OSS X-2," pp. 69–77.

14. Pirker, *Subversion*, p. 254.

15. In some literature, this type of middleman is occasionally called a "cutout," not a principal agent. However, while a cutout does facilitate clandestine contact between two parties, he or she typically remains unwitting of the identities of the individuals on at least one side, if not on both sides, to ensure that the entire group is not blown in the event that a part of the arrangement is compromised.

16. Roosevelt, *War Report*, pp. 269–270.

17. Lehrner may be identifiable with Karl Josef Lehrner (circa 1899–1983), who is buried in Vienna's Feuerhalle Simmering Cemetery (Section E13, Group 1, Number 936). However, in Fenyvesi's *The Brave Men from "Die Fledermaus"* (p. 48), Josef Lehrner was described as having graduated from the old and storied Theresian Military Academy (*Theresianische Militärakademie*) during the Habsburg era, which ended in 1918 with the conclusion of the First World War when this Karl Josef Lehrner was only 18 or 19 years old.

18. Charles Fenyvesi, "The Brave Men from 'Die Fledermaus': OSS-Istanbul and Austrian Resistance 1943/44," in *Journal for Intelligence, Propaganda and Security Studies*, Volume 3, Number 2, 2009, p. 48.

19. Fenyvesi, "Fledermaus," p. 48.

20. Philips Company, "1925–1940: The first radios, televisions and electric shavers," accessed on 22 October 2016, philips.com/a-w/about/company/our-heritage.html; The Philips Company did not respond to the author's request for any extant records of Lehrner's employment with the company.

21. Fenyvesi, "Fledermaus," p. 48.

22. Pirker, *Subversion*, p. 252.

23. Pirker, *Subversion*, pp. 254–255.

24. Fenyvesi, "Fledermaus," p. 48.

25. Fenyvesi, "Fledermaus," p. 49.

Chapter 10

1. Rubin, *Istanbul Intrigues*, pp. 163, 166.

2. Rubin, *Istanbul Intrigues*, p. 166; Jakon Hays and Maureen Watts, "Archibald Frederick Coleman—AKA 'Snapdragon,'" *The Virginian-Pilot*, 2 December 2015, accessed 21 May 2016, pilotonline.com/news/local/history/dusting-off-stones/archibald-frederick-coleman---aka-snapdragon/article_24e77609-ce00-568a-b639-b50fbbcb71e0.html.

3. Rubin, *Istanbul Intrigues*, p. 166; Hays and Watts, "Archibald Frederick Coleman."

4. Chicago Pneumatic, "History: decades of innovation," accessed on 6 September 2016, cp.com.

5. Rubin, *Istanbul Intrigues*, pp. 167–168.

6. Rubin, *Istanbul Intrigues*, pp. 167–168.

7. Rubin, *Istanbul Intrigues*, p. 168; Persico, *Piercing the Reich*, p. 313.

8. Central Intelligence Agency, Center for the Study of Intelligence, "Office of Strategic Services (OSS) Oral History Project Transcripts: Albert E. Jolis," interviewed by Siegfried Beer on 8 May 1997 (College Park, Maryland: U.S. National Archives), p. 66.

9. Rubin, *Istanbul Intrigues*, pp. 170–171.

10. Rubin, *Istanbul Intrigues*, p. 170.

11. Roosevelt, *War Report*, p. 271.

12. Roosevelt, *War Report*, p. 270.

13. Roosevelt, *War Report*, p. 270.

14. According to Austrian historian Siegfried Beer, who reviewed salient OSS files in the U.S. National Archives, approximately 50 Dogwood agents were operating at the beginning of 1944. (Source: *ARCEL/CASSIA/REDBIRD*, p. 80.)

15. Rubin, *Istanbul Intrigues*, p. 169.

16. Roosevelt, *War Report*, p. 271.

17. Rubin, *Istanbul Intrigues*, p. 166.

18. Roosevelt, *War Report*, p. 271.

19. Rubin, *Istanbul Intrigues*, p. 179.

20. Rubin, *Istanbul Intrigues*, p. 178.

21. Beer, "ARCEL/CASSIA/REDBIRD," p. 83.

22. Rubin, *Istanbul Intrigues*, p. 179.

23. Gerhard Peter "Gerry" Van Arkel (27 August 1907–8 October 1984) graduated from Princeton (class of 1929) and later from Harvard Law School. His Ivy League pedigree and chosen profession likely explain how he first came to OSS chief Donovan's attention.

24. Petersen, *Hitler's Doorstep*, p. 600.

Chapter 11

1. Rubin, *Istanbul Intrigues*, p. 170.

2. Persico, *Piercing the Reich*, p. 57.

3. Agostino von Hassell and Sigrid MacRae, *Alliance of Enemies: The Untold Story of the Secret American and German Collaboration to End World War II* (New York: Thomas Dunne Books, 2006), p. 189.

4. Molden, *Fires*, p. 61.

5. Gestapo, "Interrogations."

6. Broucek, *Militärischer Widerstand*, p. 163.

7. Michael Winninger, *Das Nibelungenwerk 1939 bis 1945—Panzerfahrzeuge aus St. Valentin* (Erfurt, Germany: Sutton Verlag, 2009), pp. 65, 89, 97.

8. Stehle, "Pfarrhaus."

9. Fenyvesi, "Fledermaus," pp. 54–55; Aronson, "OSS X-2," p. 98; Rubin, *Istanbul Intrigues*, pp. 198–199.

10. Feed material includes both disinformation—concocted or altered information—and authentic information presented in a misleading way (e.g., by omitting certain details or context, or by exaggerating the importance of lower-priority information).

11. Rubin, *Istanbul Intrigues*, p. 171.

12. Rubin, *Istanbul Intrigues*, p. 170.

13. Rubin, *Istanbul Intrigues*, p. 198.

14. Such incongruous conclusions may have resulted from flaws in the analyses of the involved USAAF appraisals, not in the appraisals themselves. However, the cited studies' findings—which were the work of experienced researchers—are consistently inconsistent, and this observation alone suggests a lack of clarity in some of the original material.

15. Persico, *Piercing the Reich*, p. 57.

16. Roosevelt, *War Report*, p. 270.

17. Roosevelt, *War Report*, p. 271.

18. Rubin, *Istanbul Intrigues*, p. 169.

19. Vienna International Airport (VIE) now operates from the site of the Luftwaffe's Schwechat base, which during the war was sometimes called "Schwechat-Heidfeld Airfield."

20. Rubin, *Istanbul Intrigues*, p. 198.

21. Jean-Denis G.G. Lepage, *Aircraft of the Luftwaffe, 1935–1945: An Illustrated Guide* (Jefferson, North Carolina: McFarland & Company, 2009), p. 228.

22. John Killen, *The Luftwaffe: A History* (South Yorkshire, England: Pen & Sword Military Classics, 2003), p. 239.

23. Rubin, *Istanbul Intrigues*, p. 198.

24. Rubin, *Istanbul Intrigues*, p. 199.

25. Fenyvesi, "Fledermaus," p. 55.

26. Fenyvesi, "Fledermaus," pp. 54–55.

27. Fenyvesi, "Fledermaus," p. 54; Continental AG, "Continental AG History," accessed on 26 October 2016, fundinguniverse.com/company-histories/continental-ag-history/.

28. Fenyvesi, "Fledermaus," p. 55.

Chapter 12

1. Schafranek and Hurton, "Netz."

2. Winston S. Churchill, *The Gathering Storm* (New York: Houghlin Mifflin Harcourt, 1985), pp. 93–94.

3. Schafranek and Hurton, "Netz."

4. Schafranek and Hurton, "Netz."

5. Schafranek and Hurton, "Netz."

6. Schafranek and Hurton, "Netz."

7. Schafranek and Hurton, "Netz."

8. Josef Rüdiger/G.J. Rüdiger, signed affidavit in which Rüdiger described CASSIA's activities and his role therein, submitted to the

Magistrate of the City of Vienna, 9 January 1956 (Vienna: DÖW archives).

9. Rüdiger, "Affidavit."

Chapter 13

1. *Auszugsweise Abschrift aus dem Urteil des Volksgerichtshofes Berlin, 5. Senat, Geschäftszahlen* (Vienna: DÖW archives, 28 October 1944).

2. *Volksgerichtshof-Urteil*, p. 4.

3. Helene Legradi (Sokal), *Das andere Wien: Erlebtes aus den Jahren 1944/45*, ed. Dr. Gerhard Schäffer and Erika Thurner (Vienna-Salzburg: Geyer Edition, 1989), p. 11.

4. Francis Spirago and James J. Baxter, eds., *Anecdotes and Examples Illustrating the Catholic Catechism* (New York: Benziger Brothers, 1904), p. 398.

5. Patrick Leigh Fermor, *A Time of Gifts* (New York Review of Books, 2005), p. 170.

6. Gestapo, "Interrogations."

7. Gestapo, "Interrogations."

8. Gestapo, "Interrogations."

Chapter 14

1. Gestapo, "Interrogations."

2. *Volksgerichtshof-Urteil*, p. 4.

3. Thoma, *Mahner-Helfer-Patrioten*, p. 149.

4. *Volksgerichtshof-Urteil*, p. 4.

5. *Volksgerichtshof-Urteil*, p. 4; This same German court document (*Volksgerichtshof-Urteil*, p. 4) suggested that Wyhnal might not have completed all of the requirements for his medical degree before he was conscripted in 1941, but several other reliable sources, to include Neugebauer's *The Austrian Resistance* (p. 168), refer to Wyhnal as "a doctor of medicine."

6. *Volksgerichtshof-Urteil*, p. 4.

7. *Volksgerichtshof-Urteil*, pp. 4–5.

8. Court documents from 1944 (*Volksgerichtshof-Urteil*, p. 1) list Ritsch's place of birth as Brez, but in *Verfolgung und Widerstand in Vorarlberg 1933–1945* (p. 343) Ritsch's place of birth appears as Nüziders, Vorarlberg. It is likely that he was born in South Tyrol and, at the age of about three, moved with his family to Vorarlberg.

9. *Volksgerichtshof-Urteil*, p. 1.

10. *Volksgerichtshof-Urteil*, p. 4.

11. *Volksgerichtshof-Urteil*, p. 5.

12. The ouster of the Austrian monarchy after the First World War ended the privileges of the nobility, but many titled families continued to use nobiliary prepositions such as *von* and *zu*. Some references assert that Austria further abolished all use of such particles in 1919, even as nominal parts of surnames, but many Viennese gravestones refute these claims. For consistency, this study refers to von Pausinger's name as it has appeared in several other works and as it was carved into his headstone—with its nobiliary preposition. Also, famed British author and adventurer Patrick Leigh Fermor once reported his firsthand observations from early 1934: Although Austria had proscribed the use of titles, most of its citizens simply ignored the edict. (Source: *A Time of Gifts*, p. 167.)

13. *Volksgerichtshof-Urteil*, p. 6.

14. *Volksgerichtshof-Urteil*, p. 1.

15. *Volksgerichtshof-Urteil*, p. 6.

16. *Volksgerichtshof-Urteil*, p. 6.

17. *Volksgerichtshof-Urteil*, p. 6.

18. *Volksgerichtshof-Urteil*, p. 6.

19. *Volksgerichtshof-Urteil*, pp. 9–10.

20. *Volksgerichtshof-Urteil*, p. 5.

21. Schafranek and Hurton, "Netz"; *Volksgerichtshof-Urteil*, p. 8.

22. *Volksgerichtshof-Urteil*, p. 8.

23. *Volksgerichtshof-Urteil*, pp. 15–16.

24. *Volksgerichtshof-Urteil*, pp. 14–17; *Auszugsweise-Urteil*; Gestapo, "Interrogations."

25. Steyr is a city in the state of Upper Austria with a long history of manufacturing. It is about 100 miles—165 kilometers—west of Vienna.

26. Schafranek and Hurton, "Netz"; Gestapo, "Interrogations"; *Volksgerichtshof-Urteil*, p. 11.

27. Beer, "ARCEL/CASSIA/REDBIRD," p. 84.

28. Mürzzuschlag, a town in northeastern Styria state, is located about 60 miles—100 kilometers—southwest of Vienna. Bleckmann Steelworks was founded in Mürzzuschlag in the 19th Century. In the early 1920s Bleckmann merged with Schoeller Steelworks of Ternitz, a town approximately 21 miles—34 kilometers—east-northeast of Mürzzuschlag. Mürzzuschlag and Ternitz each have fewer than 10,000 residents.

29. Gestapo, "Interrogations"; *Volksgerichtshof-Urteil*, pp. 12–13.

30. Beer, "ARCEL/CASSIA/REDBIRD," p. 83.

31. Thoma, *Mahner-Helfer-Patrioten*, pp. 149–150; *Volksgerichtshof-Urteil*, pp. 9–11.

32. These examples comprise only excerpts from the three original flyers, which were longer and more detailed.

33. *Volksgerichtshof-Urteil*, pp. 10–11; Thoma, *Mahner-Helfer-Patrioten*, pp. 149–150.

Chapter 15

1. Thoma, *Mahner-Helfer-Patrioten*, p. 152.

2. "Dulles...placed an inconspicuous sign outside his door [at Herrengasse 23 in Bern]: 'Allen W. Dulles, Special Assistant to the American Minister.' The flat had a back entrance that people could use when they came to see him at night. For those who might come to Dulles's front door in the evening, he pulled some strings and had the streetlight opposite his front door turned off for the duration of the war." (Greg Bradsher, "A Time to Act: The Beginning of the Fritz Kolbe Story, 1900–1943, Part 3," *Prologue Magazine*, Spring 2002, Vol. 34, No. 1, accessed on 30 September 2016, archives.gov/publications/prologue/2002/spring/fritz-kolbe-3.html.)

3. Roosevelt, *War Report*, p. 273.

4. Petersen, *Hitler's Doorstep*, p. 238.

5. Petersen, *Hitler's Doorstep*, pp. 238–239.

6. Persico, *Piercing the Reich*, p. 57.

7. Roosevelt, *War Report*, pp. 274–275.

8. Petersen, *Hitler's Doorstep*, pp. 2, 5–6.

9. Roosevelt, *War Report*, p. 274.

10. Petersen, *Hitler's Doorstep*, pp. 2–5.

11. Petersen, *Hitler's Doorstep*, pp. 11–12.

12. Petersen, *Hitler's Doorstep*, pp. 238, 549.

13. Four or five times a week Dulles also placed a scrambled telephone call—for which the Swiss had the encryption key—to OSS chief Donovan and gave him a ten-minute intelligence update. (Source: *War Report of the OSS*, Volume 2, p. 274.) According to Evan Thomas's 2011 Vanity Fair Article *Spymaster General*, "President Roosevelt was so impressed [by OSS-Bern's intelligence] that he had himself patched into Dulles's nightly radio [sic] calls to Donovan."

14. Petersen, *Hitler's Doorstep*, p. 6.

15. Roosevelt, *War Report*, p. 274.

16. According to a 1944 Nazi court document (*Volksgerichtshof-Urteil*, pp. 11–12), Maier suggested that Messner may have not limited his meetings to Grimm and Dulles: "Messner maintained contact with Hollitscher in Switzerland, to whom, in December 1943 in Zurich, Messner confided Maier's plans for the [CASSIA] group." However, it appears that Maier provided this name for purposes of misdirection, to downplay Grimm's role and to avoid revealing CASSIA's contact with Dulles. Hans Jakob Hollitscher was a Jewish lawyer who had fled Austria in 1938 and who worked in Zurich as an economist and journalist. He was already known in opposition circles and as such Maier may have viewed him as a "safe" target for misdirection. In fact, it was no great secret in Austria that in 1939 Hollitscher had written a book under the pseudonym Erich Hans Wolf in which he observed—among other things—that Austrian economic deflation had helped the Nazis to gain popular support for the Anschluss. (Source: Erich Hans Wolf, *Katastrophenwirtschaft: Geburt und Ende Österreichs, 1918–1938* [Zurich: Europa Verlag, 1939].). Unknown to Maier, however, Hollitscher was cooperating with British intelligence in Switzerland. Through his Zurich-based SOE handler, Elizabeth "Bessie" Hodgson, Hollitscher served as link to resistance-minded individuals in Austria and used his connections with a Liechtenstein prince to communicate secretly with his correspondents in Vienna. (Source: Peter Pirker, *Subversion deutscher Herrschaft*, pp. 167–168.).

17. Thoma, *Mahner-Helfer-Patrioten*, p. 151.

Chapter 16

1. Schafranek and Hurton, "Netz"; Aronson, "OSS X-2," pp. 71–73, 92–93; Rubin, *Istanbul Intrigues*, p. 192; Friling, "Istanbul-Networks," p. 126; Szita, *Trading in Lives*, p. 71.

2. Schafranek and Hurton, "Netz."

3. Schafranek and Hurton, "Netz"; Rubin, *Istanbul Intrigues*, p. 192; Szita, *Trading in Lives*, p. 71.

4. Per findings in a study by Shlomo Aronson from *Secret Intelligence and the Holocaust* (p. 71), Klausnitzer's first name may have been Alfred. This same study—which cites Schwarz's correspondence (p. 72)—suggests that Laufer may not have had a criminal record: He was born in Prague in 1900, studied at an agricultural school, later worked in his father's company and ran the family estate, and then managed the textiles section of a department store in Prague; the store sent him to its branch in Belgrade, and he later moved to Budapest and ran an import business. But when reading this version of Laufer's background, one must remember that Schwarz was duped by Laufer and that he always tried to cast his sub-sources in the best possible light.

5. Friling, "Istanbul-Networks," p. 127; Szita, *Trading in Lives*, p. 71.

6. Rubin, *Istanbul Intrigues*, p. 192.

7. Szita, *Trading in Lives*, p. 71; Aronson, "OSS X-2," pp. 92–93; Schafranek and Hurton, "Netz."

8. Friling, "Istanbul-Networks," p. 126.

9. Per *Secret Intelligence and the Holocaust* (pp. 72), OSS and Zionist groups also used Laufer as a courier.

10. Schafranek and Hurton, "Netz"; Rubin, *Istanbul Intrigues*, p. 192.

11. Friling, "Istanbul-Networks," p. 127; Rubin, *Istanbul Intrigues*, p. 192.

12. Rubin, *Istanbul Intrigues*, p. 192; Schafranek and Hurton, "Netz"; According to *Secret Intelligence and the Holocaust* (p. 127), Laufer brought this funding—the equivalent of U.S.$5,000 (purchasing value in 2016 of around $84,000)—*to* Istanbul to fund Czech underground operations.

13. Friling, "Istanbul-Networks," p. 127.

14. Fenyvesi, "Fledermaus," p. 53.

15. Aronson, "OSS X-2," pp. 86, 93.

16. Aronson, "OSS X-2," p. 72.

17. Aronson, "OSS X-2," p. 93.

18. Rubin, *Istanbul Intrigues*, p. 192.

19. Friling, "Istanbul-Networks," p. 127; Rubin, *Istanbul Intrigues*, p. 192.

20. According to Fenyvesi's *The Brave Men from "Die Fledermaus"* (p. 54), Gestapo-Vienna destroyed its files—to include those involving the CASSIA case—before the Red Army began its Vienna Offensive in April 1945. As such, the full scope of investigative methodologies that the Gestapo used against the group is unknown.

21. Sokal, "Widerstandstätigkeit," p. 3.

Chapter 17

1. Posch, "Caldonazzi."

2. DÖW, doew.at.

3. DÖW, doew.at.

4. The master harpooner in Herman Melville's *Moby Dick*.

5. Persico, *Piercing the Reich*, p. 179.

6. According to Neugebauer's *The Austrian Resistance* (p. 168), the value of 100,000 Reichmarks in 1944 would be equivalent in purchasing power to U.S.$400,000 in 2016. A reference in preceding chapter *The Merchant* illustrates how much Germany's currency had devalued as the war dragged on: Seven years earlier (1937), 100,000 Reichmarks were equivalent to more than $650,000 in 2016. Further, in an OSS cable dated 5 February 1944, MacFarland told OSS chief Donovan that OSS-Istanbul could purchase 100,000 Reichmarks for less than U.S.$6,000—about $81,500 in 2016 buying power. (Source: Siegfried Beer, *ARCEL/CASSIA/REDBIRD*, p. 96.) Apparently, at this stage of the war, if MacFarland's calculations are to be believed, the value of Reichmarks on the black market in Istanbul had twisted into a death spiral.

7. Rubin, *Istanbul Intrigues*, pp. 194, 196.

8. Petersen, *Hitler's Doorstep*, p. 600; Beer, "ARCEL/CASSIA/REDBIRD," p. 83; Rubin, *Istanbul Intrigues*, p. 194; Fenyvesi, "Fledermaus," pp. 51–52.

9. Beer, "ARCEL/CASSIA/REDBIRD," p. 85.

10. Friling, "Istanbul-Networks," p. 127.

11. Aronson, "OSS X-2," pp. 86–87.

12. Friling, "Istanbul-Networks," p. 127.

13. Kövess is likely a variation of Hungarian surname Kövesces, derived from the name of a village that Hungary ceded to Slovakia under the terms of the 1920 Treaty of Trianon. The Slovakian name of the village is Štrkovec.

14. Rubin, *Istanbul Intrigues*, p. 187.

15. Von Hassell and MacRae, *Alliance of Enemies*, p. 181.

16. Rubin, *Istanbul Intrigues*, p. 187.

17. Breitman, "Other Responses to the Holocaust," p. 52.

18. Fenyvesi, "Fledermaus," p. 51; Breitman, "Other Responses to the Holocaust," p. 52.

19. Friling, "Istanbul-Networks," p. 125; Szita, *Trading in Lives*, p. 72; Aronson, "OSS X-2," p. 88.

20. Friling, "Istanbul-Networks," pp. 125–126.

21. Rubin, *Istanbul Intrigues*, p. 192.

22. Breitman, "Other Responses to the Holocaust," p. 53.

23. Roosevelt, *War Report*, pp. 270–271.

24. Rubin, *Istanbul Intrigues*, p. 196.

25. Von Hassell and MacRae, *Alliance of Enemies*, p. 182.

26. Rubin, *Istanbul Intrigues*, p. 187.

27. Rubin, *Istanbul Intrigues*, p. 194; Neugebauer, *Resistance*, p. 168.

28. Rubin, *Istanbul Intrigues*, p. 194; Petersen, *Hitler's Doorstep*, pp. 238–239.

29. Rubin, *Istanbul Intrigues*, p. 194.

30. Roosevelt, *War Report*, p. 277.

31. Beer, "ARCEL/CASSIA/REDBIRD," p. 97.

32. At a time when the Reich had requisitioned many private vehicles and was strictly rationing gasoline, Messner's routine automobile trip to Budapest attests to his professional standing in wartime Austria and the privileges that he enjoyed.

33. Fenyvesi, "Fledermaus," p. 53.

34. DÖW, doew.at.

35. After the war, in the manuscript *Widerstandstätigkeit der Gruppen Legradi-Sokal in Verbindung mit der Gruppe Dr. Heinrich Maier* (p. 3), Sokal wrote that in her recollection Maier was arrested around 25 March. Other accounts (e.g., doew.at) have suggested that he was taken on 29 March. However, Gestapo-Vienna's first interrogation report on Maier was dated 28 March, and subsequent reports

consistently cited 28 March as the date of his arrest.

36. Gestapo, "Interrogations"; Thoma, *Mahner-Helfer-Patrioten*, p. 154.

37. On 19 January 2016, in response to a request for archived personnel records on Palme, Semperit Group Head of Communications Martina Büchele advised, "we are not able to trace this information anymore." Based on research into Vienna burial records for appropriately aged women named Hilde Palme, the former Semperit secretary may be identifiable with Hildegard Wilhemine Georgine Palme (1904–1984).

38. Rubin, *Istanbul Intrigues*, p. 196; Beer, "ARCEL/CASSIA/REDBIRD," p. 78; Rüdiger, "Affidavit."

39. Fenyvesi, "Fledermaus," pp. 53–54; Schafranek and Hurton, "Netz"; Thoma, *Mahner-Helfer-Patrioten*, p. 154.

40. Roosevelt, *War Report*, p. 271.

41. Thoma, *Mahner-Helfer-Patrioten*, p. 154.

42. Beer, "ARCEL/CASSIA/REDBIRD," pp. 85, 88.

43. Sokal, "Widerstandstätigkeit," p. 3.

44. Clemens von Pausinger, "Bestätigung, Dr. Clemens von Pausinger," 11 June 1945, *Gefangenhausdirektion des Landesgerichtes für Strafsachen Wien* (Vienna: DÖW archives).

45. Beer, "ARCEL/CASSIA/REDBIRD," p. 87.

46. Beer, "ARCEL/CASSIA/REDBIRD," p. 87.

47. While Hitler himself distracted Regent Miklós Horthy with discussions in Salzburg, the Wehrmacht marched into Hungary. Hitler had ordered the occupation after learning—from multiple sources, to include from double agents such as Hatz and György—that the Hungarian leadership had been negotiating with the Allies toward a possible armistice.

48. Rubin, *Istanbul Intrigues*, p. 196; Schafranek and Hurton, "Netz."

Chapter 18

1. To stretch the stagecraft analogy to its breaking point, a spike is a marked spot to which an actor must move during a performance.

Chapter 19

1. Tom Appleton, "Nachrichten vom Eingang zur Hölle," *Telepolis*, 14 July 2008, accessed 14 September 2016, heise.de (article may no longer be posted on-line).

2. Appleton, "Nachrichten."

3. Dieter Klein, Martin Kupf, and Robert Schediwy, eds., *Stadtbildverluste Wien—Ein Rückblick auf fünf Jahrzehnte* (Vienna: LIT Verlag, 2004), p. 121.

4. Klein, Kupf, and Schediwy, *Stadtbildverluste Wien*, p. 121.

5. Colette M. Schmidt, "Was an die Gegenwart erinnert," 13 June 2015, *Der Standard*, accessed on 17 October 2016, derstandard.at/2000017383087/Was-an-die-Gegenwart-erinnert.

6. Schmidt, "Gegenwart."

7. Jack Hedrick Taylor, Lieutenant, USNR, "DUPONT MISSION, J.H. Taylor, October 13, 1944—May 5, 1945," 30 May 1945, *U.S. National Archives*, declassified on 13 February 1999; the full text of Taylor's debriefing report appears on a number of internet sites, to include jewishvirtuallibrary.org/jsource/ww2/dupont.html.

8. Taylor, "DUPONT MISSION."

9. Taylor, "DUPONT MISSION."

10. Stefan Zweig, *The Royal Game*, trans. B.W. Huebsch (London: Pushkin Press, 2001).

11. Molden, *Star*, p. 92.

12. Molden, *Star*, p. 95.

13. Molden, *Star*, p. 93.

14. Molden, *Star*, pp. 93–94.

15. Molden, *Star*, p. 94.

16. Molden, *Star*, p. 94.

17. Molden, *Star*, p. 94.

Chapter 20

1. Thoma, *Mahner-Helfer-Patrioten*, p. 158.

2. Schafranek and Hurton, "Netz"; Gestapo, "Interrogations."

3. Gestapo, "Interrogations"; In an earlier statement to the Gestapo, Maier claimed that Messner had introduced him to "Hans" Rüdiger in Vienna in late 1942, and that at this meeting Rüdiger had revealed his connection to attorney Hans Jakob Hollitscher, a prominent Austrian exile who had fled to Zurich in 1938 because of his Jewish faith. Maier had then suggested that Rüdiger, through Hollitscher, had contacted the British on CASSIA's behalf. Maier later recanted his statements about Rüdiger, explaining—under great duress—that he had attempted to protect the people and methods that the group had actually used to reach the Allies.

4. Gestapo, "Interrogations."

5. Gestapo, "Interrogations."

6. Gestapo, "Interrogations."

7. Gestapo, "Interrogations."

8. More details on Oflag XVII-A may be found in *Five Years Behind Hitler's Barbed Wire: A Diary of French Officers in A German Prison Camp, 1940–1945* by Henri Natter and Adam Réfrégier, translated by Jacqueline Vautrain Collins (Jefferson, North Carolina: McFarland & Company, 2015).
9. Gestapo, "Interrogations."
10. Stehle, "Pfarrhaus."
11. *Volksgerichtshof-Urteil*, p. 19.
12. *Volksgerichtshof-Urteil*, p. 19.
13. Stehle, "Pfarrhaus."
14. DÖW, "Gestapo Activities and Methods," accessed on 18 October 2016, doew.at/english/memorial-room-for-the-victims-of-the-gestapo-vienna/gestapo-activities-and-methods#torture.
15. DÖW, "'They Took the Other Road'—Organized Resistance in Austria," accessed on 18 October 2016, doew.at/english/memorial-room-for-the-victims-of-the-gestapo-vienna/they-took-the-other-road-organized-resistance-in-austria-3.
16. DÖW, "They Took the Other Road,"—5.
17. DÖW, "They Took the Other Road,"—5.
18. DÖW, "They Took the Other Road,"—5.
19. DÖW, "They Took the Other Road,"—6.
20. DÖW, "They Took the Other Road,"—6.
21. DÖW, "They Took the Other Road,"—6.
22. Neugebauer, *Resistance*, p. 169; Sokal, "Widerstandstätigkeit," p. 4.
23. Sokal, "Widerstandstätigkeit," p. 4.

Chapter 21

1. Thoma, *Mahner-Helfer-Patrioten*, p. 156.
2. Stehle, "Pfarrhaus."
3. Persico, *Piercing the Reich*, p. 313.
4. Rubin, *Istanbul Intrigues*, p. 196; In an e-mail dated 6 November 2016 and during a conversation in Vienna on 29 November 2016, Rüdiger's firstborn son, Thomas, advised the author that he was unaware of his father's defection. However, he noted that he was only two years old in fall 1944 and that his father had never spoken to his children about his wartime resistance activities.
5. Beer, "ARCEL/CASSIA/REDBIRD," p. 87; Austrian scholar Siegfried Beer suggested that, to facilitate Rüdiger's exfiltration from Istanbul, OSS may have assigned him the alias "Frank H. Rediker." Perhaps casting some doubt on this theory, in 1925 an individual named Frank Howard Rediker (born 13 April 1901) was serving as a U.S. vice consul in Hamburg, Germany. He had been appointed to the U.S. Department of State in Minnesota, his home state (he was born in West Concord, a small town 69 miles—111 kilometers—south of Minneapolis). Although Rediker had moved from a clerk job to a vice consul position on 15 September 1921 while serving in Nantes, France, it was not until 28 April 1923 that he was formally commissioned as a consular officer. (Source: *Register of the Department of State, January 1, 1925* [Washington Government Printing Office, 1925], pp. 58, 171.) Vice Consul Rediker may have been assigned to the U.S. Consulate in Istanbul in 1944 and his name on the diplomatic list may have prompted such speculation. It is also possible—particularly if Rediker and Rüdiger were of similar appearance—that OSS used Rediker's name (and possibly even his passport, although Rüdiger was seven years older than Rediker) to spirit Rüdiger to Cairo.
6. Neugebauer, *Resistance*, p. 43.
7. *Auszugsweise-Urteil.*
8. *Auszugsweise-Urteil.*
9. *Auszugsweise-Urteil.*
10. Thoma, *Mahner-Helfer-Patrioten*, p. 160; Stehle, "Pfarrhaus."
11. Roosevelt, *War Report*, p. 277; Persico, *Piercing the Reich*, p. 314.
12. Sartorti, *Biographie-Messner*, p. 7; Stehle, "Pfarrhaus."
13. *Auszugsweise-Urteil.*
14. Thoma, *Mahner-Helfer-Patrioten*, p. 158.
15. Hans Rieger, *Das Urteil wird jetzt vollstreckt* (Vienna: Europa Verlag, 1977); referenced excerpts viewed on 11 October 2016 at "Bericht Hans Rieger," denkmalpflege.blogsport.de/stadtspaziergang/bericht-hans-rieger/.
16. Neugebauer, *Resistance*, p. 168; The Vienna Regional Court (*Landgericht Wien*) still stands at Landesgerichtsstrasse 11 in Vienna's 8th District but has been renamed the Vienna Regional Criminal Court (*Landesgericht für Strafsachen Wien*).
17. Rieger, *Das Urteil wird jetzt vollstreckt*; "Bericht Hans Rieger."
18. Photographs of this guillotine appear in Neugebauer's book *The Austrian Resistance* (p. 45) and at doew.at/english/memorial-room-for-the-victims-of-the-gestapo-vienna/they-took-the-other-road-organized-resistance-in-austria.
19. Posch, "Caldonazzi."

20. DÖW, "Maier Heinrich," result from "victim search" tool, doew.at.

21. Thoma, *Mahner-Helfer-Patrioten*, p. 161.

22. Neugebauer, *Resistance*, p. 168.

23. Peter Diem and Ingeborg Schinnerl, eds., "Maier, Heinrich," accessed on 18 October 2016 austria-forum.org/af/Wissenssammlungen/Biographien/Maier,_Heinrich.

24. Thoma, *Mahner-Helfer-Patrioten*, p. 164.

25. *Auszugsweise-Urteil.*

26. Rieger, *Das Urteil wird jetzt vollstreckt*; "Bericht Hans Rieger."

27. Neugebauer, *Resistance*, p. 168.

28. *Auszugsweise-Urteil.*

29. Neugebauer, *Resistance*, p. 168; According to *Mahner-Helfer-Patrioten* (p. 162), Pastor Rieger recorded that Wyhnal was beheaded first, then Maier, and lastly Klepell.

30. Neugebauer, *Resistance*, p. 169.

31. *Volksgerichtshof-Urteil*, p. 7.

32. *Volksgerichtshof-Urteil*, p. 27.

33. *Volksgerichtshof-Urteil*, p. 7; Maier's Gestapo interrogator suggested that Legradi had delivered a different message to Karrer: "We still live and await the right moment that the call for assistance will come to us."

34. Gestapo, "Interrogations."

35. Neugebauer, *Resistance*, pp. 42–44.

36. *Volksgerichtshof-Urteil*, pp. 26–27.

37. *Volksgerichtshof-Urteil*, p. 27.

38. *Volksgerichtshof-Urteil*, pp. 1–3, 16–17.

39. *Volksgerichtshof-Urteil*, p. 17; Von Pausinger, "Bestätigung."

40. *Volksgerichtshof-Urteil*, pp. 9–10.

41. *Volksgerichtshof-Urteil*, pp. 27–28.

42. To protect his business interests in the Reich, Messner belonged to two Nazi-affiliated groups: In March 1938 he joined the *Nationalsozialistische Volkswohlfahrt* ("National Socialist People's Welfare," a social welfare organization established in 1933 after the Nazis rose to power in Germany), and in May 1938 he joined the *Deutsche Arbeitsfront* ("German Labor Front," the collective trade union that the Nazis established after dissolving all other unions). (Source: Sartorti, *Biographie-Messner*, p. 3.)

43. *Volksgerichtshof-Urteil*, pp. 5–6.

44. *Volksgerichtshof-Urteil*, pp. 5, 18–19.

45. Roosevelt, *War Report*, p. 277.

46. Sartorti, *Biographie-Messner*, p. 6; the primary source material for this passage, DÖW document 20000/W19, which includes Wagner's postwar testimony and a corroborating letter from Semperit, noted that Wagner (born 25 January 1921) was released from confinement on 5 April 1945 by advancing Soviet Red Army troops. According to Sartorti's *Biographie-Messner*, after the war Wagner married an Englishman named Reynolds and moved to Lincoln, England, a city of about 100,000 residents located approximately 140 miles (225 kilometers) north of London.

47. Ernst Martin, "Gedächtnisprotokoll" (Vienna: DÖW archives). Martin drafted this aide-mémoire after attending the 8 May 1946 interview of *SS-Oberscharführer* Josef Niedermayer at the U.S. Military Court, Dachau. The document included Niedermayer's verbatim statement about Messner; Niedermayer had been in charge of the Mauthausen "bunker," or prison block, where Messner had been held. Anti-Nazi Martin had been imprisoned at Mauthausen concentration camp where he had worked as a "prisoner-functionary" camp clerk. He later served as a witness at the war-crimes trials in Dachau.

48. Sartorti, *Biographie-Messner*, p. 6.

49. Martin, "Gedächtnisprotokoll."

50. According to Sartorti's *Biographie-Messner* (p. 6), at some point during the February/March 1945 time-frame, Messner may have been held—for unspecified reasons and for an undefined duration—at the regional court in Neunkirchen, a town of about 11,000 residents in the state of Lower Austria, about 40 miles (65 kilometers) south-southwest of Vienna.

51. Taylor, "DUPONT MISSION."

52. Persico, *Piercing the Reich*, p. 225.

53. Persico, *Piercing the Reich*, p. 225; Taylor, "DUPONT MISSION."

54. DÖW, doew.at.

55. Taylor, "DUPONT MISSION."

56. Taylor, "DUPONT MISSION."

57. Taylor, "DUPONT MISSION."

58. Martin, "Gedächtnisprotokoll."

59. Taylor, "DUPONT MISSION."

60. Taylor, "DUPONT MISSION."

61. The trade name of a cyanide product that was developed in Germany in 1922, originally for use as a pesticide.

62. Taylor, "DUPONT MISSION."

63. Sartorti, *Biographie-Messner*, pp. 6–7.

64. Taylor, "DUPONT MISSION."

65. Martin, "Gedächtnisprotokoll."

66. According to Taylor, the camp's SS guards had left in early May and had been replaced by members of the "Vienna fire-police."

67. Taylor, "DUPONT MISSION."

Chapter 22

1. U.S. Federal Bureau of Investigation, "Nazi Saboteurs and George Dasch," accessed

on 19 September 2016, fbi.gov/history/famous-cases/nazi-saboteurs-and-george-dasch.

2. FBI, "Nazi Saboteurs."
3. FBI, "Nazi Saboteurs."
4. FBI, "Nazi Saboteurs."
5. FBI, "Nazi Saboteurs."
6. Thoma, *Mahner-Helfer-Patrioten*, p. 156.
7. FBI, "Nazi Saboteurs."
8. FBI, "Nazi Saboteurs."
9. Francis MacDonnell, *Insidious Foes: The Axis Fifth Column and the American Home Front* (Oxford: Oxford University Press, 1995), p. 133.
10. FBI, "Duquesne Spy Ring," 12 March 1985; a scanned copy of this 16-page document is available on-line at vault.fbi.gov.
11. FBI, "Duquesne Spy Ring."
12. FBI, "Duquesne Spy Ring."
13. FBI, "Duquesne Spy Ring."
14. FBI, "Duquesne Spy Ring."
15. FBI, "Duquesne Spy Ring."
16. FBI, "Duquesne Spy Ring."
17. Peter Duffy, *Double Agent: The First Hero of World War II and How the FBI Outwitted and Destroyed a Nazi Spy Ring* (New York: Scribner, 2014), pp. 137, 181, 225, 319.
18. Duffy, *Double Agent*, pp. 150–151.
19. FBI, "Duquesne Spy Ring."
20. FBI, "Duquesne Spy Ring."
21. FBI, "Duquesne Spy Ring."
22. Boryanabooks, "Fritz Joubert Duquesne: Boer Avenger, German Spy, Munchausen Fantasist," 1 April 2014, accessed on 19 September 2016, boryanabooks.com/index.php?s=boer.
23. Duffy, *Double Agent*, p. 272.

Chapter 23

1. The Red Army's Vienna Offensive lasted from 2 to 13 April 1945.
2. Neugebauer, *Resistance*, pp. 168–169.
3. Sokal, "Widerstandstätigkeit," p. 1; Neugebauer, *Resistance*, p. 169.
4. The Johann-August-Malin Society, ed., *Verfolgung und Widerstand in Vorarlberg 1933–1945* (Bregenz, Vorarlberg: Fink's Verlag, 1985), pp. 101–102.
5. Persico, *Piercing the Reich*, p. 314; Stehle, "Pfarrhaus."
6. Persico, *Piercing the Reich*, p. 314.
7. Persico, *Piercing the Reich*, p. 313.
8. Stehle, "Pfarrhaus."
9. Persico, *Piercing the Reich*, p. 314.
10. Persico, *Piercing the Reich*, p. 314; Although this concert in Vienna may have been Issakides's last, an article on a website hosted by *Österreichischer Rundfunk* (ORF, the Austrian Broadcasting Corporation) recorded that Issakides had three postwar performances—at the Vienna Konzerthaus, at an unspecified venue in London, and at the Vienna Musikverein, possibly in that order. (Source: Kurt Scholz, "Gedanken für den Tag," 29 October 2015, accessed on 20 October 2016, oe1.orf.at/programm/418828.)
11. Rotter-Felix may be identifiable with Margarethe Felix (10 December 1908–27 July 1969), who is buried in Vienna's Ottakring Cemetery (Group 21, Row 1, Number 9). Also buried in this grave is Johann Felix, who may have been her husband.
12. Nohl may be identifiable with Egon Wenzel Nohl, born on 1 September 1914, who was buried in Vienna's Central Cemetery (Group 3, Row 45, Number 7) on 16 August 1989.
13. Beer, "ARCEL/CASSIA/REDBIRD," pp. 85–86.
14. U.S. National Archives, "Cable reporting that the Russians seized two people from the USDIC guards escorting the pair from Vienna to the American Zone in Austria for questioning, February 3, 1946," Record Group 226, Box 11, Entry 211, WN# 23562.
15. Beer, "ARCEL/CASSIA/REDBIRD," p. 85, citing "Detailed Interrogation Reports of Margarethe Felix née Rotter and Egon Nohl, 22 March 1946," *U.S. National Archives*, Record Group 226, Box 279, Entry 108A.
16. Persico, *Piercing the Reich*, p. 314.
17. *Volksgerichtshof-Urteil*, p. 3.
18. Thoma, *Mahner-Helfer-Patrioten*, p. 156.
19. Gestapo, "Interrogations."
20. Thoma, *Mahner-Helfer-Patrioten*, pp. 139, 156.
21. Persico, *Piercing the Reich*, p. 314; Fenyvesi's *The Brave Men from "Die Fledermaus"* (pp. 55–56) cites a 12 December 1945 SSU report that proposed giving Maier's surviving relatives U.S.$1,000. Perhaps the final amount that Ulmer passed—$2,500—represents payments of $1,000 each to Katharina and Elfriede, plus $500 in other unspecified considerations for the family.
22. Fenyvesi, "Fledermaus," p. 58.
23. Trudi is possibly identifiable with Trudi Fulterer (née Scheffknecht), who was born on 14 January 1921 and who died in Lustenau, Vorarlberg, on 7 January 2007.
24. Johann-August-Malin Society, *Verfolgung und Widerstand in Vorarlberg*, pp. 102, 292.
25. Molden, *Fires*, Figure 38 and caption.
26. Persico, *Piercing the Reich*, p. 315.

Chapter 24

1. Molden, *Star*, p. 180; Frederiksen, "Papers," Box 1, Folder 8.
2. Frederiksen, "Papers," Box 1, Folder 8.
3. Neugebauer, *Resistance*, p. 197.
4. Frederiksen, "Papers," Box 1, Folders 3, 8.
5. Frederiksen, "Papers," Box 1, Folders 3, 8.
6. Frederiksen, "Papers," Box 1, Folders 3, 8.
7. Molden, *Star*, pp. 224–225.
8. Frederiksen, "Papers," Box 1, Folder 8.
9. Frederiksen, "Papers," Box 1, Folder 8.
10. Wien Geschischte Wiki, "Eduard Jakob Sekler," *Stadt Wien*, accessed on 17 December 2015, wien.gv.at/wiki/index.php/Eduard_Jakob_Sekler.
11. Eduard Jacob Sekler is buried in Section 2, Group 8, Number 12. The headstone bears no dates and only one name, "Lenchen," possibly a nickname or term of endearment for his wife, Elisabeth, who died two years before he did.
12. The J. Paul Getty Trust and Eduard F. Sekler, "Spirit and Project: Art History Oral Documentation Project," an interview of Eduard F. Sekler by Richard Candida Smith, 25 February 1994, *Getty Research Institute*, Los Angeles, accessed on 30 September 2016, archive.org/stream/spiritprojectedu00sekl/spiritprojectedu00sekl_djvu.txt; Austria-Forum, ed., "Sekler, Eduard F.," accessed on 21 October 2016, austria-forum.org/af/AEIOU/Sekler%2C_Eduard_F.
13. Possibly identifiable with Father Willibald Berger of Schottenstift.
14. J. Paul Getty Trust and Sekler, "Spirit and Project."
15. In his oral history interview for The J. Paul Getty Trust's "Spirit and Project" series, Sekler explained that, if a high school graduate passed the *matura*, the Austrian exit examination that qualified students to apply for university-level education, and if the graduate immediately volunteered for military service (i.e., did not wait to be drafted), he would be required to serve for only one year, not for the regular conscript's two years.
16. J. Paul Getty Trust and Sekler, "Spirit and Project."
17. J. Paul Getty Trust and Sekler, "Spirit and Project."
18. Neugebauer, *Resistance*, pp. 214–215.
19. J. Paul Getty Trust and Sekler, "Spirit and Project"; According to Neugebauer's *The Austrian Resistance* (p. 215), the betrayal was perpetrated "by, among others, the proprietor of a well-known 'Maturaschule' or private tutoring institute."
20. Neugebauer, *Resistance*, pp. 214–215.
21. J. Paul Getty Trust and Sekler, "Spirit and Project."
22. J. Paul Getty Trust and Sekler, "Spirit and Project."
23. The Sudetenland comprised parts of former Czechoslovakia that in the prewar years had a majority of German-speaking residents. The area was ceded to Germany in 1938 under the terms of the controversial Munich Agreement. In the spring of 1939, Germany invaded and occupied the rest of Czechoslovakia.
24. Sokal, "Widerstandstätigkeit," p. 1 (source of all names in this section).
25. Sokal, "Widerstandstätigkeit," pp. 4–6 (source of all names in this section).
26. Sokal, "Widerstandstätigkeit," pp. 4–6 (source of all names in this section).
27. Johann-August-Malin Society, *Verfolgung und Widerstand in Vorarlberg*, pp. 102, 343.
28. Molden, *Fires*, pp. 69–71; Parlamentarischen Unterlagen des Vorarlberger Landtags, "Linder Anton (1880–1958) (Biografie)," accessed on 21 October 2016, suche.vorarlberg.at/vlr/vlr_gov.nsf/0/F38F71914EE63A37C125757700489613.
29. In his *OSS Oral History Project* interview (p. 15), former OSS officer Albert Jolis noted that Ed Lindner (1918–2007), a native of Vienna, found his way first to Algeria and later to the OSS. While he was stationed in Italy, Lindner worked on OSS propaganda operations directed against the Reich, and thus may have been indirectly involved with CASSIA through OSS-Istanbul or OSS-Bern.
30. Gestapo, "Interrogations" (source of all names in this section).
31. Rüdiger, "Affidavit" (source of preceding names in this section).
32. Thomas Rüdiger, e-mail message to author, 6 November 2016; Rüdiger, "Affidavit."
33. According to Neugebauer's *The Austrian Resistance* (p. 90), in the early years of the war Holzmeister worked in Turkey with resistance-minded fellow architects Herbert Eichholzer and Margarete Schütte-Lihotzky, who were functionaries of the Austrian Communist Party. In late 1940 Eichholzer and Schütte-Lihotzky returned to Vienna on a resistance operation and in early 1941 they were betrayed and arrested. Eichholzer (1903–1943) was executed and Schütte-Lihotzky (1897–2000) was sent to prison.
34. Beer, "ARCEL/CASSIA/REDBIRD," p. 80.
35. *Volksgerichtshof-Urteil*, p. 20.
36. Possibly identifiable with Regina Böhm

(1874–1956), who is buried in Vienna's Jedlesee Cemetery (Group 3, Row 1A, Number 17).

37. Beer, "ARCEL/CASSIA/REDBIRD," p. 77.

38. Although some references spell her name Wilma, a 1 August 1945 Semperit document, which bears her typewritten name and her signature, recorded her preferred spelling as Vilma. (Source: DÖW archives.)

39. Beer, "ARCEL/CASSIA/REDBIRD," p. 78.

Chapter 25

1. Rubin, *Istanbul Intrigues*, p. 178.
2. Neugebauer, *Resistance*, p. 151.
3. While scores of books have been written on persuasion, many of these were intended for people involved in marketing and sales, and as such their content is sometimes not readily transferable to the work of field intelligence operations. However, in his 25 years of experience in the practical application of persuasion, the author discovered one recent title that merits singling out: Jim Randell's *The Skinny on the Art of Persuasion: How to Move Minds* (Westport, Connecticut: Rand Media, 2010). This slender book describes in simplified but effective terms "the principles, techniques, and strategies" (from its introduction) involved in the practice of successful persuasion—although, of course, some inimitable human qualities are also required to make these techniques work. Further, Randell's distinction between manipulation and persuasion (item 31 in the book) tracks perfectly with what the author has observed and experienced over the years, and the final sentence of the referenced paragraph reflects this shared opinion.
4. While every word has different meanings and shades of meaning, consider the two definitions, which were drawn from the Merriam-Webster dictionary: manipulate—"to control or play upon by artful, unfair, or insidious means especially to one's own advantage"; and persuade—"to cause (someone) to do something by asking, arguing, or giving reasons."
5. Stewart Alsop and Thomas Braden, *Sub Rosa: The OSS and American Espionage* (New York: Harcourt, Brace & World, 1964), p. 10.
6. Evan Thomas, "Spymaster General: The adventures of Wild Bill Donovan and the "Oh So Social" O.S.S.," *Vanity Fair* (on-line version), 3 March 2011, accessed 13 September 2016, vanityfair.com/culture/2011/03/wild-bill-donovan201103.
7. Roosevelt, *War Report*, pp. 271–272.
8. Roosevelt, *War Report*, pp. 271–272.

Chapter 26

1. Persico, *Piercing the Reich*, p. 57.
2. Fenyvesi, "Fledermaus," p. 55.
3. CIA, "Oral History Project: Jolis," p. 30.
4. CIA, "Oral History Project: Jolis," p. 68.
5. Roosevelt, *War Report*, p. 272.
6. Roosevelt, *War Report*, p. 272.
7. Rubin, *Istanbul Intrigues*, p. 224.
8. Rubin, *Istanbul Intrigues*, p. 224.
9. Roosevelt, *War Report*, p. 269.
10. Roosevelt, *War Report*, p. 272.
11. Rubin, *Istanbul Intrigues*, p. 224; Cedric Seager (1902–1959) was the eldest son of British subject Walter Seager (1876–1934), the founder of an eponymous telecommunications-supply company in Istanbul. Cedric's great-grandfather Edward (1809–1854) had left Britain in the late 1840s and had settled with his family in Istanbul (at the time known as Constantinople), where he had worked in the shipping industry. Cedric acquired U.S. citizenship in 1942 through marriage and began work with OSS that same year. (Source: "Seager Family of Bebek: Four Generations," accessed 23 January 2017, levantineheritage.com/seager.htm.)
12. Rubin, *Istanbul Intrigues*, p. 226.
13. Thomas N. Moon and Carl F. Eifler, *The Deadliest Colonel* (New York: Vantage Press, 1975), pp. 337–338; while there are many published references to OSS Detachment 101's Presidential Distinguished Unit Citation, this book includes a copy of the document.
14. Roosevelt, *War Report*, p. 273.
15. Roosevelt, *War Report*, p. 271.
16. Fenyvesi, "Fledermaus," p. 43.
17. Fenyvesi, "Fledermaus," p. 48.
18. Fenyvesi, "Fledermaus," p. 43.
19. Breitman, "Other Responses to the Holocaust," p. 53.
20. Rubin, *Istanbul Intrigues*, p. 170.
21. Roosevelt, *War Report*, p. 271.
22. Rubin, *Istanbul Intrigues*, pp. 189–190.
23. Breitman, "Other Responses to the Holocaust," p. 53.
24. Von Hassell and MacRae, *Alliance of Enemies*, p. 182.
25. Von Hassell and MacRae, *Alliance of Enemies*, p. 182.
26. Fenyvesi, "Fledermaus," p. 55.
27. Fred Herok may be identifiable with Alfred Herok (1903–1986), who is buried in Vienna's Feuerhalle Simmering Cemetery (Section 7, Ring 3, Group 6, Number 28).

28. Fenyvesi, "Fledermaus," p. 55.
29. Beer, "ARCEL/CASSIA/REDBIRD," p. 87.
30. Breitman, "Other Responses to the Holocaust," p. 52.
31. Fenyvesi, "Fledermaus," p. 54.
32. Roosevelt, *War Report*, p. 271.
33. Petersen, *Hitler's Doorstep*, pp. 238–239.
34. Petersen, *Hitler's Doorstep*, p. 285.

Chapter 27

1. Karsten Damen, e-mail message to author, 15 March 2016; Frederiksen, "Papers," Box 1, Folder 3.
2. Frederiksen, "Papers: Biographical note"; Frederiksen, "Papers," Box 1, Folder 8.
3. Frederiksen, "Papers: Biographical note"; Frederiksen, "Papers," Box 1, Folder 8.
4. Frederiksen, "Papers," Box 1, Folder 8.
5. Frederiksen, "Papers: Biographical note"; Frederiksen, "Papers," Box 1, Folder 8.
6. Frederiksen, "Papers: Biographical note"; Frederiksen, "Papers," Box 1, Folder 8.
7. Frederiksen, "Papers: Biographical note."
8. Frederiksen, "Papers: Biographical note."
9. Frederiksen, "Papers: Biographical note."
10. Frederiksen, "Papers: Biographical note"; Death Certificate for Harald Frederiksen, 9 August 1970 (issued on 12 August 1970 by Leesburg Hospital, Leesburg, Virginia), State File Number 70 024919, Commonwealth of Virginia, Department of Health, Bureau of Vital Records and Health Statistics, Richmond, Virginia (Karsten Damen provided the author a scanned image of the original document on 20 March 2017).
11. Karsten Damen, e-mail message to author, 18 January 2017, citing the memories of his late mother, one of Frederiksen's Danish cousins; and Karsten Damen, e-mail message to the author, 20 March 2017.
12. Neugebauer, *Resistance*, p. 152.
13. Siegfried Beer, conversation with author, 13 August 2016.
14. Gerald Spitzner/Venite-Austria, "Heinrich Maier Oratorium," accessed on 26 October 2016, venite-austria.jimdo.com/heinrich-maier-gedenken/.
15. Michael T. Calvert, "Austria Turns 1,000 in 1996," *Encyclopædia Britannica*, accessed on 4 October 2016, britannica.com/topic/Austria-turns-1000–1011929.
16. Sartorti, *Biographie-Messner*, p. 8.
17. George Howe, *Call It Treason* (New York: The Viking Press, 1949), p. 5.
18. Neugebauer, *Resistance*, p. 259.
19. Standesamtsverband Pottenstein (Pottenstein, Austria), e-mail messages to author, 27/28 October 2015; Sartorti, *Biographie-Messner*, p. 2.
20. In Neugebauer's *The Austrian Resistance* (p. 167), Sokal's birthdate appears as 26 May 1903. However, other documents—some that Sokal herself drafted—and her published memoir of the war's final year, *Das andere Wien: Erlebtes aus den Jahren 1944/45*, record her birth month as March.
21. Legradi (Sokal), *Das andere Wien*, p. 9.
22. Neugebauer, *Resistance*, p. 168.
23. Legradi (Sokal), *Das andere Wien*, p. 9.
24. Legradi (Sokal), *Das andere Wien*, p. 9.
25. Jan von Flocken and Eberhard Vogt, "STASI: Wolfs Prinzessin in Wien," *Focus*, Number 10, 1999, accessed on 12 November 2015, focus.de/politik/deutschland/stasi-wolfs-prinzessin-in-wien_aid_176067.html.
26. The East-West Trade Bureau's address has also appeared as Pacassistrasse 85 in Vienna's 13th District.
27. Von Flocken and Vogt, "STASI."
28. Von Flocken and Vogt, "STASI."
29. Von Flocken and Vogt, "STASI."
30. The author viewed a copy of the death announcement among the papers that Erika Thurner graciously lent.
31. Although primarily a women's camp, the Ravensbrück complex included a small camp for men, which the SS opened in 1941.
32. Encyclopædia Britannica, ed., "Karl Seitz: Austrian Politician," accessed on 26 October 2016, britannica.com/biography/Karl-Seitz.
33. Helga Maria Wolf, "Fellinger, Karl," ed. Ingeborg Schinnerl, accessed on 12 November 2015, austria-forum.org/af/Wissenssammlungen/Biographien/Fellinger%2C_Karl.
34. As of 2016, Aristides (born 1923) lived in the Principality of Monaco but remained a majority owner of the family rug store, Orient-Teppiche Issakides, at Fleischmarkt 13 in Vienna.
35. Beer, "ARCEL/CASSIA/REDBIRD," p. 88.
36. Wolf, "Fellinger."
37. Wolf, "Fellinger."
38. Wolf, "Fellinger."
39. Handwritten letter by Barbara Fellinger, 4 March 1975, addressed to "Herr Professor," DÖW archives.
40. Persico, "Papers," Box 27, Folder 40 (Issikides [sic], Barbara).
41. Wolf, "Fellinger."
42. Persico, "Papers," Box 27, Folder 40.
43. For more on the Ephrussi family, the author recommends *The Hare with Amber Eyes*,

a memoir by Edmund de Waal, Ignace von Ephrussi's great-great-grandson.

44. Rathkolb, *The Paradoxical Republic*, pp. 243–244.

45. Rathkolb, *The Paradoxical Republic*, pp. 243–244.

46. Feldman, *Austrian Banks*, p. 391.

47. "Stink in the Creditanstalt," *Time* (magazine), 18 August 1952.

48. Semperit AG, *Partner: the international Semperit magazine*, Issue 1, 2015, pp. 9–10.

49. Peter Diem, "Caldonazzi, Walter," ed. Ingeborg Schinnerl, accessed on 12 November 2015, austria-forum.org/af/Wissenssammlungen/Biographien/Caldonazzi%2C_Walter.

50. Thomas Rüdiger, e-mail message to author, 6 November 2016.

51. Semperit Gummiwerke AG, certification letter for "Josef G. Ridiger" (sic), 1 August 1945, signed by Semperit officials Vilma Heindl, Franz Schuster, Karl Klose, Erwin Rind, and Viktor Horwitz (Vienna: DÖW archives).

52. Thomas Rüdiger, e-mail message to author, 6 November 2016.

53. Thomas Rüdiger, e-mail message to author, 6 November 2016.

54. Thomas Rüdiger, e-mail message to author, 6 November 2016.

55. Thomas Rüdiger, e-mail message to author, 6 November 2016.

56. Thomas Rüdiger, e-mail message to author, 6 November 2016.

57. Thomas Rüdiger, e-mail message to author, 6 November 2016.

58. Rubin, *Istanbul Intrigues*, p. 201.

59. Rubin, *Istanbul Intrigues*, Preface, pp. xiii–xv.

60. "Lanning MacFarland Dies at 73," *Chicago Tribune*; Law Bulletin Publishing Company, "About the Law Bulletin Publishing Company," accessed on 26 September 2016, lawbulletin.com/company.

61. Rubin, *Istanbul Intrigues*, pp. 135–136; "Lanning MacFarland Dies at 73," *Chicago Tribune*.

62. "Lanning MacFarland Dies at 73," *Chicago Tribune*.

63. "Lanning MacFarland Dies at 73," *Chicago Tribune*; Montana Historical Society Research Center Archives, "Historical Note," in *Intermountain Lumber Company photograph collection, 1947–1962*, Helena, Montana, accessed on 30 September 2016, archiveswest.orbiscascade.org/ark:/80444/xv51760.

64. "Lanning MacFarland Dies at 73," *Chicago Tribune*.

65. "Lanning MacFarland Dies at 73," *Chicago Tribune*.

66. Hays and Watts, "Archibald Frederick Coleman."

67. According to *Istanbul Intrigues* (p. 166), Coleman was "a Treasury agent" in Mexico in the 1930s.

68. Hays and Watts, "Archibald Frederick Coleman."

69. Hays and Watts, "Archibald Frederick Coleman."

70. Breitman, "Other Responses to the Holocaust," p. 50.

71. Rubin, *Istanbul Intrigues*, p. 166.

72. Hays and Watts, "Archibald Frederick Coleman."

73. Hays and Watts, "Archibald Frederick Coleman."

74. Hays and Watts, "Archibald Frederick Coleman."

75. Hays and Watts, "Archibald Frederick Coleman"; WHRO-TV, the PBS-member station that services the Hampton Roads area of southern Virginia (essentially Norfolk, Portsmouth, and Newport News).

76. Hays and Watts, "Archibald Frederick Coleman."

77. Schafranek and Hurton, "Netz."

78. *Auszugsweise-Urteil.*

79. *Auszugsweise-Urteil.*

80. Pressespiegel (a German news-monitoring and -collection service), a synopsis of German-language newspaper articles on the coverage and aftermath of the Rechnitz Massacre trial, *Burgenländische Freiheit*: 27 June 1948, 4 July 1948, 18 July 1948, and 25 July 1948 issues; *Fries Burgenland*: 2 July 1948, 9 July 1948, 16 July 1948, 24 June 1951, and 1 July 1951 issues; *Der Abend*: 24 July 1948, and 26 July 1948 issues; *Burgenländische Volksblatt*: 30 June 1951 and 28 July 1951 issues; accessed on 30 September 2016, kreuzstadl.net/downloads/pressespiegel_1948_51.pdf.

81. Pressespiegel, Rechnitz Massacre articles.

82. Pressespiegel, Rechnitz Massacre articles.

83. Stefan Klemp, "Good comrades," 29 October 2007, signandsight.com/features/1591.html, accessed on 25 September 2016.

84. Pressespiegel, Rechnitz Massacre articles.

85. Pressespiegel, Rechnitz Massacre articles.

86. Sacha Batthyany, "Das Grauen von Rechnitz," *Süddeutsche Zeitung Magazin*, Munich: issue 16/2010, sz-magazin.sueddeutsche.de/texte/anzeigen/33506/2, accessed on 25 September 2016.

87. Batthyany, "Das Grauen von Rechnitz."

88. Fulterer Drawer Slide Systems, accessed on 26 October 2016, fulterer.at/en/.

89. Rubin, *Istanbul Intrigues*, p. 197.

90. Schafranek and Hurton, "Netz."

91. Aronson, "OSS X-2," p. 95.

92. Persico, *Piercing the Reich*, p. 312; Tom Hawkins, "America's First SEa, Air, Land Commando—Lieutenant Jack Taylor, USNR," *BLAST Magazine* (UDT-SEAL Association), Third Quarter Edition, September 2002, accessed on 30 September 2016, 11tharmoreddivision.com/history/first_seal_jack_taylor.htm.

93. Persico, *Piercing the Reich*, pp. 312–313.

94. Hawkins, "America's First SEa, Air, Land Commando."

95. Taylor, "DUPONT MISSION."

96. Hawkins, "America's First SEa, Air, Land Commando."

97. Jewish Virtual Library, "Franz Ziereis," accessed on 26 October 2016, jewishvirtuallibrary.org/jsource/biography/Ziereis.html.

98. Persico, *Piercing the Reich*, p. 277.

99. Tomaz Jardim, *The Mauthausen Trial: American Military Justice in Germany* (Cambridge: Harvard University Press, 2012), pp. 219–221.

100. Jardim, *The Mauthausen Trial*, p. 75.

101. Jardim, *The Mauthausen Trial*, p. 198.

102. Christoph Freyer, "Eduard F. Sekler," *Architektenlexikon Wien 1770–1945*, 1 October 2013 (updated 19 December 2014), accessed on 26 October 2016, architektenlexikon.at/de/1433.htm.

103. Freyer, "Eduard F. Sekler."

104. Freyer, "Eduard F. Sekler."

105. Munroe Center for the Arts, "Pat Sekler, Watercolorist, Photographer, Art Historian," accessed on 26 October 2016, munroecenter.org/patricia-sekler-watercolor photography.html.

106. Bruno Maldoner, "Architekt Sepp Stein: 1920–2008," in *Kunstruktiv 269: Amtliche Nachrichten*, September/October 2008 issue, p. 30.

Afterword

1. On 1 April 1944 James G. O'Conor assumed control of OSS-Istanbul from MacFarland. O'Conor left Istanbul on 30 May 1944 and appointed a fairly junior OSS officer, Robert Miner, to serve as acting chief until 15 June 1944, when Frank Wisner (1909–1965), who had overseen OSS's southeastern Europe operations, became chief of OSS-Istanbul, which by that time had seen its staff reduced by some 50 percent. Wisner, a staunch opponent of DOGWOOD, focused largely on eliminating all of the cases that the errant agent network had tainted. After the war Wisner rose to the senior ranks of CIA, serving as the head of the Directorate of Plans (today's Directorate of Operations) and as Chief of Station LONDON. After a long battle with mental illness, he retired from CIA in the early 1960s and a few years later died by his own hand.

2. Rubin, *Istanbul Intrigues*, p. 201.

3. "Lanning MacFarland Dies at 73," *Chicago Tribune*.

4. Rubin, *Istanbul Intrigues*, Preface, pp. xiv–xv.

5. Rubin, *Istanbul Intrigues*, Preface, p. xiv.

6. J. Ted Hartman, *Tank Driver: With the 11th Armored from the Battle of the Bulge to VE Day* (Bloomington: Indiana University Press, 2014), p. 111.

7. Stefan Zweig, *The World of Yesterday*, trans. Anthea Bell (Lincoln: University of Nebraska Press, 2013), p. 191.

Appendix I

1. K.S. may be the initials of Kaiser's given names, or may be an acronym for Gestapo rank *Kriminalsekretär*, which is often translated as detective major; *Kriminalsekretär* was essentially equivalent to a sergeant major in the Wehrmacht. It is possible that Kaiser is identifiable with Gestapo-Vienna officer Rudolf Kaiser. Volume four of Franz Weisz's exhaustive *Die geheime Staatspolizei Staatspolizeileitstelle Wien: 1938–1945; Organisation, Arbeitsweise und personale Belange* (University of Vienna, 1991) documented Gestapo-Vienna officer Rudolf Kaiser's severe mistreatment of prisoners and his involvement in the deaths of prisoners during detention.

2. It is possible—though perhaps unlikely—that this summary, which lacks Kaiser's customary signature at its end, is missing its concluding passage(s).

3. According to Doew.at, about 80 percent of the officers and employees of Gestapo-Vienna had previously served with the Austrian police; it is therefore probable that Kaiser was originally an Austrian police officer.

4. "DRA." appears to refer to Maier's citizenship, the Third Reich, which in German is rendered *Drittes Reich*. "Rk." is an unknown abbreviation.

5. A town in the Austrian state of Styria known for its history of mining and for the Gösser beer brewery. It is about 100 miles—160 kilometers—southwest of Vienna.

6. As noted previously, Maier received his doctorate in philosophy in 1930, and his doctorate in theology in 1942. Kaiser transposed the degrees and got the second date wrong.

7. A misspelled reference to Schwarzau am

Steinfeld, a small town in Lower Austria approximately 40 miles—65 kilometers—south of Vienna.

8. A small town about 19 miles—31 kilometers—west of Schwarzau am Steinfeld, at the foot of the Rax Mountains.

9. A town of around 20,000 residents approximately 8.5 miles—some 14 kilometers—south-southwest of Vienna.

10. The *Ostmärkische Sturmscharen*, which translates loosely as "Eastern March Storm Troops," was an Austrian paramilitary organization established in 1930 to counter the ambitions of the *Heimwehr* ("Home Guard"), a nationalist/militarist group similar to Germany's *Freikorps*. The *Österreichischen Jungvolk*—literally, the "Austrian Young People"—was a national group that existed for about two years until the Anschluss; it was the youth counterpart of the *Vaterländischen Front*, the "Fatherland Front," the Austrofascist political organization founded in 1933 by Chancellor Dollfuss. As an interesting aside, in its final judgment the People's Tribunal wrote that Caldonazzi and von Pausinger had previously belonged to the *Heimwehr* and the *Vaterländischen Front*.

11. During the Second World War, Ritsch's military rank—*Obergefreiter* in German—was roughly equivalent to a senior lance corporal. (The next lowest rank, *Gefreiter*, was essentially a lance corporal. As an aside, when Adolf Hitler was demobilized after the First World War, he held the rank of *Gefreiter*.)

12. This appears to be a reference to Messner's status as a naturalized Brazilian citizen.

13. The capital of Liechtenstein.

Appendix II

1. Pirker, *Subversion*; the preceding and following details represent a translated précis of a chapter titled "Gedye und die Maier-Messner-Gruppe" (pp. 252–256), to which the author has added some minor contextual commentary for the wider CASSIA story; only direct quotes from Pirker's narrative will subsequently be cited by page number.

2. Pirker, *Subversion*, pp. 254–255.

3. Pirker, *Subversion*, p. 252.

Appendix III

1. Beer, "ARCEL/CASSIA/REDBIRD," p. 81.

2. Beer, "ARCEL/CASSIA/REDBIRD," p. 81.

3. Beer, "ARCEL/CASSIA/REDBIRD," p. 81.

4. Beer, "ARCEL/CASSIA/REDBIRD," pp. 81–82.

5. Yale Law School, "The Moscow Conference."

6. Beer, "ARCEL/CASSIA/REDBIRD," p. 82.

7. Beer, "ARCEL/CASSIA/REDBIRD," pp. 88–89.

8. To wit, "ARCEL has pledged itself to supply [OSS] currently with military, economic, and political intelligence, and to create and organize subversive groups in preparation for action at a time to be agreed upon in the future," "ARCEL undertakes by this agreement to develop a Courier service to Istanbul or other possible points, to insure a regular flow of the substantial volume of required intelligence," and "ARCEL undertakes to organize active subversive warfare against the enemy."

9. Beer, "ARCEL/CASSIA/REDBIRD," pp. 92–95.

Bibliography

Alsop, Stewart, and Thomas Braden. *Sub Rosa: The OSS and American Espionage*. New York: Harcourt, Brace & World, 1964.

Appleton, Tom. "Nachrichten vom Eingang zur Hölle." *Telepolis*, 14 July 2008. Accessed 14 September 2016. heise.de.

"Auszugsweise Abschrift aus dem Urteil des Volksgerichtshofes Berlin, 5. Senat, Geschäftszahlen," 28 October 1944. Vienna: Dokumentationsarchiv des österreichischen Widerstandes (DÖW) archives.

Bankier, David, ed. *Secret Intelligence and the Holocaust*. New York: Enigma Books, 2006.

Batthyany, Sacha. "Das Grauen von Rechnitz." *Süddeutsche Zeitung Magazin*, Munich: issue 16/2010. Accessed on 25 September 2016. sz-magazin.sueddeutsche.de/texte/anzeigen/33506/2.

Beer, Siegfried. "'ARCEL/CASSIA/REDBIRD': Die Widerstandsgruppe Maier-Messner und der amerikanische Kriegsgeheimdienst OSS in Bern, Istanbul und Algier 1943/44." *Jahrbuch 1993*. Vienna: DÖW, 1993.

Best, S. Payne. *The Venlo Incident: A True Story of Double-Dealing, Captivity, and a Murderous Nazi Plot*. New York: Skyhorse Publishing, 2010.

Boryanabooks. "Fritz Joubert Duquesne: Boer Avenger, German Spy, Munchausen Fantasist," 1 April 2014. Accessed on 19 September 2016. boryanabooks.com/index.php?s=boer.

Bradsher, Greg. "A Time to Act: The Beginning of the Fritz Kolbe Story, 1900–1943, Part 3." *Prologue Magazine*, Spring 2002, Vol. 34, No. 1. Accessed on 30 September 2016. archives.gov/publications/prologue/2002/spring/fritz-kolbe-3.html.

Breitman, Richard, et al., eds. *U.S. Intelligence and the Nazis*. Washington, D.C.: National Archives Trust Fund, 2004.

Broucek, Peter. *Militärischer Widerstand: Studien zur österreichischen Staatsgesinnung und NS-Abwehr*. Vienna: Böhlau Verlag, 2008.

Büchele, Martina, Semperit Group. E-mail message to author, 19 January 2016.

Calvert, Michael T. "Austria Turns 1,000 in 1996." *Encyclopædia Britannica*. Accessed on 4 October 2016. britannica.com/topic/Austria-turns-1000–1011929.

Central Intelligence Agency, U.S. "Office of Strategic Services (OSS) Oral History Project Transcripts: Albert E. Jolis" (interviewed by Siegfried Beer on 8 May 1997). *CIA Center for the Study of Intelligence*. College Park, Maryland: U.S. National Archives.

Central Intelligence Agency, U.S. "Office of Strategic Services (OSS) Oral History Project Transcripts: Fritz P. Molden" (interviewed by Siegfried Beer on 5 November 1996). *CIA Center for the Study of Intelligence*. College Park, Maryland: U.S. National Archives.

Chicago Pneumatic. "History: decades of innovation." Accessed on 27 September 2016. cp.com/usen/whoweare/history/.

Churchill, Winston S. *The Gathering Storm*. New York: Houghlin Mifflin Harcourt, 1985.

Coast Guard, U.S. "USS *Monticello*, AP-61." Accessed on 24 December 2016. uscg.mil/history/webcutters/AP61_Monticello.pdf.

Continental AG. "Continental AG History." Accessed on 26 October 2016. fundinguniverse.com/company-histories/continental-ag-history/.

Crankshaw, Edward. *The Fall of the House of Habsburg*. New York: Popular Library, 1963.

Creditanstalt-Bankverein—"Stink in the Creditanstalt." *Time*, 18 August 1952.

Damen, Karsten. E-mail messages to author, 15 March 2016 and 18 January 2017.

Delattre, Lucas. *A Spy at the Heart of the Third Reich: The Extraordinary Story of Fritz Kolbe, America's Most Important Spy in World War II*. Translated by George A. Holoch, Jr. New York: Grove Press, 2005.

De Waal, Edmund. *The Hare with Amber Eyes: A Hidden Inheritance*. New York: Picador, 2010.

Diem, Peter. "Caldonazzi, Walter." Edited by Ingeborg Schinnerl. Accessed on 12 November 2015. austria-forum.org/af/Wissenssammlungen/Biographien/Caldonazzi%2C_Walter.

Diem, Peter, and Ingeborg Schinnerl, eds. "Maier, Heinrich." Accessed on 18 October 2016. austria-forum.org/af/Wissenssammlungen/Biographien/Maier,_Heinrich.

Doew.at. Searchable on-line data holdings of DÖW. Accessed extensively from 15 October 2015 to 15 September 2016.

Dollfuss—"Engelbert Dollfuss: Chancellor of Austria." *Encyclopædia Britannica*. Accessed on 11 October 2016. britannica.com/biography/Engelbert-Dollfuss.

Dreyer—"Carl Ernst Dreyer." *Genealogia Pernambucana*. Accessed 24 December 2016. araujo.eti.br/familia.asp?numPessoa=44232.

Duffy, Peter. *Double Agent: The First Hero of World War II and How the FBI Outwitted and Destroyed a Nazi Spy Ring*. New York: Scribner, 2014.

Ender—"Dr. Otto Ender 1875–1960." *Vorarlberg Chronik*. Accessed 21 October 2016. apps.vol.at/tools/chronik/viewpage.aspx?viewtype=artikel&id=94&left=artikel.

Ender—"Otto Ender: Chancellor of Austria." *Encyclopædia Britannica*. Accessed on 16 September 2016. britannica.com/biography/Otto-Ender.

Epictetus. *The Golden Sayings of Epictetus*. Translated by Hastings Crossley. New York: P.F. Collier & Son, 1909.

Federal Bureau of Investigation, U.S. "Duquesne Spy Ring," 12 March 1985. vault.fbi.gov.

Federal Bureau of Investigation, U.S. "Nazi Saboteurs and George Dasch." Accessed on 19 September 2016. fbi.gov/history/famous-cases/nazi-saboteurs-and-george-dasch.

Feldman, Gerald D. *Austrian Banks in the Period of National Socialism*. Cambridge: Cambridge University Press, 2015.

Fenyvesi, Charles. "The Brave Men from 'Die Fledermaus': OSS-Istanbul and Austrian Resistance 1943/44." *Journal for Intelligence, Propaganda and Security Studies*, Volume 3, Number 2, 2009.

Fermor, Patrick Leigh. *A Time of Gifts*. New York Review of Books, 2005.

Frederiksen, Harald Sattler. "Harald S. Frederiksen Papers" and "Biographical note." *Georgetown University Library Special Collections Research Center*. Collection identifier GTM.GAMMS450. Donated by Harry P. Travis, 2002.

Freyer, Christoph. "Eduard F. Sekler." *Architektenlexikon Wien 1770–1945*, 1 October 2013 (updated 19 December 2014). Accessed on 26 October 2016. architektenlexikon.at/de/1433.htm.

Fulterer Drawer Slide Systems. Accessed on 26 October 2016. fulterer.at/en/.

Gedye, G.E.R. *Fallen Bastions*. London: Left Book Club, 1939.

Gedye, G.E.R. *Introducing Austria*. London: Methuen & Co., 1955.

Geheime Staatspolizei-Staatspolizeileitstelle Wien. Interrogation reports and related documents on Heinrich Maier, prepared by Gestapo-Vienna officer K.S. Kaiser, dated 28 March 1944, 29 March 1944, 5 April 1944, 7 April 1944, 25 April 1944, 27 April 1944, 5 June 1944, 10 June 1944, and 22 June 1944. Vienna: DÖW archives. Originally retrieved circa 2010 by Austrian author Hans Schafranek from Bundesarchiv Berlin, Aussenstelle Dahlwitz-Hoppegarten.

Gisevius, Hans Bernd. *To the Bitter End.* Translated by Richard and Clara Winston. Boston: The Riverside Press, 1947.

Glaubauf, Karl. "Forstwirt Widerstamdskämpfer Walter Caldonazzi." Accessed on 15 January 2016. austria-forum.org/af/Wissenssammlungen/Biographien/Caldonazzi,_Walter.

Graber, Renate. "Ein übertypischer Österreicher." *Der Standard*, 30 November 2006. Accessed on 6 October 2016. derstandard.at/2678171/Ein-uebertypischer-Oesterreicher.

Hartman, J. Ted. *Tank Driver: With the 11th Armored from the Battle of the Bulge to VE Day.* Bloomington: Indiana University Press, 2014.

Hawkins, Tom. "America's First SEa, Air, Land Commando—Lieutenant Jack Taylor, USNR." *BLAST Magazine* (UDT-SEAL Association), Third Quarter Edition, September 2002. Accessed on 30 September 2016. 11tharmoreddivision.com/history/first_seal_jack_taylor.htm.

Hays, Jakon, and Maureen Watts. "Archibald Frederick Coleman—AKA 'Snapdragon.'" *The Virginian-Pilot*, 2 December 2015. Accessed on 21 May 2016. pilotonline.com/news/local/history/dusting-off-stones/archibald-frederick-coleman—-aka-snapdragon/article_24e77609-ce00–568a-b639-b50fbbcb71e0.html.

Hornbostel, Caleb. *Construction Materials: Types, Uses and Applications.* New York: John Wiley & Sons, 1991.

Howe, George. *Call It Treason.* New York: The Viking Press, 1949.

Ingrao, Charles, and Franz A.J. Szabo, eds. *The Germans and The East.* West Lafayette, Indiana: Purdue University Press, 2007.

Issakides, Barbara. Handwritten letter by Barbara Fellinger (née Issakides) to "Herr Professor" (former DÖW director Herbert Steiner), 4 March 1975. DÖW archives.

Italy, Government of. *Astat info*, No. 38, 06/2012. (Population census, 2012.)

Jardim, Tomaz. *The Mauthausen Trial: American Military Justice in Germany.* Cambridge: Harvard University Press, 2012.

The Johann-August-Malin Society, ed. *Verfolgung und Widerstand in Vorarlberg 1933–1945.* Bregenz, Vorarlberg: Fink's Verlag, 1985.

Killen, John. *The Luftwaffe: A History.* South Yorkshire, England: Pen & Sword Military Classics, 2003.

Klein, Dieter, Martin Kupf, and Robert Schediwy, eds. *Stadtbildverluste Wien—Ein Rückblick auf fünf Jahrzehnte.* Vienna: LIT Verlag, 2004.

Klemp, Stefan. "Good comrades," 29 October 2007. Accessed on 25 September 2016. signandsight.com/features/1591.html.

Kniefacz, Katharina, and Herbert Posch. "Heinrich Maier." *Gedenkbuch für die Opfer des Nationalsozialismus an der Universität Wien 1938.* Accessed on 10 October 2016. gedenkbuch.univie.ac.at/.

Korotin, Ilse, ed. *biographiA: Lexicon österreichischer Frauen, Band 02, I-O.* Vienna: Böhlau Verlag, 2016.

Lasinger-Guserl, Anna, Semperit Group. E-mail message to author, 25 October 2016.

Law Bulletin Publishing Company. "About the Law Bulletin Publishing Company." Accessed on 26 September 2016. lawbulletin.com/company.

Legradi (Sokal), Helene. *Das andere Wien: Erlebtes aus den Jahren 1944/45.* Edited by Gerhard Schäffer and Erika Thurner. Vienna-Salzburg: Geyer Edition, 1989.

Lepage, Jean-Denis G.G. *Aircraft of the Luftwaffe, 1935–1945: An Illustrated Guide.* Jefferson, North Carolina: McFarland, 2009.

"Linder Anton (1880–1958) (Biografie)." *Parlamentarischen Unterlagen des Vorarlberger Landtags.* Accessed on 21 October 2016. suche.vorarlberg.at/vlr/vlr_gov.nsf/0/F38F71914EE63A37C125757700489613.

MacDonnell, Francis. *Insidious Foes: The Axis Fifth Column and the American Home Front.* Oxford: Oxford University Press, 1995.

MacFarland—"Lanning MacFarland Dies at 73." *Chicago Tribune*, Wednesday edition, 13 October 1971, Section 2A, p. 6.

Maldoner, Bruno. "Architekt Sepp Stein: 1920–2008." *Kunstruktiv 269: Amtliche Nachrichten.* September/October 2008.

Marcuse, Harold. "Historical Dollar-to-Marks Currency Conversion Page," 19 August 2005 (updated 9 February 2013). Accessed on 4 November 2016. history.ucsb.edu/faculty/marcuse/projects/currency.htm.

Martin, Ernst. "Gedächtnisprotokoll." Vienna: DÖW archives.

Maximiano, Cesar Campiani, and Ricardo Bonalume Neto. *Brazilian Expeditionary Force in World War II.* Oxford: Osprey Publishing, 2011.

Meßner, Franz (Josef). "Die Grundlagen des Kaffeebaues im brasilianischen Bundesstaat Sao Paulo, eine wirtschaftsgeographische Studie." PhD dissertation, University of Vienna, 1934. ("Universität Wien Philosophischer Rigorosenakt 12155." *VERZEICHNIS: über die seit dem Jahre 1872 philosophischen Facultät der Universität in Wien eingereichten und approbierten DISSERTATIONEN, Band I.* Nendeln, Liechtenstein: Kraus Reprint, 1972.)

Messner, Franz Josef. Archived record: "PH RA 12155; 1934.04.24–1934.05.04." Archivinformationssystem, Archiv der Universität Wien. Accessed on 27 September 2016.

Molden, Fritz. *Exploding Star: A Young Austrian Against Hitler.* Translated by Peter and Betty Ross. New York: William Morrow & Company, 1979.

Molden, Fritz. *Fires in the Night.* Translated by Harry Zohn. Boulder: Westview Press, 1989.

Montana Historical Society Research Center. "Intermountain Lumber Company photograph collection, 1947–1962: Historical Note." *Montana Historical Society Research Center Archives,* Helena, Montana. Accessed on 30 September 2016. archiveswest.orbiscascade.org/ark:/80444/xv51760.

Moon, Thomas N., and Carl F. Eifler. *The Deadliest Colonel.* New York: Vantage Press, 1975.

Mugrauer, Manfred. "Eine 'Bande von Gaunern, Schwindlern und naiven Leuten': Die Widerstandsbewegung O5 und die Kommunistische Partei Österreichs." *Jahrbuch 2016.* Vienna: DÖW, 2016.

National Archives, U.S. "Cable reporting that the Russians seized two people from the USDIC guards escorting the pair from Vienna to the American Zone in Austria for questioning, February 3, 1946." Record Group 226, Box 11, Entry 211, WN# 23562.

Natter, Henri, and Adam Réfrégier. *Five Years Behind Hitler's Barbed Wire: A Diary of French Officers in A German Prison Camp, 1940–1945.* Translated by Jacqueline Vautrain Collins. Jefferson, North Carolina: McFarland, 2015.

Neufeld, Michael J. *The Rocket and the Reich: Peenemunde and the Coming of the Ballistic Missile Era.* Washington, D.C.: Smithsonian Books, 2013.

Neugebauer, Wolfgang. *The Austrian Resistance: 1938–1945.* Translated by John Nicholson and Eric Canepa. Vienna: Edition Steinbauer, 2014.

Olson, James M. *Fair Play: The Moral Dilemmas of Spying.* Washington, D.C.: Potomac Books, 2007.

Österreichischer Cartellverband. *Hundert (100) Jahre Nibelungia: Festschrift zum hundertsten Stiftungsfest der Katholisch-Österreichischen Studentenverbindung Nibelungia zu Wien im ÖCV.* Vienna: ÖCV, 2008.

Paikert, G.C. *The Danube Swabians: German Populations in Hungary, Rumania and Yugoslavia, and Hitler's impact on their Patterns.* New York: Springer Publishing, 1967.

Pascal, Blaise. *Pascal's Pensées.* Translated by W.F. Trotter. New York: E.P. Dutton & Co., 1958.

Persico, Joseph E. "Papers of Joseph E. Persico." *M.E. Grenander Department of Special Collections and Archives,* State University of New York at Albany. Collection identifier APAP-030.

Persico, Joseph E. *Piercing the Reich: The Penetration of Nazi Germany by American Secret Agents During World War II.* New York: Barnes & Noble Books, 1997.

Petersen, Neal H., ed. *From Hitler's Doorstep: The Wartime Intelligence Reports of Allen Dulles, 1942–1945.* University Park: Pennsylvania State University Press, 1996.

Philips Company. "1925–1940: The first radios, televisions and electric shavers." Accessed on 22 October 2016. philips.com/a-w/about/company/our-heritage.html.

Pirker, Peter. *Subversion deutscher Herrschaft: Der britische Kriegsgeheimdienst SOE und Österreich*. University of Vienna Press, 2012.

Posch, Roman. "Walter Caldonazzi." *Katholische Österreichische Hochschulverbindung (KÖHV) Amelungia*. Accessed on 20 December 2015. amelungia.org/site/pages/view/12.

Pottenstein (Austria), Standesamtsverband. E-mail messages to author, 27/28 October 2015.

Pressespiegel. Excerpts on "Rechnitz Massacre" in German newspapers: *Burgenländische Freiheit*: 27 June 1948, 4 July 1948, 18 July 1948, and 25 July 1948 issues; *Fries Burgenland*: 2 July 1948, 9 July 1948, 16 July 1948, 24 June 1951, and 1 July 1951 issues; *Der Abend*: 24 July 1948, and 26 July 1948 issues; *Burgenländische Volksblatt*: 30 June 1951 and 28 July 1951 issues. Accessed on 30 September 2016. kreuzstadl.net/downloads/pressespiegel_1948_51.pdf.

Randell, Jim. *The Skinny on the Art of Persuasion: How to Move Minds*. Westport, Connecticut: Rand Media, 2010.

Rathkolb, Oliver. *The Paradoxical Republic: Austria 1945–2005*. Translated by Otmar Binder. New York/Oxford: Berghahn Books, 2014.

Rieger, Hans. *Das Urteil wird jetzt vollstreckt*. Vienna: Europa Verlag, 1977.

Roosevelt, Kermit, et al., eds. *War Report of the OSS* (Volume 1). Washington, D.C.: U.S. Government Printing Office, 1949; New York: Walker and Company, 1976.

Roosevelt, Kermit, et al., eds. *War Report of the OSS, Volume 2: The Overseas Targets*. Washington, D.C.: U.S. Government Printing Office, 1949; New York: Walker and Company, 1976.

Rubin, Barry. *Istanbul Intrigues: Espionage, Sabotage, and Diplomatic Treachery in the Spy Capital of WWII*. New York: Pharos Books, 1992.

Rüdiger, Josef (G.J. Rüdiger/Gustav Rüdiger). Affidavit submitted to the Magistrate of the City of Vienna, 9 January 1956. Vienna: DÖW archives.

Rüdiger, Josef Wenzel and Margaretha Eugenia Maria Rüdiger (née Ender). "Trauungs-Schein" (revised marriage certificate that regularized Rüdiger's surname and supplanted the original 21 August 1941 certificate), 7 April 1952. Stephansdom Parish, Vienna.

Rüdiger, Thomas M. E-mail messages to author, 6 November 2016 and 4 January 2017.

Sartorti, Volker. *Biographie Dr. Franz Josef Messner*. Elmshorn, Germany: Eigendruck, 2003.

Schafranek, Hans, and Andrea Hurton. "Im Netz der Verräter." *Der Standard*, 5/6 June 2010. Accessed 28 October 2015. derstandard.at/1271378203933/Im-Netz-der-Verraeter.

Schmidt, Colette M. "Was an die Gegenwart erinnert." *Der Standard*, 13 June 2015. Accessed on 17 October 2016. derstandard.at/2000017383087/Was-an-die-Gegenwart-erinnert.

Scholz, Kurt. "Gedanken für den Tag," 29 October 2015. *Österreichische Rundfunk* (ORF). Accessed on 20 October 2016. oe1.orf.at/programm/418828.

Schorske, Carl E. *Fin-de-Siècle Vienna: Politics and Culture*. New York: Vintage Books, 1981.

Seager, Cedric—"Seager Family of Bebek: Four Generations." *Levantine Heritage Foundation*. Accessed 23 January 2017. levantineheritage.com/seager.htm.

Seitz—"Karl Seitz: Austrian Politician." *Encyclopædia Britannica*. Accessed on 26 October 2016. britannica.com/biography/Karl-Seitz.

"Sekler, Eduard F." *Austria-Forum*. Accessed on 21 October 2016. austria-forum.org/af/AEIOU/Sekler%2C_Eduard_F.

Sekler, Eduard F., and The J. Paul Getty Trust. "Spirit and Project: Art History Oral Documentation Project" (interview by Richard Candida Smith on 25 February 1994). *Getty Research Institute*, Los Angeles. Accessed on 30 September 2016. archive.org/stream/spiritprojectedu00sekl/spiritprojectedu00sekl_djvu.txt.

Sekler, Eduard Jakob—"Eduard Jakob Sekler." *Stadt Wien*. Accessed on 17 December 2015. wien.gv.at/wiki/index.php/Eduard_Jakob_Sekler.

Sekler, Pat—"Pat Sekler, Watercolorist, Photographer, Art Historian." *Munroe Center for the Arts*. Accessed on 26 October 2016. munroecenter.org/patricia-sekler-watercolor photography.html.

Semperit AG. *Partner: The International Semperit Magazine*, Issue 1, 2015.

Semperit Gummiwerke AG. Certification letter for "Josef G. Ridiger" (sic), 1 August 1945. Signed by Semperit officials Vilma Heindl, Franz Schuster, Karl Klose, Erwin Rind, and Viktor Horwitz.

Sokal-Legradi, Helene. "Widerstandstätigkeit der Gruppen Legradi-Sokal in Verbindung mit der Gruppe Dr. Heinrich Maier," unpublished manuscript dated circa 1963. Vienna: DÖW archives, catalogue entry DOeW01553.

Spirago, Francis, and James J. Baxter, eds. *Anecdotes and Examples Illustrating the Catholic Catechism*. New York: Benziger Brothers, 1904.

Spitzner, Gerald. "Heinrich Maier Oratorium." Accessed on 26 October 2016. venite-austria.jimdo.com/heinrich-maier-gedenken/.

Stehle, Hans Jakob. "Die Spione aus dem Pfarrhaus." *Die Zeit*, Number 02/1996, 5 January 1996. Accessed on 28 October 2015. zeit.de/1996/02/Die_Spione_aus_dem_Pfarrhaus.

Steininger, Rolf. *South Tyrol: A Minority Conflict of the Twentieth Century*. Piscataway, New Jersey: Transaction Publishers, 2003.

Szita, Szabolcs. *Trading in Lives?: Operations of the Jewish Relief and Rescue Committee in Budapest 1944–1945*. Translated by Sean Lambert. New York: Central European University Press, 2005.

Taylor, Jack Hedrick, Lieutenant, USNR. "DUPONT MISSION, J.H. Taylor, October 13, 1944—May 5, 1945," 30 May 1945. *U.S. National Archives*. Declassified on 13 February 1999.

Thoma, Helga. *Mahner-Helfer-Patrioten: Porträts aus dem österreichischen Widerstand*. Klosterneuberg, Austria: Edition VA bENE, 2004.

Thomas, Evan. "Spymaster General: The adventures of Wild Bill Donovan and the "Oh So Social" O.S.S." *Vanity Fair*, 3 March 2011. Accessed 13 September 2016. vanityfair.com/culture/2011/03/wild-bill-donovan201103.

Thurner, Erika. *National Socialism and Gypsies in Austria*. Translated by Gilya Gerda Schmidt. Tuscaloosa: University of Alabama Press, 1998.

"Urteil des Volksgerichtshof, 5. Senat," 28 October 1944. Vienna: DÖW archives. (A scanned copy of this document, labeled *Volksgerichtshof-Urteil*, is also available at doew.at.)

U.S. Allied Commission for Austria (USACA). Industry Report 22: "Semperit Gummiwerke A.G.," November 1947, two-page attachment on Semperit's foreign subsidiaries as of 1943. (A scanned copy of this document is available at fold3.com.)

U.S. Department of State, *Register of the Department of State, January 1, 1925*. Washington Government Printing Office, 1925.

Von Flocken, Jan, and Eberhard Vogt. "STASI: Wolfs Prinzessin in Wien." *Focus*, Number 10, 1999. Accessed on 12 November 2015. focus.de/politik/deutschland/stasi-wolfs-prinzessin-in-wien_aid_176067.html.

Von Hassell, Agostino, and Sigrid MacRae. *Alliance of Enemies: The Untold Story of the Secret American and German Collaboration to End World War II*. New York: Thomas Dunne Books, 2006.

Von Pausinger, Clemens. "Bestätigung, Dr. Clemens von Pausinger," 11 June 1945. *Gefangenhausdirektion des Landesgerichtes für Strafsachen Wien*. Vienna: DÖW archives.

Washington, George. Letter to John Armstrong, 26 March 1781. *U.S. Library of Congress*. Available at memory.loc.gov/cgi-bin/query/r?ammem/mgw:@field(DOCID+@lit(gw210400)).

Weisz, Franz. *Die geheime Staatspolizei Staatspolizeileitstelle Wien: 1938–1945; Organisation, Arbeitsweise und personale Belange*. University of Vienna, 1991.

Winninger, Michael. *Das Nibelungenwerk 1939 bis 1945—Panzerfahrzeuge aus St. Valentin*. Erfurt, Germany: Sutton Verlag, 2009.

Wolf, Erich Hans (Hollitscher, Hans Jakob). *Katastrophenwirtschaft: Geburt und Ende Österreichs, 1918–1938*. Zurich: Europa Verlag, 1939.

Wolf, Helga Maria. "Fellinger, Karl." Edited by Ingeborg Schinnerl. Accessed on 12 November 2015. austria-forum.org/af/Wissenssammlungen/Biographien/Fellinger%2C_Karl.

Yale Law School, ed. "The Moscow Conference; October 1943." *The Avalon Project: Documents in Law, History and Diplomacy*, Lillian Goldman Law Library. Accessed on 27 October 2016. avalon.law.yale.edu/wwii/moscow.asp.

Zahn, Gordon. *In Solitary Witness: The Life and Death of Franz Jägerstätter*. Springfield, Illinois: Templegate Publishers, 1986.

Ziereis—"Franz Ziereis." *Jewish Virtual Library*. Accessed on 26 October 2016. jewishvirtuallibrary.org/jsource/biography/Ziereis.html.

Zweig, Stefan. *The Royal Game*. Translated by B.W. Huebsch. London: Pushkin Press, 2001.

Zweig, Stefan. *The World of Yesterday*. Translated by Anthea Bell. Lincoln: University of Nebraska Press, 2013.

Index

Numbers in ***bold italics*** indicate pages with illustrations

www.ingramcontent.com/pod-product-compliance
Ingram Content Group UK Ltd.
Pitfield, Milton Keynes, MK11 3LW, UK
UKHW040309200726
13851UKWH00026BB/111